MATCH FIT FOR TRANSFORMATION

Realising the Potential of Everyday Heroes

Nigel Adams

MATCH FIT FOR TRANSFORMATION
Realising the Potential of Everyday Heroes

First published in Australia by Hetton Advisory Pty Ltd 2019
www.hettonadvisory.com

Copyright © Nigel Adams 2019
All Rights Reserved

A catalogue record for this
book is available from the
National Library of Australia

NATIONAL
LIBRARY
OF AUSTRALIA

ISBN: 978-0-6486578-0-4 (pbk)
ISBN: 978-0-6486578-1-1 (ebk)

Typesetting and design by Publicious Book Publishing
Published in collaboration with Publicious Book Publishing
www.publicious.com.au

TABLE OF CONTENTS

ABOUT THE AUTHOR

Originally from Leeds in the United Kingdom, Nigel has spent the last 25 years living in Melbourne, Australia, with his wife, two children and a German Shepherd.

He is a passionate and innovative senior executive specialising in service operations management, known for driving performance and rapid transformational change, while leading large, award-winning teams in complex delivery networks distributed across many countries and locations.

Nigel's career path started in management consulting, where he worked across a wide range of functions and industries from sales to finance, and from the public sector to automotive manufacturing. He subsequently transitioned to financial services operations, where he spent considerable time exploring the "black box" of payments. He is known for challenging received wisdom and for being an industry thought leader in operational excellence.

Nigel now spends his time consulting, training, coaching and blogging.

FOREWORD

In this volume, Nigel Adams has documented what amounts to a guiding handbook of how to do a critically important initiative well that most organisations will face. That challenge involves how to go through a transformation such as digitisation, while still effectively running the ongoing business. Challenges like these have numerous aspects, many of which are tricky and easy to get wrong, which would be at great cost. Indeed, the evidence shows that most such transformations don't go very well.

Based on deep knowledge and decades of practical executive experience, Nigel Adams has provided a thorough and structured approach to how the issues can be addressed, from the top floor issues to the shop floor issues. Tools, useful frameworks and checklists are provided that will help readers to assess their readiness—match fitness—to take on a digital transformation while still cranking the handle effectively on 'business as usual'. These are inherently different tasks, one requiring stability and consistent productivity and service quality of operations, and the other being all about change and progress of new processes and technologies. There are many challenges and topics covered here from quality to leadership, from change management to metrics and control and from innovation to human skills. To effectively run a business and simultaneously transform it is both multidimensional and extremely non-trivial! I particularly like the approach to quality and operational excellence provided herein that many other books and practitioners under-emphasise.

This book also pays good and due attention to the human issues in stable existing processes and digital transformation processes, which we see as also presenting major challenges in practice, for example in our larger banks. Avoiding a problematic mismatch of existing skills and required capabilities needs good planning and action, and this book documents how such matters can be assessed, led and managed. Skills and tasks are very different in the old world and the new digitalised world. This is particularly evident in services businesses that are mature, that might have a myriad of legacy systems patched together, and that involve some inefficient and wasteful processes that must be overturned prior to their automation. People need to be fully onboard with the change agenda, otherwise we are lost.

Readers will find this book thought provoking and rigorous, yet practical; reflective of the author's background. For those who are contemplating the necessary and potentially onerous journey of a digital transformation, which is often attractive in concept and painful in implementation, you will be better informed and much better prepared by this book's approach.

I commend this volume to all those executives who wish to transform to a new digitalised organisation form. Digitisation is essentially a must do, and I hope and fully expect this book will help readers to do it well. It is rich with wisdom, insights and practical advice and tools.

Professor Danny Samson
University of Melbourne

Part 1 – The Need for Match Fit

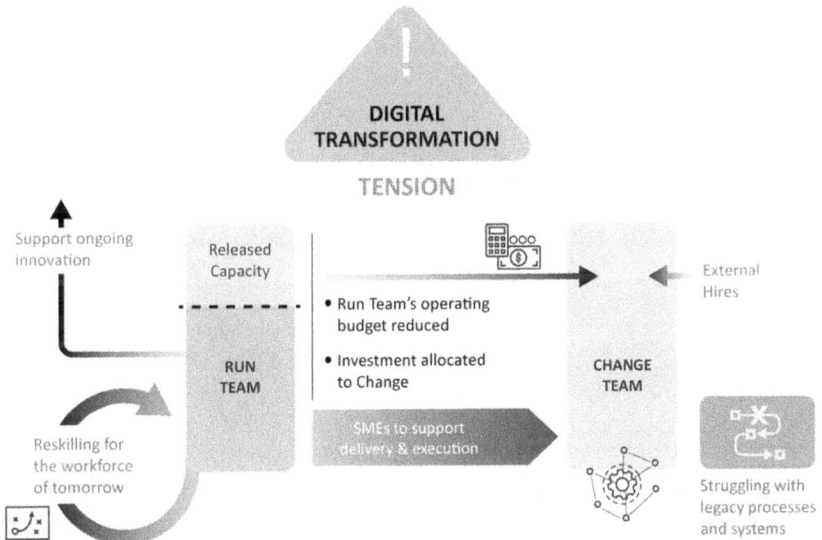

DIGITAL TRANSFORMATION

TENSION

Support ongoing innovation

Released Capacity

- Run Team's operating budget reduced
- Investment allocated to Change

RUN TEAM

SMEs to support delivery & execution

Reskilling for the workforce of tomorrow

CHANGE TEAM

External Hires

Struggling with legacy processes and systems

Chapter 1
Digital – An Existential Crisis

"As Gregor Samsa awoke one morning from uneasy dreams he found himself transformed in his bed into a gigantic insect." — *Franz Kafka, Metamorphosis*

If you work in an organisation, there's a very good chance you are being transformed as we speak. Somewhere between 80–90% of organisations currently have a transformation agenda. For some, this is exciting. It provides an opportunity for growth—both personal and organisational. For others, it's just the latest fad. It keeps the transformation team busy and will go away with the next round of executive change. But it fills many people with trepidation.

Organisations have been transforming for years, but the scale, breadth, pace and intensity of organisational transformation, particularly digital transformation, has risen to a whole new level. Whatever your perspective, the transformation in your organisation will have an impact on your working life. For many of you responsible for keeping the day to day going—chasing sales, fulfilling service requests, answering enquiries, supporting teams—you know the impact of today's transformation will be profound and potentially life-changing.

But with so much executive attention on the transformation, your part of the organisation may be flying under the radar. The impact of the pressure you are under may be going unnoticed. Your team members keep customers satisfied and the revenue rolling in, so surely they merit executive attention? How can you voice your concerns without appearing to undermine the strategy? How do you demonstrate the value your team bring, without appearing negative? How do you convey to the transformation team the complex and unique workarounds needed for highly valued customers, and not seem to be alarmist or difficult? How do your team get their fair share of executive attention? How can you convince the decision makers that the transformation is likely to fail unless your team members continue to meet the demands of business as usual (BAU)? How do you stay positive and achieve your goals when your budget is under pressure and your customers are more demanding than ever? And how do you do all this knowing that, in all likelihood, your role won't exist in the workforce of the future?

The simple answer is you need to get Match Fit for Transformation.

But first it will help to get a better understanding of what's going through the minds of the CEO and their executive team.

The CEO's agenda

Hardly a day goes by without the launch of a new start-up threatening to disrupt whole industries or a new technology coming to market that will revolutionise our current way of living, thinking, behaving and operating. Fuelled by technology innovation, changing customer expectations and competitor behaviour, the threat of disruption and disintermediation strikes fear in the heart of the most seasoned executive. Report after report supports this position. A recent survey of over 800 CEOs, directors and senior executives worldwide found that the number one rated risk is that existing operations will not be able to keep up with those "born digital" (North Carolina State University's ERM Initiative; Protiviti, 2018). According to a 2018 KPMG survey of 220 leaders across Australia, digital transformation is the number one issue keeping leaders up at night. At the same time, 86% of Australian CEOs are feeling overwhelmed by it (the corresponding figure for international CEOs is 65%).

This is hardly surprising. The language alone is enough to test the mettle of the most resilient corporate veteran. It is full of jargon, acronyms and technical references depicting new ways of working and new technologies in often the most abstract, conceptual way. Just when you think you have understood a new idea, along comes something else. Some terms and what they represent are entirely new. Others are an enhancement on something that's been around for a while but given a new label. Other terms are nothing more than a re-branding exercise—game-changing at first glance, but thoroughly depressing when you scratch below the surface—or as one former colleague put it, "I like out-of-the-box solutions, but the problem with this one is there is nothing in the box!" Then there are the buzzwords, which to misquote Sir Winston Churchill, are "a riddle, wrapped in a mystery, inside an enigma".

However, it's not just about language. What's driving this level of executive angst is the very real, existential threat that the new breed of digital competitors poses. Over the last 80 years, the average lifespan of an American S&P 500 company has fallen from 67 to 15 years, and 76% of UK FTSE 100 companies have disappeared in the last 30 years (Hill, et al., 2018). This level of corporate demise is only set to accelerate, and incumbent CEOs know that their legacy and the future of the organisation they lead will depend on how they embrace the digital Zeitgeist.

More than likely, this is what is occupying the mind of your CEO. They are not worrying about the issues you face because they're trying to keep the ship afloat as the digital transformation team turn the organisation upside down. They are worrying about how to increase the likelihood that the big bet they've made on transformation will pay off (and not leave your organisation in the corporate graveyard). This is a Catch-22 situation; doing nothing will almost certainly see the organisation fail, however, the success rate of business transformations, particularly digital transformations, is so low (c. 27% according to McKinsey research and only 5% according to Bain & Company research), there is a very good chance that the organisation will invest heavily in something that is doomed to fail anyway.

With this in mind, the executive team are focussed on outcomes. They want to simplify their business; they want it to be fit-for-purpose in a digital age. The desired outcome is clear. Getting to the outcome is not, and from an executive perspective that's what they pay their transformation team for: figuring out "how to get there".

This is where you come in. You may not be officially part of the transformation team, but you can play a major role in ensuring it succeeds. Match Fit for Transformation will show you how to do just that.

What is business transformation?

Before we move into the "how", it will help to understand a little more about the nature of business transformation. While there is no agreed definition it typically refers to a very fundamental change to how the organisation currently goes about its business. This can be quite operational in terms of changing existing systems, processes and the way people interact with them. It can also involve changing the operating model, for example newspaper publishers switching from paper to digital. Finally, it can include changing the essence of the company, for example Nokia moving from mobile phones to networking.

For any mature organisation to go through such a fundamental change has far-reaching consequences. Existing ways of working—all the received wisdom from prior years, stalwart products and services, the shortcuts, tips and tricks, checklists, skills, techniques and workarounds that have served a business so well in the past—are destined for the annals of corporate history and not part of the future. This can be very challenging, when the future, in particular the role you and your team play in the future, is so uncertain.

While the transformations underway today will take various forms, digital transformation and the concepts underpinning it have been gaining momentum over the last two decades. As new technologies emerge, they are enabling new business models, a tsunami of innovation, a swathe of start-ups and the emergence of tech giants like Google, Amazon, Apple and Alibaba. Unencumbered by legacy, the success of these businesses and others such as Uber, Netflix, Airbnb, Spotify, etc. have, at their core, a cluster of technologies: mobile (smart phones), cloud computing, social networking, big data and Application Programming Interfaces (APIs). These are now being enhanced by artificial intelligence (AI), robotics, the internet of things, Blockchain, virtual reality and 3D printing. It is these technologies that are fundamentally changing how organisations do business.

For a transformation with technology at its core, it's not just about technology. Alongside the technology sit new management techniques and methodologies, such as Agile and design thinking, which are creating new ways of working. Collectively, they are transforming how organisations design and build business models, how they conceive, design and bring products and services to market, and how they scale their businesses by delivering services at a fraction of the cost of more mature organisations. Most telling is the pace at which this happens. Within the time frame it takes many mature organisations to develop a business case, new start-ups have designed, tested, launched and started to scale brand new products and services.

And it's not just the new kids on the block. Amidst this digital maelstrom, there are now examples of mature organisations making huge leaps forward in terms of customer satisfaction and productivity. Companies such as Burberry, Nike and Starbucks are digital masters, not digital companies (Westerman, et al., 2014). The subsequent impact on earnings and share price multiples has captured the imagination of investors and hedge funds alike. Whether it's a consequence of detailed analysis, peer pressure or fear of missing out, no CEO wants to appear a Luddite[1]. As such, they are now either dipping a tentative toe in the foaming digital torrent or have dived in headfirst and are now truly submerged in its raging waters.

Business transformations today are different

The response to this challenge by so many senior teams is to embark on a transformational journey. At first glance, today's transformations are no different to their predecessors. The outcomes the CEO is looking for are eminently reasonable:

- A superior customer experience.
- Revenue-driven growth.
- A step change in productivity and efficiency.
- Better risk management.

With these stated goals, the initial response is certainly no different:

1. A degree of restructuring by creating new roles with new senior appointments, including a smattering of external hires.
2. Internal communications focussed on creating the case for change and a bright vision of the future supported by carefully chosen facts and data to mobilise the workforce.

1. Someone opposed to new technology or ways of working. It is a term, derived from an organisation of English textile workers in the nineteenth century renowned for destroying textile machinery.

3. A painful reprioritisation of the capital program to find funds for the new initiative, typically allocating a "haircut" but not stopping any of the other programs underway.

So why is business transformation today—particularly digital transformation—different?

It's one thing to reimagine your business when it's a start-up, but for a large, mature organisation, it's a completely different proposition:

1. A digital transformation is far more pervasive and intrusive. It goes to the very heart of how an organisation creates and delivers value, turning the received wisdom, processes, relationships, systems, roles, capabilities, policies and all the other artefacts that comprise the "way things get done around here" on their head. Organisations that have evolved over many decades of technology change, mergers and acquisitions, divestments, geographic and market expansion, and channel and product proliferation are now held together by tens, if not hundreds of thousands of process fragments. Trying to digitise this is not for the fainthearted.

2. Many of the skills required to execute the transformation are not readily available in-house (e.g., data scientists, AI "Python" coders, Agile coaches, scrum masters, human-centred design (HCD) specialists and ecosystem curators). Finding and hiring the talent is difficult and expensive. But for them to be productive, they need to be supplemented by subject matter experts (SMEs) drawn from the business, as the new hires have no understanding of how the current organisation works.

3. Addressing the underlying complexity is a critical success factor. A program of radical product rationalisation, simplification and an agenda to industrialise residual processes is a pre-requisite to the technology change. This is neither a task for the timid, nor the new hires. It requires significant numbers of SMEs drawn from the Run Team.

4. Not only are the SMEs required to pave the way for the technology transformation, but it's highly likely that the same resources will also be sought after to support the remediation

agenda that so many large, mature organisations have underway, addressing the policy and design sins of the past.

5. The tendency to adopt Agile as the transformation methodology has changed how those directly involved with the transformation interact with those responsible for continuing to run day-to-day activities. Previously, there would be a series of workshops to gather requirements and then the project team would go away for several months, or years, before requesting support to test the new services. Now change comes off the Agile change production line every two weeks and needs to be absorbed into BAU operations.

6. Customers' expectations are being shaped by their digital experiences with the tech giants and speed to market of new start-ups. Organisations cannot wait 10 years for the digital transformation to finish before the new experience is revealed. Customer experience innovation is a day-to-day proposition, and this will mean having to accommodate legacy technology and fragmented processes. These processes will more than likely have finite capacity for change, long backlogs and a stream of demand filling the pipeline from other areas (e.g., regulatory and compliance requirements).

7. The negative impact on jobs that moving to a digital model would potentially have has been commented on extensively. There has been more discussion recently of new roles being created that will be supplemented by technology, and the workforce of the future will look very different and require very different skills to succeed. Many of the people required to support the transformation will not have a role to go back to once it is finished. The fear that this engenders and how the organisation handles it will determine whether these people are pivotal to the transformation's success or directly responsible for undermining it.

8. These new ways of working also set the business up for a culture clash. For many organisations, the energy and focus during a digital transformation is on the team chosen to deliver the transformation. The fact that there is both a run-the-business team (Run Team) and a change-the-business team (Change Team) is problematic. Immediately there is an "us" and "them" conflict. Executive attention appears

focussed on the new hires—with their new digital skills—who are well versed in the jargon but not well versed in how the organisation currently operates. Run Teams are expected to find efficiencies and do more with less: fewer people and less investment. Many believe that bonuses and rewards are skewed towards those that have a transformation story to tell rather than those who merely ran their team well. At the same time, the volume and pace of poorly executed change under a minimum viable product (MVP) and fail-fast mind-set can have a dramatic impact on the workload of those charged with running BAU. This breeds resentment.

9. Finally, all of the above points mean the transformation will be expensive. It will consume all discretionary resources. It will suck up investment funding and drain the organisation of the most talented SMEs. To pay for this, the Run Team will see their operating budgets cut, revenue targets stretched and their access to investment capital severely constrained. At the same time, customers expect more and want it right now. The Run Team will need to find ways to fund continuing innovation and address the insatiable needs of the regulators.

Embarking on any transformation is fraught with danger. While there are different implementation pathways, there is no easy option. If you must migrate your customer base, either one customer journey at a time or by building a greenfield business and then transitioning them en masse, it will be hard. To paraphrase the opening Franz Kafka quote—be careful what you wish for!

Run v Change

Of all the points raised underlining the difficulty of embarking on transformation, for me, the most fundamental one to address is the conflict between the Run and Change Teams. In many organisations, there is a clear distinction between the Run Team and the Change Team. The Run Team are responsible for BAU activities: generating leads, closing deals, processing applications, delivering product, fulfilling service requests, keeping the systems running, etc. The Change

Team are responsible for designing and developing change initiatives and delivering them to the Run Team. Alignment between the two is typically quite loose, becoming tighter if they have a specific initiative in common and drifting apart when there is little overlap.

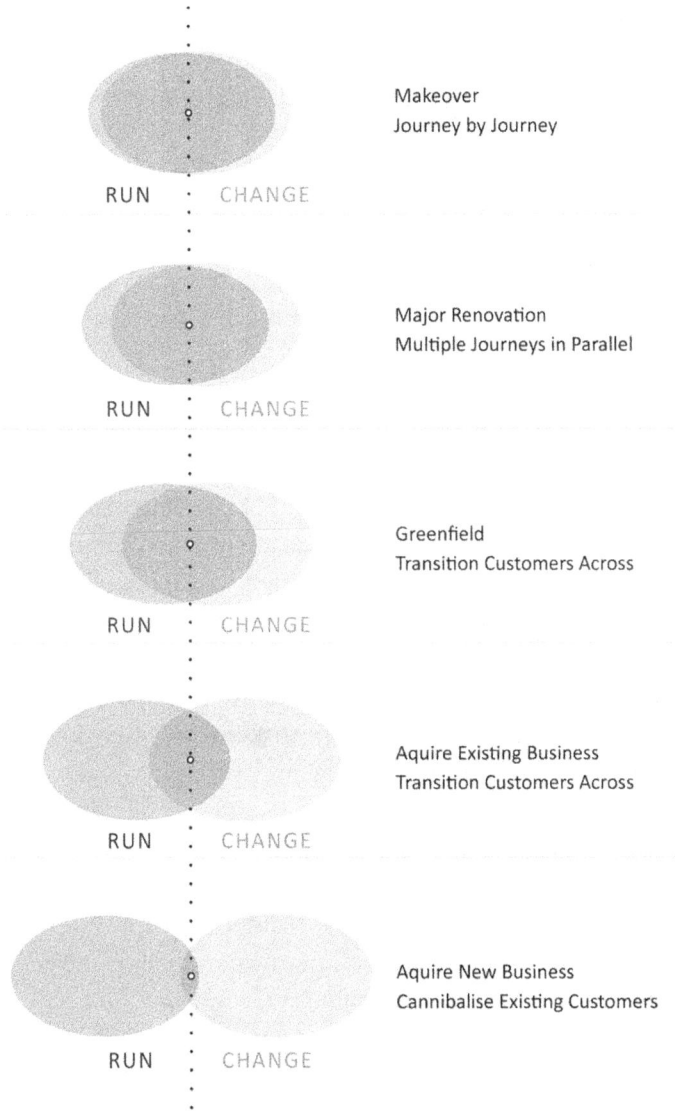

Figure 1 – Collaboration required between teams to deliver digital transformation for alternative pathways.

With today's transformation, in particular digital transformation, there are a finite number of implementation pathways (Figure 1):

1. **Makeover** – Transforming end-to-end customer journeys, journey by journey.
2. **Major renovation** – Transforming end-to-end customer journeys, with multiple journeys in parallel.
3. **Greenfield transition** – Building a new business from scratch and transitioning customers from the old to the new.
4. **Acquire transition** – Acquiring an existing business and transitioning customers from the old to the new.
5. **Cannibalise** – Building a new business from scratch or acquiring an existing business, and then cannibalising customers from the old business.

All options, except cannibalise, require extensive collaboration. But it's not just a question of supplementing the new hires in the Change Team with a few SMEs from the business. The fates of the Run and Change Teams are now inextricably interlinked. The relatively loose, historic relationship between the Run and Change Teams will not work. The role of the Change Team, broadly speaking, remains the same—albeit with far wider and more frequent engagement. It is the role of the Run Team that must change.

The implication of this is that the Run Team needs to do far, far more with far, far less. Not only to keep the ship steady, but also to play a major role in supporting and, in some areas, leading the transformation, e.g., paving the way for technology change by simplifying and industrialising existing processes.

This is where we get to the heart and soul of this book. Many of the larger consulting practices have digital transformation as one of their core offerings, and there is a mountain of information publicly available on how to succeed with a digital transformation. A Google search for "critical success factors for a digital transformation" yields page after page of results, but none of the links I followed provided any guidance for a Run Team leader.

As the complications inherent within this type of change bear out, for the transformation to be successful, the Run Team and the Change Team must be collectively responsible for delivering the outcome. They just play different roles. The Run Team must free up sufficient capacity to loan out SMEs to the Change Team, fund ongoing innovation, maintain sales and service standards, deliver productivity savings, consolidate, simplify and standardise existing processes to make them easier to transform and prepare the team for the workforce of the future (Figure 2). It is not an incremental 5–10% p.a. improvement—it is more like 20–30% p.a. without investment funding!

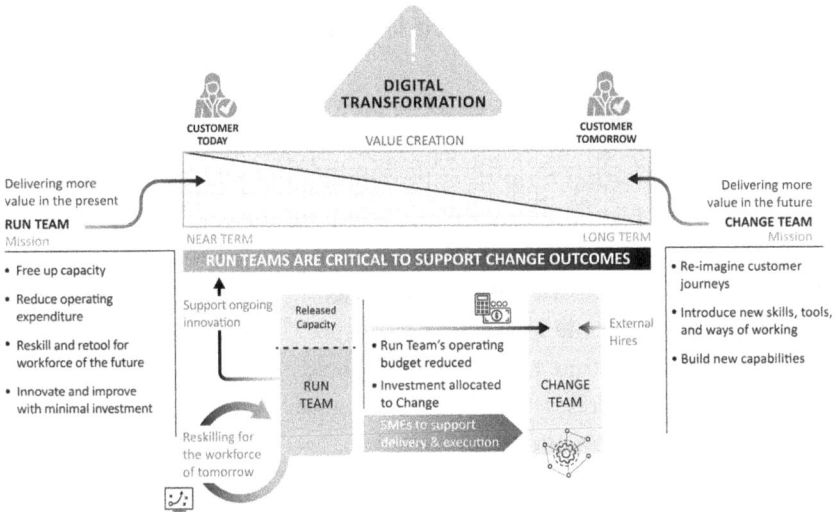

Figure 2 – Run Teams and Change Teams are jointly responsible for delivering a digital transformation.

The vast majority of people working in an organisation work in the Run Team. Just asking them to triple their rate of improvement is not going to work. They are already struggling to cope with targets that appear to be more fantasy than fact. The team may be feeling resentful because they are starved of management attention and their bonuses are being repurposed to support the Change Team. They are fielding constant requests for resources to move across to the Change Team, who are struggling to come to terms with the underlying complexity of how the organisation actually works. They are also a team that will more than likely be impacted by the transformation, with many of them potentially losing their jobs. To triple their rate of improvement they need to do things differently.

That's what this book is about. How do you lead a team that is being transformed? How do you lead a team that is potentially going to be impacted by the transformation? How can you achieve seemingly impossible targets? How can you keep the team focussed and motivated? How can you ensure your team members continue to deliver day-to-day services with far fewer resources? How can you prepare your team to be part of the workforce of the future? How can you keep up with customer expectations when you have little to no investment funding? How do you avoid being a victim and take control?

As I said at the start of the book, the answer to these questions is that your team need to be Match Fit for Transformation.

What does it mean to be Match Fit?

Match Fit is a sporting term used to describe the process of getting the players ready to play and ready to win. It is about preparation: mental, physical and technical. While the focus is always on the players in the squad, as anyone who has listened to a victory speech will attest, there is a whole raft of people in support to ensure the players are in the best shape possible every time they take to the field.

To do this requires a pattern. Each season comprises three phases: pre-season, mid-season and end of season.

- **Pre-season** – Where they set themselves up for the season ahead.
- **Mid-season** – Where they finesse and fine-tune their performance during the season.
- **End of season** – Where they reflect on lessons learned from the season just completed and lock them in so that the team become more than a one-title wonder.

Towards the end of each season, the pace and rhythm intensify as teams jockey for position to determine the winners and losers. This intensity takes its toll. Without the right conditioning, players succumb to injuries; they show signs of fatigue and their performance drops.

In many sports, the season is topped off with a major event every four years, such as the Olympics or a World Cup. As teams build a rhythm throughout a single season, they also build a rhythm around a four-year cycle. If the intensity builds throughout the course of a normal season, it is taken to a whole new level during an Olympics or World Cup year. The pressure, both on and off the field, is overwhelming.

Whether it is a pre-season friendly or a World Cup final, champion teams (teams that consistently win) go into every game Match Fit—ready to play and ready to win.

To win consistently requires versatility and bench strength. It's not just the players who walk onto the field that count—the depth of talent in the squad from which the team of the day is selected is also very important. This squad is supported by coaching staff, medical staff, conditioning staff, analysts, media trainers, transport crews, board members, management teams, selection committees and many, many more. Not only are they ensuring the team are running through their established drills, but they are also scouting the world and looking for new technology, new skills, new techniques and new ways of playing that will give the team the performance edge.

But it's the day-to-day results that truly count. A team may have the best players on paper and the best coaching and support staff, but if they are not Match Fit and not playing together as a team, they will not win. A team that have forgotten how to win will not be able to adapt their strategy and game plan to win at the highest levels.

The more Match Fit the team are, the more resilient they are and the more they are able to adopt innovative practices. Their base conditioning is so good that their body will be able to function to its maximum potential. They are mentally strong enough to stay calm no matter what is thrown at them and how far behind they are on the scoreboard. Technically, their skill level is such that they rarely make mistakes, from the start of the game to the final whistle. This level of conditioning gives them the ability to adapt their game plan to match-day circumstances, irrespective of who they play.

This is what it means to be Match Fit.

How does this relate to business transformation?

And so it is with business transformation. Adapting to the new ways of working and adopting the new technology requires the team on the field—the Run Team—to be Match Fit. They must be resilient, prepared and conditioned to go into every day ready to play and ready to win, knowing that at some stage in the future they will need to embed the changes driven by the transformation.

Delivering the digital transformation will be intense. The early stages will see quick wins, but as the transformation progresses and it gets to the more complex and difficult part of the change, the Run Team will have to be leaner and fitter to ensure they are continuing to satisfy customers while providing more and more resources to the Change Team to ensure the transformation is successful.

The pre-season is where the squad comes together for the first time since the end of the previous season. The players reconnect, catch up on off-season news and get to know the new players. A tailored regime is put in place for each player to resolve any niggling issues and get them back up to peak performance. The coaches and captains provide the pep talk, outline the goals and objectives, and go through any rule changes, which all set the scene for the season ahead. They repeat drills, try out new set pieces and relearn how to play together as a team. They also focus on the competition and the match schedule, understanding individual strengths and how they expect to select the team to beat each rival.

In an organisational context, this is about bringing the team together and getting the people basics right. The team need to understand the strategic context and the part they play in it, as well as determine what success looks like and how their performance will be measured. It is also about understanding customers, what they value, how to deliver quality and make sure they have the right people, at the right time, to fulfil customers' requests (Figure 3).

Sporting Perspective		Organisational Perspective
Pre-season pep talk	⇒	Setting the context
Bringing the squad together	⇒	Putting the people basics in place
League ladders and the trophy room	⇒	Getting the scorecard right
Know the rules. Read the game	⇒	Understanding service quality
Skills clinic	⇒	Quality essentials
Picking the team	⇒	Managing capacity

Figure 3 – Pre-season training focus (Part 2).

The mid-season equivalent is to focus on problem solving, finesse performance for each individual game and adapt tactics for the next adversary. This will involve reviewing what's going well and what can be improved, finding out the small changes the players think they need to make for next week's game, and making sure they have a plan to peak at the right time towards the end of the season. Preparations will also be underway for the next World Cup (or its equivalent), and some players will be involved with those plans. At the same time, players will also be starting to think about next season. Will they continue, potentially transfer to another club or be looking towards life after sport?

From an organisational perspective, this is about change and leading through change. Some changes are small and are issues, problems or opportunities that the team have the resources to fix themselves. Other changes will need a more concerted plan and effort but are still well within the capability of the team itself. For the bigger changes—and digital transformation is one example—the team will play more of a supporting role. SMEs will go on secondment to help connect the Change Team with the Run Team. Finally, they will need to prepare for what comes next, building resilience and getting the skills and capabilities they will need to be part of the workforce of the future (Figure 4).

Sporting Perspective		Organisational Perspective
Go for the gap, find the opportunity	⇨	The need for change
The 1 percenters	⇨	DIY problem-solving
Timing the peak	⇨	DIY redesigning
Reinvent your game	⇨	Supporting transformational change
A game of hard knocks	⇨	Resiliency and workforce of the future

Figure 4 – Mid-season focus (Part 3).

Finally, the question is how to make it sustainable. How do you take a good team and make it a champion team? What can be learned from the previous year's performance that needs to be incorporated permanently into the team's DNA for next year? What changes to the game plan will be required as the transformation intensifies? What role does the board and management team play? How will the selection committee improve its processes? How do they develop a rhythm to ensure this happens day in and day out, year in and year out?

A Run Team that are Match Fit will be more resilient to the change heralded by digital transformation and deliver far better performances along the way, with better outcomes for the business and the team and a far more collaborative relationship with the Change Team.

Bringing this all together, the book is structured in four parts (Figure 5).

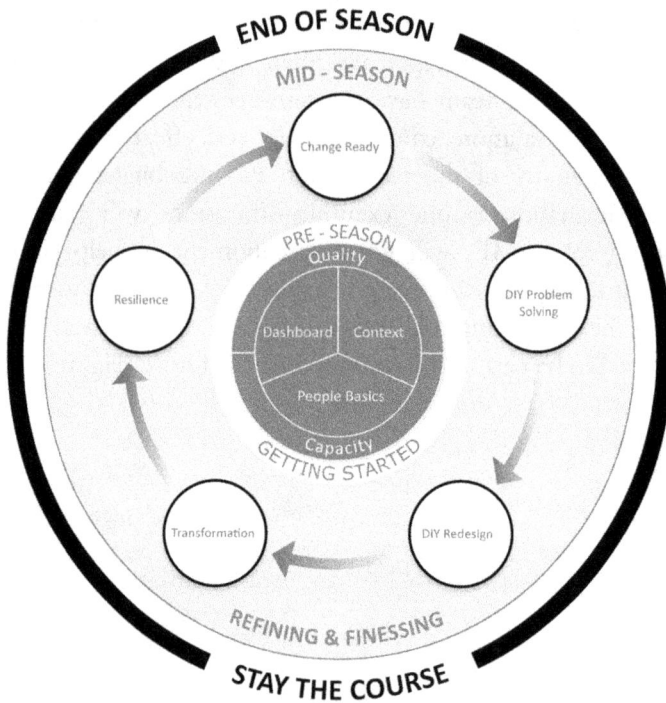

Figure 5 – Match Fit for Transformation structure.

What's in it for me?

As a leader or team member on the Run side of the organisation, the onus is on you to help free up capacity to support the wider digital agenda and equip yourself and/or your team to operate in the workforce of the future.

This will require you to learn some new skills, refine existing skills and dust off skills that you may have practiced once but have not used in a while. It will more than likely require you to adapt your style and change the way you work and interact with your team and your wider organisation. In some ways, organisations going through this type of transformation are asking the impossible of their BAU teams. The "deliver more with less" mantra seems like a walk in the park in comparison to the scale of the BAU challenge now. It may be perceived as unfair, but the opportunity to achieve this level of performance uplift with fewer resources is more than attainable. Of all the service organisations I've visited and worked in, I've always seen the opportunity to free up 15–25% of capacity by fixing the basics and a further 20–30% p.a. by getting the improvement mind-set and skills right. And with freed up capacity comes choices about how you invest it.

The good news is that the tools and techniques required to deliver this improvement are not expensive or complicated. They can be learned very quickly—albeit mastering them may take a lifetime—and put to immediate use with immediate benefits, not least of which are the benefits accruing to you. Not only will you learn new ways to help yourself achieve your goals and targets, but in doing so, you will also reduce the pressure on the team. It also ensures you are visibly connected and aligned to the strategic agenda and sets you up for whatever the future holds.

Finally, it is great for your confidence. It will help create a workplace you can feel proud of. A sense of team. A place where everyone works together. A place underpinned by trust. A team with a "can-do" attitude. A team ready to adapt, take control and win. Again and again. A champion team. This is transformation with a difference. It delivers.

A word of caution

This book is very much a "what-to-do" guide. It is very broad and, to keep the narrative flowing, where there are lists that benefit from a more detailed explanation, I have incorporated the list in a diagram and added the detail to an appendix. At the end of each chapter is a checklist to provide readers with a simple to-do list of actions to take their team through a Match Fit for Transformation journey.

For each subsection of a chapter, there may be books, articles and essays on that topic. This book does not aim to match the depth that those works bring to the subject. I have listed multiple sources in the references towards the back of the book, which are there for further reading if a topic proves to be of special interest. The value in the book is bringing together all these areas, so even a relatively new leader, with little technical management expertise, can materially transform the day-to-day running of their team, work collaboratively and effectively with the Change Team and prepare their team for the future.

If you do this, not only will you get Match Fit, you will also build a champion team.

Chapter summary

The digital revolution is posing an existential threat for many large, mature organisations. The emergence of the tech giants—in many cases with new business models supported by a whole host of new technologies—is disrupting and disintermediating mature organisations at an alarming rate.

The response to this context by most organisational leaders is to embark on a transformation journey. It is a transformation, yes, but it is also unlike any other transformation in terms of depth, breadth and pace. The traditional separation of Run Team and Change Team is being challenged. As the Change Team acquire new, external resources, the Run Team must do so much more with so much less to support the transformation.

Unless the organisation is prepared to take a cannibalisation approach, the Run Team and Change Team will need to collaborate far more than in the past. The success of the transformation is co-dependent on each team. The Change Team will help reimagine creating value for customers and leveraging the new technologies. The Run Team will free up resources (both financial and human) to fund the change, consolidate, standardise and simplify existing processes to make them easier to transform, supplement the new hires with technical expertise to help transition customers and prepare their team members for the workforce of the future.

For the Run Team, the bar has been set far higher than ever before. If they are to be successful, there is a lot that can be learned from the world of sport. The focus and attention is on preparation and planning to ensure every player in the squad is at the top of their game—mentally, physically and technically—ready to play and ready to win: Match Fit.

But above all, this is a book that stands up for the Run Team and the leaders who are often overlooked but contribute so much to underwriting their organisation's long-term success by doing far, far more, with far, far less. It will give them a playbook of what they need to do to get Match Fit and to survive and thrive in a digital transformation.

Checklist:

Checklist Item	Status
Is business/digital transformation on your CEO's agenda and do your team know about it?	❏
Do your team understand what a business/digital transformation is?	❏
Do your team understand how a business/digital transformation is different to other transformations and how it impacts them?	❏
Is there a dedicated transformation team, do your team know about them and are resources being redirected towards them?	❏
Do your team understand what Match Fit means?	❏
Do your team know how Match Fit applies to them, and do they have the tools, techniques and skills to get Match Fit?	❏
Do your team know how Match Fit will benefit them?	❏

Part 2 – Pre-Season: Getting Match Fit

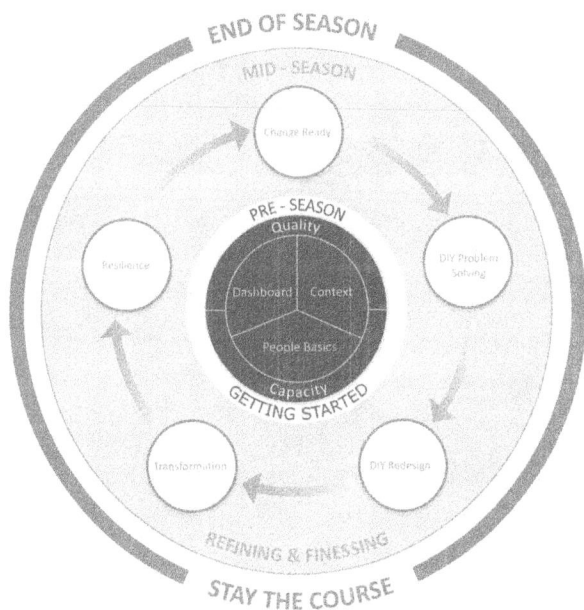

END OF SEASON

MID - SEASON

PRE - SEASON

GETTING STARTED

REFINING & FINESSING

STAY THE COURSE

Change Ready

DIY Problem Solving

DIY Redesign

Transformation

Resilience

Quality

Dashboard | Context

People Basics

Capacity

Chapter 2

Pre-Season Pep Talk – Setting the Context

"Electric communication will never be a substitute for the face of someone who with their soul encourages another person to be brave and true." — *Charles Dickens, The Wreck of the Golden Mary*

Throughout pre-season training, the coach and team are working on communication and alignment. This covers everything from setting the game plan, goals, and objectives for the season, to what the schedule looks like, how they will communicate with each other—both on and off the field—how they will work together to reach the goals and objectives, who makes what decisions, what their immediate priorities are, expectations about how players will behave, what to do if they're not happy about specific decisions, and time spent together outside of the work environment to tighten the bond between squad members.

Of course, this is not a one-off action during pre-season. It is a critical building block that is reinforced throughout the season. Language, rites, rituals, symbols, responsibility and purpose are all part of and permeate the culture. As new players join the squad and others retire or move, storytelling and communication tighten the bond between the current players and the history of the club, reinforcing and enhancing the culture. It is culture that acts as a leading light to help guide the players through everything they do. It provides the clarity that is required to ensure the squad know exactly what is expected of them. Focussing on this aspect in pre-season allows the coach to refresh memories since the last season and reset expectations before the real work gets underway.

In the context of an organisation going through a digital transformation, there is nothing more critical. There has been so much publicity about the impact of digital technologies on the workforce, such as robotics and AI, that many people on the team will be fearing for their jobs. In the absence of good communication, this has the potential to spin out of control, with rumour heightening the level of anxiety.

As a minimum, you need to ensure your team understand your organisation's purpose, strategy, operating model, priorities and the role the team play in this.

Clarifying the purpose

In recent years, many mature organisations have made a concerted effort to clarify their purpose and have energised their teams around that purpose. Without a common, clear understanding of why the organisation exists, it is very hard to win the clichéd "hearts and minds" and gain the discretionary effort that all businesses ultimately depend on to survive and thrive.

A purpose statement aims to encapsulate the very essence of why the organisation was founded, in a succinct way. It helps transcend the day to -day and provides staff with a leading light—the "North Star" in the current vernacular. It strives to create a clear, emotional connection between what the individual holds dear and to be true, and the stated intent of the organisation. It helps an individual answer why they joined an organisation, at a deeper level than just the economic benefits, and hopefully plays a major part in staff retention. By association, it helps define who the individual is, and the collection of individuals with a common purpose help define the organisation.

As such, it goes far beyond a simple mantra plastered on posters and mastheads. Ideally, it courses through the veins of the organisation and is deeply entrenched in the organisational culture and psyche. For example, TED has a mission to "spread ideas" and Tesla aims to "accelerate the world's transition to sustainable energy". Both missions are broad and deep, yet they are also high level enough to adapt to a rapidly changing environment.

For mature organisations with a rich history, this may be challenging. When Fusajiro Yamauchi (Nintendo) started producing and marketing Hanafuda playing cards in 1889, he presumably had no idea that the company he founded would be entertaining and delighting customers with video games over a century later. Similarly, the founders of Royal Dutch Shell, which started as an antiques dealer specialising in shells from the Far East, or Nokia, which started life manufacturing paper, rubber tires and boots, may have had no inkling that their organisations would evolve into the institutions we know today. Hence, crafting a purpose statement that will stand the test of time is not a trivial matter.

The first part of getting Match Fit is to establish the "why" for your team. It's one thing to know why the organisation exists, but it's another to know why your team exist and the role they play in helping fulfil the organisation's purpose. The purpose also acts as a reference point. Clarifying how the digital transformation connects to the organisation's purpose and helps fulfil it is a critical point of understanding. This is particularly the case if there are apparent conflicts between the purpose and the outcomes expected from the transformation. For example, if the purpose statement focusses on creating opportunities for the organisation's people, but an expected outcome of the digital transformation is a reduction in roles, how the organisation reconciles this inherent conflict will play a significant role in establishing the trust required to execute a program like digital transformation.

If you work in an organisation that has already established and communicated its purpose, you are off to a good start. If not, you will still need to answer "why" when you talk to your teams. This can be quite tricky. Crafting a purpose statement is usually the responsibility of the CEO, and it may be a little presumptuous for a team leader or manager to embark on this task. However, in the absence of an official purpose statement, by researching the organisation's history, talking to key stakeholders—such as your line manager, peers, customers and suppliers—and asking their views, you can at least answer the question of what the company means for you. Why does it exist in your mind, why did you join and how do your values align? Using this as a start is better than nothing.

In either scenario, the role of the leader is to make it "real" for their team. In a large, diverse organisation, spanning multiple products, divisions and countries, a purpose statement written for the organisation needs to embrace all aspects of the organisation, so a leader of a specific team must translate this to make it relevant. What does the purpose mean for our day-to-day roles and responsibilities—the customers we support, the services we provide and the processes we run? It needs to be communicated in language the team understand. This is an exercise launched by the leader, but it is best completed in conjunction with a small number of representatives from the team.

Once you have agreed on what it means, write it down and share it with the wider team, including commentary from the team members who drafted it and any explanatory notes (e.g., the process you went through to draft it). It must be:

- Clear and succinct.
- Credibly optimistic.
- In language the team will understand.
- Connected to the organisation's purpose statement.

I imagine that if you are part of TED's technology delivery team, understanding that the team's purpose is to "make platforms available to spread ideas" would be far more powerful than telling the team that they will be measured on systems uptime.

Sharing the strategy

If the purpose provides the "why", the strategy provides the "what". It is basically a high-level plan of what the organisation will focus on and the actions it will take. These decisions are derived from a set of assumptions it has made about the nature of the operating environment it will face. It can take many months to craft an appropriate strategy, but the success of a strategy will depend on execution. For it to be successful, the strategy will not only need to be acceptable, suitable and feasible, it must be understood. That means it will need to be simple to communicate and communicated well.

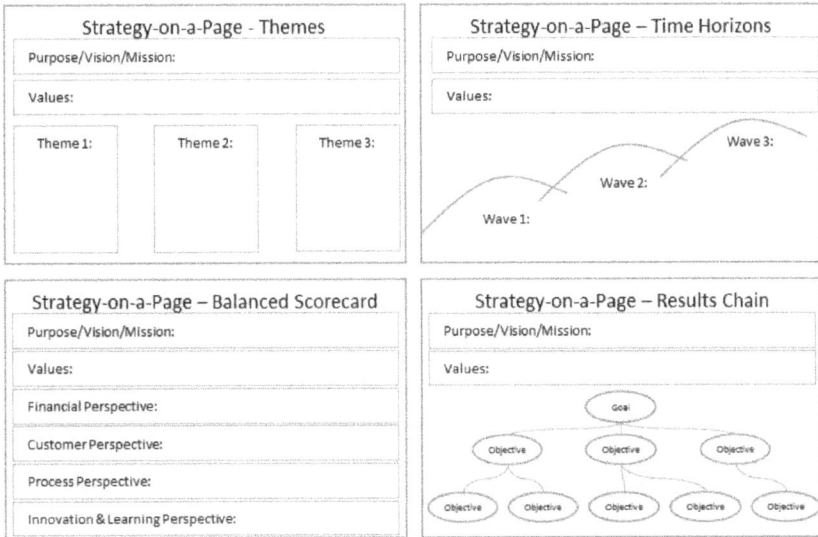

Figure 6 – Typical strategy.

A "strategy-on-a-page" approach, typically with the purpose of making the linkage between strategy and purpose transparent, is effective. There are several different formats in practice (see Figure 6 for some examples). Irrespective of the format, it should include something like: "Our purpose is to [insert purpose statement] and over the next [insert time frame] we will achieve [insert goals/objectives] by [insert strategic themes]." This document is brief and concise and can be shared with all the stakeholders of an organisation: customers, staff, suppliers, regulators, etc.

The role of the line manager is to make the strategy relevant for the specific team. The manager must explain how the strategy-on-a-page format relates to the team and clarify the team's role in executing that strategy. This is the NASA janitor moment. When President John F. Kennedy was touring the NASA facility in 1961, he introduced himself to a janitor who was mopping the floor and asked him what he did at NASA. The janitor replied, "I'm helping put a man on the moon".

Writing a strategy-on-a-page that speaks to everyone about their specific role in that strategy is extraordinarily difficult in a small organisation. In an organisation with tens, if not hundreds of thousands of people, it is impossible. That's the job of the line manager—to translate and communicate it to the team.

A key communication from the CEO—the strategy on a page— will focus on what will change. For an organisation undergoing a digital transformation, that means the strategy on a page will be about digital transformation. When a Run Team leader shares the strategy on a page, if it's just emailed out or printed and stuck up on a wall, the team may conclude that the strategy is about what the Change Team are doing. The Run Team may then decide to keep going the way they've always worked, perhaps with a sense of relief (i.e., no change is a good thing). Alternatively, it will create fear and uncertainty about the future. In either case, there has been a communication failure.

In this context, the role of the Run Team leader is to create the linkages between day-to-day delivery and change. This is the second step in creating the context, and it must focus on how day-to-day activity needs to change to support the larger change (i.e., the digital transformation). The strategy on a page may focus on the larger change, but there is still a role for the BAU team to play in delivering that change. Their role is to free up capacity and do more with less so that the difference can be invested in day-to-day innovation and change, freeing up both financial and human resources to work on the digital transformation. You need to be able to communicate this in words that make sense to you and your team.

Working through the operating model

If the purpose gives you the "why" and the strategy gives you the "what", the operating model shows "how" the various elements of the organisation come together to deliver and create value.

Along with purpose and strategy, many leaders may be asked for input into the operating model design process, but the task of crafting and designing the operating model is allocated to a small number of people in the organisation. For most leaders, their role is to communicate the operating model and translate it into something relevant to their specific team. This is a cascading process. An operating model is typically put together at an enterprise level. It cascades down through the layers of the organisation with words, phrases or sections highlighted that have specific meaning or relevance for the leader's team. The role of the team member is to understand where and how they fit into this bigger picture. This also provides context for their role.

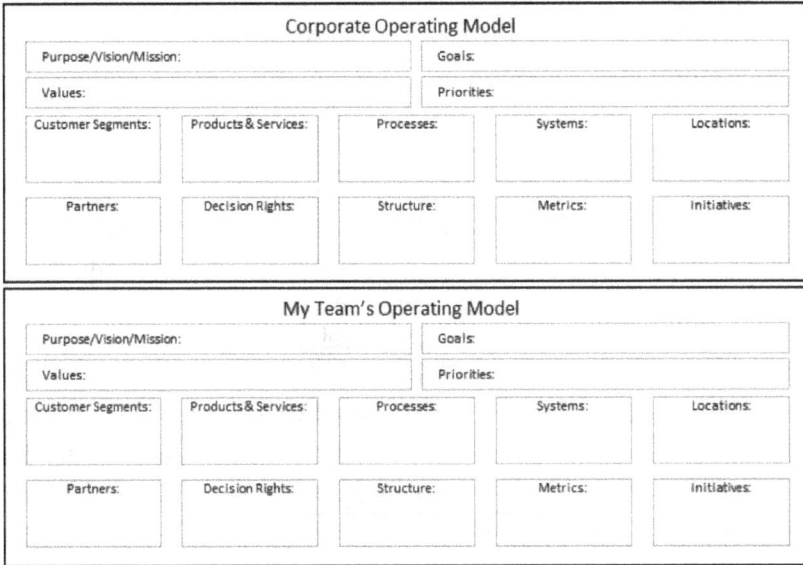

Figure 7 – Operating model example.

The simpler the operating model, the better. There is no one right way to define an operating model, but it should cover at least the following (Figure 7):

- **Customers**[2] – What are the principal segments targeted by the organisation?
- **Products and services** – What are the products and services offered to these segments?
- **Processes** – What are the core processes required to deliver these services?
- **Locations** – From which locations are the services provided? Where are the main service centres and distribution points?

---

2. Customers, products and services are generally captured within the business model. Rather than add another document for the team to understand in terms of context, I prefer to see them added to the operating model.

- **Technology** – What platforms, systems and technology are critical to executing these processes?
- **Decision rights** – How will we run the organisation, how are decisions made and who has what authority?
- **Structure** – How are the team organised?
- **Suppliers** – Who are the key suppliers and what do they provide?
- **Performance measures** – What are the critical performance metrics?

Like purpose and strategy, if the operating model has already been communicated by the CEO's executive team, it will be much easier to share the relevant parts with your team. At team leader level, you will:

- Take the enterprise operating model and highlight the elements that are relevant to your team.
- Create a two-page "operating model on a page". Page 1 is the enterprise model and page 2 uses the enterprise model as a watermark (i.e., a faded version) with "call out" text boxes to adapt and translate into your team's language.

If your organisation doesn't have a formal operating model, you will need to draft a team operating model. This is a critical tool to help create context and clarity around a team member's role and where they "fit" in the organisation. In the absence of anything at an organisational level, once again, something is better than nothing.

Setting the priorities and initiatives

The final element of setting the context is to clarify priorities. The strategy will typically articulate the high-level list of things to do and allocate them to a time horizon: short, medium and long term. The initiatives are the programs of work that are tasked with delivering these priorities. For those items falling into the short-term horizon, there is a "drill down" process to define the activities in more detail, which become the key priorities for that period.

This approach ensures that items to be delivered in the short term are articulated with greater clarity and remain anchored to the end game. An interesting side note here is the role Agile, as a project methodology, is playing in speeding up the delivery cycle, using epics and sprints to distinguish between the long term and the short term but maintaining the relationship between the two.

It will come as no surprise for most leaders that their role is to translate these enterprise priorities into something that is meaningful for their team. The questions to consider are:

- Which priorities will impact the team?
- How will they impact the team?
- When will they impact the team?
- What will it mean for someone within the team?
- Will any of the priorities change or impact a team member's job?
- What must the team do to support the priorities?

From a simple change management perspective, given the amount of information about the impact of digital transformation on jobs, the key question for many team members will be, "Will I have a job at the end of this?"

As well as managing this concern, you will more than likely be faced with the task of extolling the virtues of doing more with less. This may be interpreted as, "You want me to work harder so that the project team can finish faster and bring forward my redundancy date."

This is where true leaders demonstrate their credibility.

Telling the story

The purpose of this chapter is to focus on setting the context. Asking your team to follow you when they don't know why they are following you will invariably lead to failure. Some workplaces are much more accepting of a command-and-control style, adopting the "tell me to jump and I'll ask you how high" approach. Others will question every decision and need to understand why.

Even in the most hierarchical and bureaucratic environment, I have never been criticised for explaining why we are doing something. People need context, and it is the role of the leader to provide context and the role of the team member to ask for it. The elements outlined in this chapter are those that are critical to providing context—who we are, why we exist, what we are striving to achieve, how we will go about it, how we will organise ourselves to achieve these goals and what our immediate priorities are.

Throughout the chapter, I have referred to the need to "translate" and make the enterprise elements relevant to the team. This is not just about modifying PowerPoint templates and then emailing them out. This is about effective communication. The context is so critical and so easy to misinterpret that I cannot overemphasise just how important two-way communication is. Setting the context is not about issuing an edict, it is about explaining why and for people to understand why, they need to be able to ask questions.

For the "why" to be accepted, it needs to be delivered in a credible, authentic way. Simply forwarding the link in an email is not enough. Reading from a script is not enough. Delegating to your managers is not enough. A quick teleconference is not enough.

If the organisation's purpose is, "Doing the right thing for all of our stakeholders", you must identify for the team who those stakeholders are. If the strategy includes, "Dramatically improving our most critical processes", identify for the team the processes they use that will be improved.

By translating, you will help the team to understand and heighten the credibility of the leader delivering the message. Someone reading from a script using words they would never use on a day-to-day basis will never sound real. There is obviously a risk here that the "translator" gets the translation wrong and doesn't interpret the cascaded message correctly. This is where the translator's line manager plays a key role to ensure that it is translated and applied appropriately to maintain the integrity of the message.

Setting the context can be done in a formal roundtable or town hall arrangement, but— depending on the team—it can also be done in a creative way:

- Through an interactive game, such as charades.
- By acting out the strategy.
- By running brainstorming sessions to figure out the implications of the strategy.

The key point is that all members of the team leave the session knowing what the context is, how it affects them and what they need to do to support it. How it's delivered must be perceived as credible and authentic by the audience—the exact method may well differ by team.

Much has been written on effective communication, which is well beyond the scope of this book. It doesn't matter how many books or articles you read or speakers you listen to, for many people, standing up in front of a crowd of people and speaking is an extraordinarily difficult thing to do. Of all the research I have read on the subject, storytelling appears to be one of the most effective ways of communicating the message. We all have different preferences for receiving information: some people like pictures, some are more comfortable with charts and tables, and some like written text. It is hard to get the format just right for each member of the audience, but most people remember stories. Crafting a message into a personal story is a very powerful way of communicating something you need your team to remember and something you are likely to feel far more comfortable with. The story doesn't need to be capable of winning the Nobel Prize for literature, it just needs to be personal and related from the soul.

The final point on this topic is around your plan to communicate. You cannot cover these topics in a single briefing session and then forget about them for the next few years or until the next major initiative is launched. You need a communications plan. It needs to cover:

- Who the audience is.
- Where the audience is (especially if teams are based in multiple locations).
- How you will connect with people on secondment or long-term absentees.
- Who will deliver the briefing.
- What the briefing format will be.
- Where and when it will be communicated.
- How questions and answers will be handled.
- What the follow-up will be.
- Where team members go for more information.

In terms of frequency, you need to keep communicating and providing updates—daily, weekly, monthly, quarterly, biannually and annually—and it should form part of the induction program for new team members. The long-dated updates may be more detailed and more staged, but never waste an opportunity to connect what the team are doing on a day-to-day basis to the strategy. And always provide an opportunity for the team to ask questions and seek clarity.

Chapter summary

This chapter focussed on the importance of setting context. In the sporting analogy, it is the pre-season pep talk. It draws a line under the past and introduces the goals and objectives for the future and a high-level plan of how the team are going to attain those goals. To make this real for the team and establish an emotional connection between the players and the club, there is always a call to action that draws on the spirit of the club, what the founders said, why the club was established in the first place and how that intent is manifested today.

In an organisational context, this is really about purpose, strategy, the operating model and priorities. For many organisations, the audience is wide and diverse. It is difficult to craft these statements in a way that speaks directly to a specific role within the organisation. The purpose is typically far-reaching and aspirational. The strategy is high level and broken down into three to five key themes. The operating model covers broad customer segments, major processes, critical applications, key suppliers and the top two to three layers of the organisational structure. The priorities focus on a handful of major actions across the enterprise.

The role of the line manager is to translate these elements "on a page" into something that is simple to understand for the individual team member. This helps them understand how their role fits into the grand plan and what they need to do to contribute to the project's success.

Given the potential impact on the Run Team's livelihoods, this requires effective communication. It must be a dialogue that is authentic, honest and credible. The leader must provide examples using language and terminology that he/she uses in their normal day-to-day interactions with the team and provide the opportunity for the team to ask questions. This is not a one-off exercise. The leader needs to be available to provide reminders of the context and answer questions as they arise. Using storytelling techniques to make the message more personal enhances authenticity.

The pep talk is the foundation of your success.

Checklist:

Checklist Item	Status
Do your team have a clear purpose statement and understand how their work supports it?	❏
Do your team understand their role in executing your organisation's strategy?	❏
Do your team understand how they fit into your organisation's operating model?	❏
Do your team understand the organisation's priorities and how they support them?	❏
Do you have a clear communications plan to share the context frequently with your team in an authentic way?	❏

Chapter 3
Selecting the Squad – The People Basics

"We tend to meet any new situation by reorganising, and a wonderful method it can be for creating the illusion of progress while producing confusion, inefficiency and demoralisation." — *Petronius Arbiter, a Roman official at the time of Emperor Nero*

There is a vast difference between a champion team and a team of champions. In most sporting codes, you can buy a team of champions, but you can't buy a champion team—it must be built. A champion team may not have the best players on paper but will still consistently beat teams that do. A champion team are a team that performs, year in and year out.

The All Blacks are New Zealand's rugby union team and the most successful major sporting team in history. They have won more than 77% of their games since first setting foot on the field. What is even more remarkable is that the team are drawn from a population of just over 4.5 million people. Their ability to snatch victory from the jaws of defeat, and their consistency, commitment, humility, leadership approach, physicality, technical prowess and depth of talent are without doubt. The place they hold in New Zealand's psyche, embodying a nation's hope and civic pride, is without parallel. They have been the subject of many books, such as *Legacy* (Kerr, 2013) and *Behind the Silver Fern* (Johnson, et al., 2017), which extrapolate lessons from the playing field to leadership and management. Yet the team have had setbacks. They have had to transform and adapt to their environment and have done so in such a sustainable way that the accolades have kept on flowing, the air of invincibility has grown and every other rugby-playing nation knows that there is no such thing as an easy game against the All Blacks.

It is not just about the team of players who run out onto the field, it is about the depth of talent in the whole squad—the bench strength— that gives them the resilience and flexibility to field the best team, selected specifically to face their adversary, irrespective of the strengths that adversary can muster. They don't have a good year or two and then fade into oblivion; their success continues through decades. Given that the average tenure of an elite athlete in many team sports is 10 to 15 years, and every year the team members change, how do champion teams build long-term success? It is a question that experts and armchair pundits alike have argued about for years. One thing is certain: they all get the people basics right.

Pre-season training for any club lays the foundation for next year's success. It is during pre-season training that coaching staff:

- Set the scene by drawing on the past and identifying the future game plan.
- Introduce new players and build team spirit and camaraderie.
- Get the basics right by regaining fitness levels, fixing niggling injuries and sorting out lingering issues.
- Figure out which configuration of players in the squad works best.

In the previous chapter, we focussed on setting the context for the challenge ahead. This chapter will concentrate on who's who, building trust, getting the people basics right, organising the team and what makes individuals tick.

Who's who

The first task of the leader is to make sure that everyone knows everyone else on the team. This must extend to those people on the Change Team that the Run Team will be interacting with frequently. Even for established leaders, this is a great opportunity to bring everybody together at the start of a new financial year or when a major initiative like a digital transformation is launched. When a new leader is appointed, this is even more critical. Too many leaders take over teams and then spend the first few days buried in process maps, talking to customers or suppliers, poring over management reports and getting to know their peers but not even saying hello to their own team.

The "meet and greet" is one of the highest priority tasks a new leader has on their agenda. For small teams located in the same building, this should happen face-to-face within the first few days. For more dispersed and larger teams, a conference call to introduce yourself and an indication of when you will be visiting each location should happen within the first week. Depending on its size and geographic scope, it's hard to be prescriptive about precisely when you should get to meet all team members face-to-face, but it must be your number one priority. For a CEO or divisional leader in charge of many thousands of people, face-to-face meetings will obviously take far longer, but it is something people expect. Team members want to look their leaders in the eye and greet them in the way that is customary in their culture.

The team want to know about the leader, who they are and what they stand for, to try and get an early indication of what to expect. This is a "moment of truth" opportunity. What the leader says and doesn't say, their facial expression, stance, body language, tone, choice of words and how they respond to questions will all be analysed and interpreted by the team in the days to come.

Leaders cast a very long shadow, and as a former colleague was fond of saying, "You never get a second chance to make a first impression." This rings very true for new leaders. First impressions do count, and your preparation for this initial meet and greet is critical. The worst thing you can do is not do it. It may be difficult for introverts, but you must find a way, whether that is in small group sessions, one-on-ones (if it's a small team), large "town hall" briefings or informal floor walks. You must connect with every member of your team.

For leaders of established teams who are preparing to communicate the enterprise decision to undertake a digital transformation, you need to make sure that everyone knows each other on the team. The very nature of getting Match Fit requires everyone to know everyone else on the team.

Over time, as people come and go in mature teams, cliques and factions can develop. Conversely, people sitting a few metres apart may not know each other. Even worse, there may be people who have sat next to and disliked each other for several years, never speaking or asking to move desks, all while their direct line manager is unaware of the animosity. As the other team members essentially have to choose sides, the atmosphere would be dreadful and team performance significantly impacted.

There are many techniques to get people talking, from morning teas, lunch and learns, fast five Q&As, team-building days, off-site meetings, etc. The actual technique is less relevant. What is important is that everyone gets to know each other not just at a superficial level, but at a much more human level. It is about everybody. Everybody on the team has a role to play. Everybody is important, everyone needs to be made to feel special and you must not play favourites. It is neither expected nor realistic for everyone to become "best friends forever". It is, however, essential to establish the basis for developing a high-trust work environment.

Building trust

I have been fortunate enough to work in high-performing teams. High-performing teams feel different, and the one distinguishing factor was the level of trust. This includes trust between the team members and the leader, and trust between the team members and each other. The leader worked with the team to set the agenda and then got out of the team's way. When there was a problem, the team tried to work it out amongst themselves before turning to the leader.

One example that sticks in my mind occurred during an investment planning session. Usually a dog-eat-dog scrap for scarce investment dollars, on this occasion one team member chose to share her investment budget because she believed another team member had more opportunity to drive the overall team's performance. She went back to her team and told them that their job for the year was to "keep the ship steady". She essentially sacrificed her bonus, which was largely driven by an individual's ability to secure investment funding and transform. She put the team's goals above her individual goals and was rewarded for doing so.

Trust arrives on a tortoise but will leave on a hare. Undertaking any shared endeavour without trust is doomed to fail. Building a high-trust environment, on the other hand, is far from easy. In clichéd terms: "Say what you're going to do and do what you say." Once again, there is a huge body of work on this subject, but essentially:

- Connect people to the purpose.
- Ensure expected values and behaviours are understood, with practical examples of what they mean.
- Allow and encourage the team to speak up and hold each other to account for working in line with the values.
- Don't make promises you can't keep, and follow through on what you do promise.
- Be open, transparent and encourage information sharing.
- Trust each other and ensure people are empowered to do their job.
- Reward and recognise achievement.
- Demonstrate personal vulnerability and that it's okay to fail.

This is not achieved overnight. It is consistency that matters more than anything else. Day in and day out, every member of the team must work on these elements, and the leader must be a role model.

However, this is all irrelevant if the environment isn't right.

Getting the environment right

At the start of the chapter, I mentioned that a major objective of pre-season training was to work on the fitness of the players, address niggling injuries, refresh core skills and sort out any lingering issues. By getting these basics right, players are not distracted and devote their attention to performing at their best.

In a work context, this means getting the people basics right: do people know what their job is and what is expected of them? Do they have the skills and knowledge at the right level to do their job, are they remunerated accordingly and is this all properly recorded in a contract of employment? It is rare, when taking over a new team, to find all the above in place.

These are hygiene factors, and—like niggling injuries—if they are not corrected, they will undermine the good work done elsewhere. If you have unsafe work practices, an environment perpetuating bullying and harassment, staff without valid contracts, people not being paid appropriately, people performing the same job but with different grades or titles, vague reporting lines, an excessive number of direct reports, team members not knowing what their targets are, team members never seeing their job description or team members never having a one-on-one development conversation, it doesn't matter how inspiring and visionary a leader you are, the environment will range from dysfunctional to toxic, and you will fail.

This may appear to be too micro-focussed, but further investigation often reaps rewards for the team. A disgruntled staff member may portray their grievance in broad terms, but some forensic digging often uncovers issues related to the items highlighted in Figure 8, which is covered in more detail in Appendix 2.

People Basics

- Health & Safety ☐
- Contracts ☐
- Job Titles ☐
- Reporting Lines ☐
- Renumeration ☐
- Hours & Conditions ☐
- Grades ☐
- Secondments, Absences & Vacancies ☐
- Job Descriptions ☐
- Targets & KPIs ☐
- Individual Development Plans ☐
- Success Profiles ☐
- Employee Milestones ☐

Figure 8 – People basics (see Appendix 2 for more detail).

One example that springs to mind is where a team member was reassigned to work in a different area. The work was well within his capability, and he had done the job before. It should have been a fairly smooth transition. It was everything but! To quote one of his colleagues, every day he came to work looking like a "bulldog chewing a wasp"! He was angry all the time, snapped at colleagues, was curt with customers and was obstructive in team meetings. The team was walking on eggshells and morale was plummeting. The reason for the challenging behaviour was identified: the work requests in the new area had a different arrival pattern—the workload would peak later in the day, meaning he would finish work 30 minutes later than before. This meant he would miss his train home, and he then had an hour-long wait until the next train! He came to work knowing that he was going to miss his train and was upset about having to wait. Five minutes to ask why he was so angry, five minutes to listen, five minutes to fix—weeks of impacted performance had passed before the question was ever asked!

At face value, it's tempting to relegate the items above to the very bottom of the to-do list when faced with the monumental, game-changing challenges of a digital transformation. Asking these questions invariably creates a long list of problems to fix. But fix them you must. A team of malcontents will never go above and beyond. By getting the people basics right and fostering a high-trust environment, you are well on the way to setting the foundations of your success.

Selecting the squad

As the quote at the start of the chapter suggests, substantive restructuring is enormously disruptive. It can take many months, if not years, to execute and bed down. A restructure will distract the team, undermine engagement and significantly increase the team's risk profile. There is a time and a place for major restructuring, and a large change program like digital transformation could be one of those catalysts. However, that is for the Change Team to decide. As far as the Run Team is concerned, I would strongly advise against it.

There is no doubt, however, that taking over a new team and working with the hand you're dealt can be challenging. It would be far easier to start from scratch, hire the people you want and have, at least initially, a natural degree of loyalty. Unfortunately, this opportunity rarely presents itself to Run Team leaders. With major structural change off the table, the Run Team leader must be shrewd in how he/she goes about getting the right people into the right roles.

Logically, the approach would be:

- Design what you need.
- Assess what you have.
- Find the gaps.
- Plug the gaps.

In practice, I've found the best approach is to be iterative and in a different order:

- Assess what you have.
- Understand the limitations.
- Design what you need.
- Plug the gaps.

It also helps to take it in two stages:

1. Review the structure chart.
2. Review the people.

Structure chart review

As mentioned, this section is not about redesigning the structure top to bottom. It is about finding ways to tweak and enhance what you have. The first objective is to determine whether you have the right type and number of roles. The second objective is to ensure they are organised appropriately.

To address the first objective, you must know what your team need to do—both core tasks and support activities. Using the context documents from Chapter 2 and the process documentation that you will learn more about in Chapter 6, you must create a list of all the tasks. Then, using the existing structure chart and the relevant position descriptions (assuming that these exist!), map these tasks to the roles on the structure chart. This will highlight tasks that don't appear to be mapped to a role and roles that don't appear to have a clear connection to what the team are trying to achieve (Figure 9).

Process/Task	Role				
	A	B	C	D	E
Process 1.0					
Task 1.1	✓	✓			
Task 1.2		✓		✓	
Task 1.3					
Process 2.0					
Task 2.1	✓				✓
Task 2.2				✓	✓

Figure 9 – Mapping tasks to roles.

Over time, the nature of work changes. Given how big a job it is to redesign and restructure a team from the ground up, don't be surprised if what's written in the job description does not represent an accurate picture of what the team member does. Some tasks may no longer exist, and additional tasks may have been added but not documented. You will need the help of the team to complete this mapping exercise.

The output from the exercise is an assessment of whether you have the right type of roles to do the work that the team are expected to complete and what gaps exist. The decision tree in Figure 10 suggests a course of action to follow if you do not have the right roles.

The next question is: how many of each type of role is required? Answering this requires an understanding of capacity management. We'll cover this in Chapter 7.

The second objective requires you to analyse the structure chart in more detail by asking questions like:

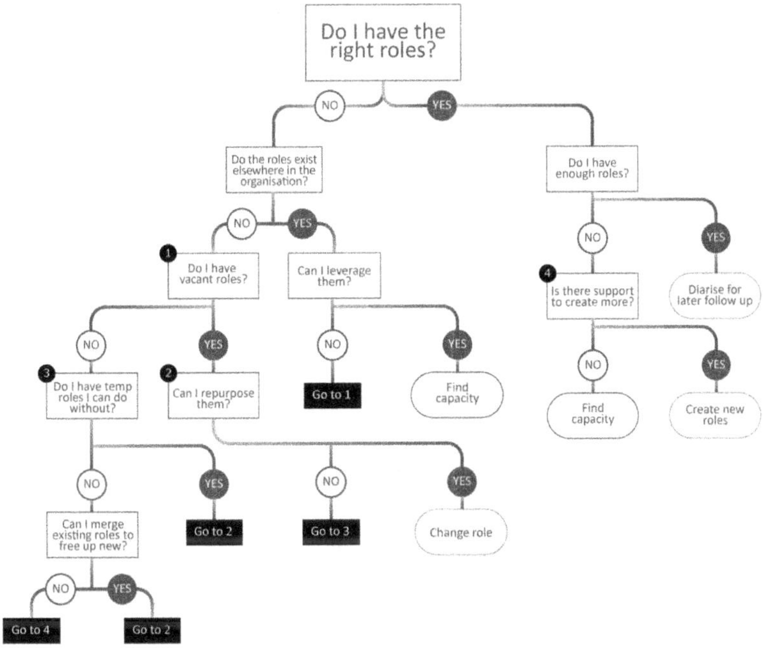

Figure 10 – Right roles decision tree.

- What is the span of control for each leader?
- Are there any very small (2–4 people) or very large teams (25+)?
- How many locations do the team operate from?
- Are all tasks performed in all locations? Do they need to be?
- Are roles that are co-dependent also co-located?
- Are there any orphaned teams?
- Are the roles aligned logically?
- Is there overlap between teams? Are the lines of demarcation clear?
- Are there support teams or do the team rely on pooled support resources?
- Can you envisage how the work flows across the team?
- Is there a dependency on other teams? How do they connect?

The structure chart will provide you more insights about the organisation and its culture than just a list of who's who on the team (Figure 11). The political games that can be reflected in structure charts are fascinating: using different fonts and bold case to imply seniority of one direct report in a team of peers, positioning boxes to be higher or bigger, not showing matrix reporting lines, not showing locations, not showing actual titles and grades, and showing a number of people in a single box. Fortunately, most people see through this and recognise it for the political skulduggery it is.

Structure Chart
Tips & Tricks

- Is there a stucture chart? ☐
- Is it readily available? ☐
- Is it current? ☐
- What format is it in? ☐
- Does it show: ☐
  - Names ☐
  - Job Titles ☐
  - Grades ☐
  - Location ☐
  - Role Type (Full Time v Part Time) ☐
  - Tenure Type (Permanent v Contract) ☐
  - Secondments ☐
  - Vacancies? ☐
- What is the span of control? ☐
- Are there any matrix reporting lines? ☐
- Is there any optical bias? ☐
  E.g. different colours, different box sizes, height placement, ect.

Figure 11 – Structure chart tips & tricks (see Appendix 3 for more detail).

This information should help you design the leadership roles—how many, where they're based and their overall responsibilities. With any luck, this may only lead to some tidying up (e.g., a leader may have too many direct reports or there may be a couple of very small teams that can be merged). How you implement these types of changes will be determined by local human resources practices, so you will need to discuss any prospective change with your human resources support partner.

Also pay particular attention to how you draft the position description and grade a role. Both can place overly burdensome constraints on how you run the team. They can limit flexibility and create unnecessary noise amongst team members. I've worked in organisations with over 16 different grades, and the difference between one grade and the next, particularly at middle and junior levels, was almost imperceptible. However, a different grade implied a different pay level and a promotion; hence, it was deemed to be material from the team member's perspective. This became an issue when there was an opportunity for a team member to gain new skills or experiences on a secondment. If the role was a slightly lower grade, they rarely took it, even if it would have rounded out their experience. Similarly, if there was an experience that would be useful for a team member at a slightly higher grade, they tended to ask for an increase in remuneration, even though it was administratively very challenging to process for only a short-term secondment. This organisation subsequently moved to four broad grades, and this increased flexibility dramatically.

The same goes for position descriptions. Where a position description is overly detailed, there are many occasions where the opportunity to lend and borrow staff to meet demand is constrained by an individual saying, "It's not in my position description." Clearly the position description needs to be detailed enough for the individual to understand what is expected of them but be careful about just how restrictive you make it in the context of flexing capacity. There will be more on this later in Chapter 7.

By the end of this review, you should have a to-do list of actions to create the right structure chart with the right roles. Remember, the intent is to minimise the changes while trying to avoid a full-scale restructure. You can "delegate" this task to the Change Team, who should have the right resources to help with such a complex task. It may mean you have to compromise, but—in my mind—it is far better than the alternative.

People review

The next step is to assess the current people in the roles. Once again, there are many questions to ask:

- Are all the roles filled?
- Are they filled with permanent staff or temporary/contractor staff?
- Are there people on secondments both seconded in and seconded out?
- Are there any long-term absences? When are they due to return?
- Are there part-time staff or staff working on flexitime?
- What is the diversity mix?

This will give you an overview of any gaps but will not help you understand the capability of the team. There are three matrixes I like to use when assessing skills and capability:

- Skills.
- Attitude v aptitude.
- Performance v potential.

It should go without saying that the information contained in these assessment tools is extremely sensitive. You must exercise extreme care when populating and using them. You should discuss the data and how you intend to use it with your human resource support partners <u>before</u> taking or communicating any specific course of action.

Skills matrix

A simple skills matrix is invaluable. You list the tasks along the top and the names of the team down the side, and then you assess each team member's ability to perform the task. You can score them out of 5, out of 10 or with Harvey Balls, just use the scoring system consistently.

Looking along a specific row will identify the skill level of a specific team member: their strengths, their gaps and the areas where they lack experience. This can then form the basis of their individual development plan (Figure 12).

| Name | Task (score out of 5) | | | | | |
	A	B	C	D	E	Total
Sarah	3	4	5	5		17
Sharon			5	3		8
Sridhar				1	2	3
Anurag	5		3			8
Mike	5		4	4		13
Helen	3			2	3	8
Total	16	4	17	15	7	

Figure 12 – Skills matrix.

Averaging and totalling a column will highlight those tasks where you have strength and depth and those areas where you are exposed. Any task that only one or two people can perform should be of concern. This is often the case with teams suffering the consequences of process proliferation. Many individuals have become extreme specialists and consequently a key person risk. If the tasks are not documented (which is usually the case and the reason for the section above), and you rely on one or two people to perform those tasks, what happens if they fall ill or leave? These SMEs are the very people that will be targeted by the digital transformation team. How will you cope without them?

A skills matrix will provide you with a great action plan for the short term: it will tell you who your "A" team is (or who should be), who needs to be developed and in what tasks, where the skills gaps are for the team, and the risks that need to be mitigated.

One of the limitations of the skills matrixes I've seen is that they tend to focus only on the technical skills or tasks. A champion team, however, is one that has depth and balance not only across the technical, but they also have the soft skills and other competencies required to build a winning team. Who is the innovator? Who always gets things done? Who keeps the team together? Who challenges the team? These are all roles that are vital to keep the team moving forward, and there is nothing stopping you from adding these into the skills matrix.

Attitude v aptitude matrix

Many organisations recognise that it's not just what you do but also how you do it. The attitude v aptitude matrix simply assesses team members based on their ability and their willingness to do the job (Figure 13). Current performance appraisals and feedback from peers, leaders and other stakeholders can be used as input to plot each team member on the matrix.

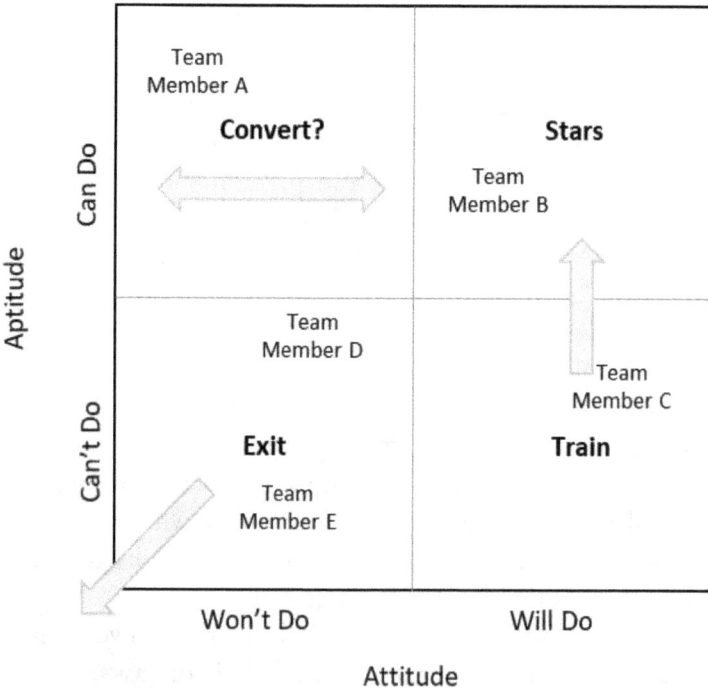

Figure 13 – Attitude v aptitude matrix.

Positioning individuals on the matrix then helps you identify a suitable action plan for each individual. For the "Stars", look for stretch opportunities. For "Train", focus on building core skills. For "Convert?", seek to understand and, if possible, address their behaviour. For "Exit", work with your human resources partner to develop a suitable plan to remove the individual from the team.

Performance v potential

A matrix that is particularly suited to assessing capability is the performance v potential matrix. In simple terms, it compares an individual's current level of on-the-job performance with their future potential (Figure 14). Succession plans are a particularly useful input, as they give an indication of the level of role the individual is being considered for and the time frame to get there. Add to this data from the most recent performance reviews, individual development plans, and feedback from peers, leaders and other stakeholders, and you have the basis for a powerful assessment tool.

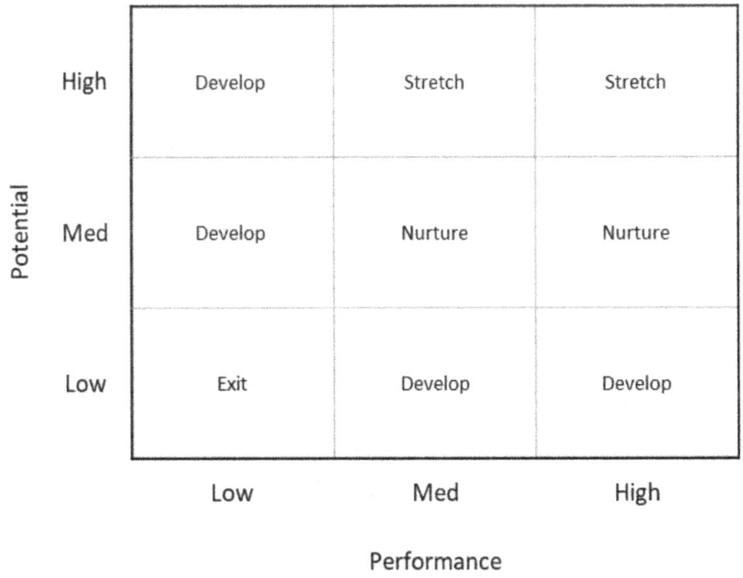

Potential	Low	Med	High
High	Develop	Stretch	Stretch
Med	Develop	Nurture	Nurture
Low	Exit	Develop	Develop

Performance

Figure 14 – Performance v potential matrix.

By positioning each member of the team on the matrix, you can implement an appropriate plan and view the overall capability of the team. For a mature team, you would expect most people to be in the "Nurture" category, with one or two people in each of the other categories.

Bringing all this together, you are now able to complete the initial assessment. For each individual, there are three options:

- Retain.
- Watch.
- Exit.

Needless to say, this is both difficult to do and very sensitive. This type of assessment has far-reaching consequences for each individual, and the information should be secure and only discussed with your line manager and human resources support partner before acting.

Bringing the reviews together

The final stage in ensuring you have the right people in the right roles is to bring the two reviews together. For each role, you must determine the right course of action. Please refer to the decision tree in Figure 15.

There is one more thing you must do before hitting the recruit button and that is to understand the short- and long-term outlook. The outlook matrix is particularly useful (Figure 16). I will cover the outlook calculation referred to in Chapter 7. In the interim, the matrix should guide your decision on whether to recruit, and if so, whether they should be permanent or contractor resources.

Bearing this in mind, the last step to getting the right people into the right roles is to execute your action plan—both in terms of the structure and the people. You may need to be patient. The benefit of not going through a restructure is that you will avoid a lot of unnecessary disruption, but the time frame may stretch out as individual action points are worked through (e.g., to allow the continued assessment of those on the watch list). It may take time to merge roles or to free up space to create new roles. It's also important not to waste an opportunity. If a team member leaves, think very clearly about what you want to do with the vacancy and refer to your original plan.

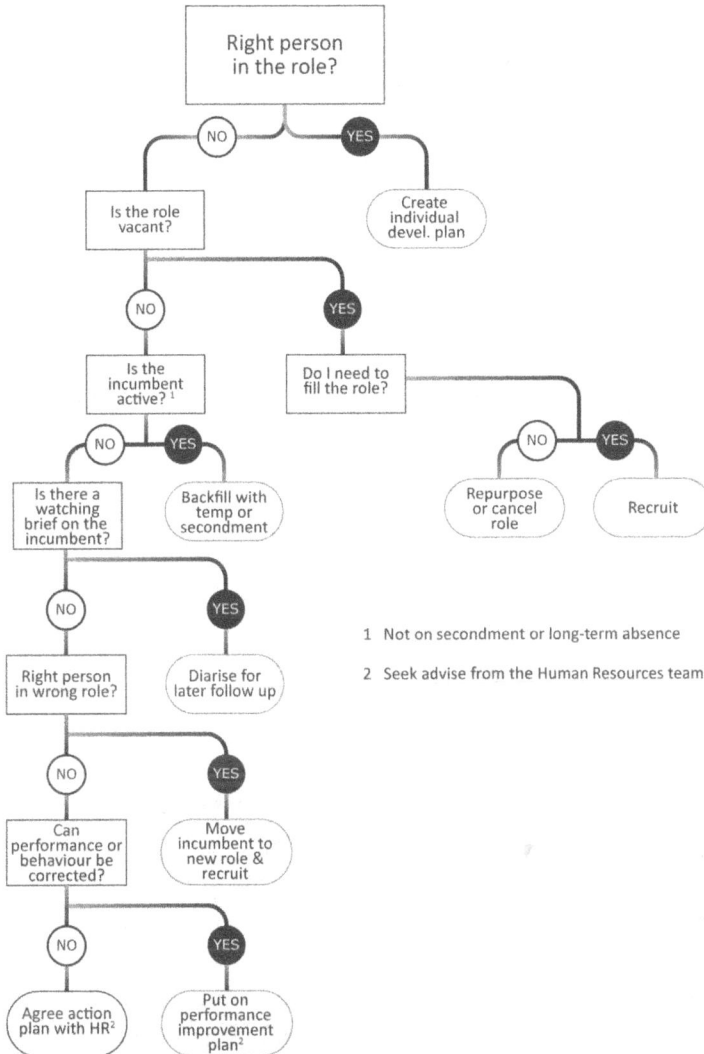

Figure 15 – Right people in right roles decision tree.

While the intent is to avoid a restructure, it may be unavoidable. You need to work very closely with your human resources team to determine what you can do as incremental change and what will require a more formal approach.

Either way, you will need to publish a new structure chart. No matter how transparent and fair the process, a new chart will throw up dozens of questions. Prepare carefully, have your written FAQs well

Short-term Outlook

		Poor (<1)	Normal (=~1)	Good (>1)
Long-term Outlook	**Poor (<1)**	Lay off staff	Delay any action X-Training	Overtime Borrow Hire temporary staff
	Normal (=~1)	Short-term secondments Leave management X-Training Projects	Do nothing	Overtime Borrow Hire temporary staff
	Good (>1)	Short-term secondments Leave management X-Training Projects	Hire Staff Automate Outsource	Hire staff Automate Outsource

$$\text{Outlook} = \frac{\text{Forecast Demand}}{\text{Forecast Capacity}}$$

Figure 16 – Outlook matrix (Slack, et al., 2015).

thought through and ensure the channels of communication are both open and accessible.

Once developed, reviewing and maintaining a current, accurate structure chart, which takes the above points into consideration and is visible to all, is a great way to build trust and stay on top of your resource position. In my experience, leaders that are reluctant to share their structure charts typically have something to hide, which in fact everybody knows or suspects, and this undermines everyone's trust.

As with the "Getting the environment right" section, reviewing the structure will create a lengthy to-do list. These types of issues may seem trivial for busy leaders with a focus on the future, but if you don't address them, the underlying issues will fester and undermine your ability to get the team Match Fit.

Finally, given the sensitivity around the topics discussed here, attention to detail is of paramount importance:

- The information must be kept safe—password protected, only printed using a secure print process and hard copies locked away.
- Work closely with your human resources support partner, and do not announce any changes without getting their input first.
- Ensure everyone that is impacted is on the distribution list. Pay particular attention to those on secondment and long-term absence.
- If there is a negative impact for anyone, they must be informed before any public announcement and be clear about their options.

Remember: the key question for most people is, "Can I see my name in a box?", which is shortly followed by, "Which box am I in?"

Managing individual differences

With the right people in the right roles, one of the great delights of leading teams is managing individual differences. Very early in my career, I was fortunate enough to work for a leader who understood this. Within 12 months, she managed to turn one of the worst-performing teams into an award-winning team. While there were many secrets to her success, at the top of the list, in my opinion, was her ability to adapt her approach to get the best out of each individual—and a mixed bunch it was, too.

Why is it that some days a staff member will handle 20 enquiries, the next day, 22 and the day after, 15? Understanding what makes an individual tick, their life outside of work, what energises them, their goals and aspirations and what you can do to help them is one of the many benefits of leading a team. For the Run Team to meet their objectives of freeing up capacity, the onus is on the leader to help everyone be as productive as possible. Given the individual differences at play, there is not a "one size fits all" approach. It is important that the leader understands the drivers of individual productivity:

- **Aptitude** – Does the individual have the skills and abilities to perform the task competently?
- **Motivation** – Is the individual motivated to perform the task to the best of their ability?
- **Opportunity** – Does the individual have enough work to do that is challenging but within their aptitude level?

With aptitude, there is no excuse for not training your people, as I will discuss in Chapter 6. Motivation can obviously play a major role in an individual's performance. This is why it is so important to spend time with your team and really get to know them. Active listening, empathy and compassion go a long way. The team must meet its goals, but a supportive culture, which recognises there is life outside of work and that occasionally it gets in the way (e.g., leaving early to collect a sick child) will pay off in the long run. Supporting a team member through a difficult situation will create social capital, and staff will go the extra mile.

Of the three factors, opportunity is the one that tends to drive the variability in productivity. I will deal with how to address this in Chapter 7. For the rest of this section, it's important to visualise how variability impacts team performance.

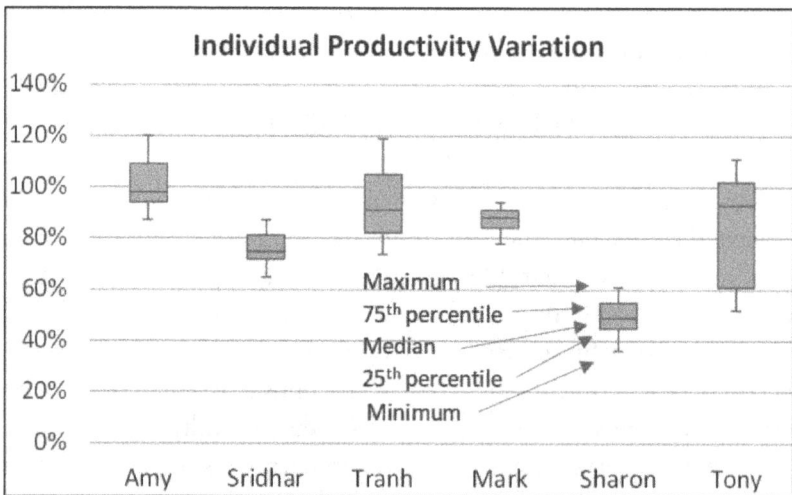

Figure 17 – Box plot of individual daily productivity.

A box-plot chart is an ideal tool for visualising what is happening. Use the last 30 days of individual productivity data as a minimum (90 days would be better), and calculate the minimum, 25th percentile[3], median, 75th percentile and maximum for each team member (see Appendix 1 Calculating Percentiles if you're not familiar with how percentiles are calculated). The shaded part that corresponds to each team member is where they typically operate. The ideal picture is a narrow range between maximum and minimum and the box positioned towards the top of the chart. In the example shown in Figure 17, Amy appears to be the better performer, but Mark is far more consistent. Sharon is either relatively new and still learning, or she is performing well below expectations. Tony is a tricky one. He is clearly capable of performing on a par with the best members on the team, but there are far too many days when his performance is amongst the lowest. Why is this? You will need to talk to Tony to dig a little deeper.

This type of chart prompts some critical questions for actively managing individual performance:

- Who are the stars, and what can they share to help others who are struggling?
- Why does an individual vary from one day to the next?

People do not have dials on their forehead that will calibrate how fast they work. The only way to answer these questions is to talk to the team. Communication "in the moment" helps the team recognise that this is important, and the immediate feedback reduces the risk of forgetting any mitigating circumstances. A low productivity day may have been caused by exceptionally challenging cases that day. There may be a personal issue that the leader needs to be aware of and acknowledge. The key here is to turn this into a positive coaching opportunity and not make people feel that they are being micro-managed. All we can ask of an individual is that they do the best they possibly can and remember that a champion team requires diversity. Not everyone will be a productivity gun. In the example above, Sridhar may be steady in terms of productivity, but if he is the go-to technical guru

---

3. Appendix 1 provides an overview of how to calculate percentiles.

that everyone seeks out for advice, the whole team's productivity may fall without him!

As surprising as it may sound, the most common reason for an individual's productivity dipping is there isn't enough work for them to do. Commonly, when you bump into team members that you haven't seen for a while and ask how they are going, "Busy" is the response. Yet, when you track what gets done you find that in times of crisis, such as a business continuity event, the team manage to do significantly more work than normal. This is Parkinson's law in action, where work expands to fill the time available. If there isn't enough work, it is a very misguided view to "give the team a rest". Use it or lose it. There are so many other things team members could be doing:

- Helping another team.
- Working on a stretch opportunity.
- Working on their individual development plan.
- Completing some training.
- Working on continuous improvement initiatives.
- Acting as a buddy to a struggling team member.

It is the leader's responsibility to make sure they understand what every team member has to offer and how the team can get the most value out of each individual—especially when volumes are below expectation. It's not enough to find something to keep the team busy. It must add value. The leader must keep an ongoing list of non-critical but value-adding activities that can be accessed at short notice. If your systems go down, what happens at your workplace? Do the team sit around chatting? Go for coffee? A Match Fit team would immediately look for the list and start working on it until the systems came back up again.

Running a champion team is a lot more complicated than just having adequate coverage on a skills matrix. It requires underlying competencies, including problem solving, communication and collaboration. There are other elements, such as the different personality types and behavioural patterns, which bring a champion team to life. A balanced team of creative people, SMEs, great communicators, planners, researchers and completers really sets the scene for building a high-performing team. Add to this diversity: diversity of gender, ethnicity, thinking style and personality, and you really are setting the team up for success in this challenging environment.

I have never seen a team's performance deteriorate by extending the level of diversity. In fact, the worst performing teams I have seen are those where the leader has recruited a team of clones or promoted a technical specialist without people leadership skills into a people leadership position. Yes, they may have the technical skills and the credibility that goes with it, but without the aptitude and training, they will not make good leaders.

One final note on this topic: I have never filled a role with an individual that ticks all the boxes in the job description. At the same time, everyone I have recruited has brought something to the team that wasn't in the job description that proved to be invaluable. This might be a specialist skill or even a personal passion (e.g., photographers and social media aficionados are great at publishing team newsletters).

Chapter summary

The aim of this chapter was to focus on getting the Run Team ready to take on the Match Fit initiative. The core components are to ensure that everyone on the team knows everyone else, that all the hygiene factors that eat away at people if they are not in place are addressed and that the team are organised appropriately to meet the challenge.

It is ironic how often the blatantly obvious is only obvious to those who know about it. Unfortunately, as career paths accelerate and management 101 is considered to be a relic of the past, many leaders are not aware of these issues. They can make or break an initiative. If that initiative is as emotive, pervasive and challenging as a digital transformation, you cannot afford to have anything detract from its likelihood of success. A disgruntled Run Team will undoubtedly have a negative impact on the likelihood of success.

For a high-level, visionary leader, these aspects can seem to be trivial, frustrating, bureaucratic, clutter issues that are not worthy of the leader's time. But if the role of the leader is to ensure the team are fit to play and play to win, players need to be physically and psychologically fit. A player with a voice in their head telling them they are being unfairly treated is not a player you want to have on the field.

Getting the right people into the right roles is critical. Restructuring is a drain on resources and a huge distraction. Don't shy away from restructures but acknowledge their impact. Work closely with human resources to do as much as possible without restructuring, recognising that it may take some time to get the "dream team" in place. Also be aware that this is highly sensitive and confidential information and should be handled carefully.

Finally, with the right people in the right roles, one of the great joys of leading teams is helping individuals achieve their goals and aspirations. There isn't a one-size-fits-all approach, and individual differences must be acknowledged and worked with. When you analyse individual productivity, in most cases, you will find that insufficient work drives the variability. Each leader must have a list of value-adding, non-time-critical activities that the team can turn to when there isn't enough core work to do.

Checklist:

Checklist Item	Status
Do you know your entire team, and do they know each other?	❏
Do you know the level of trust in your team and do you have a plan to enhance it?	❏
Have you addressed all hygiene factors on your team?	❏
Have you identified the roles and skills required, designed an appropriate structure, assessed the current capability of your team and made a plan to address any gaps?	❏
Does each individual on your team have a plan showing them how they can enhance the team's success?	❏

Chapter 4

League Ladders and the Trophy Room – Getting the Scorecard Right

> "Would you tell me, please, which way I ought to go from here?"
> "That depends a good deal on where you want to get to."
> "I don't much care where."
> "Then it doesn't matter which way you go."
> — *Lewis Carroll, Alice in Wonderland*

Not so long ago, if you went to a sporting event, all you would see was the score and the clock. Now there are statistics for pretty much everything: time in the opponent's half, shots on goal, passes, missed tackles, scrums won, contested marks, hit outs, service speed, break points converted, aces and second service points, win percentage, etc. Behind the scenes, the coaches will be aggregating and analysing the relevant statistics to understand past performance and what changes should be made to improve future performance.

But the statistics you see on the screen are only the tip of the iceberg. For all the data captured about an individual player's on-field performance, there is even more at the organic level, such as the player's body fat percentage, calorific intake, VO2 max, lactate thresholds and recovery rates. Data is captured about specific events, playing conditions, stadiums, weather patterns and relative performance. Statistics are gathered about competitors, commercial deals, transfer markets, agents, sporting goods suppliers, technology innovation, etc. Some of this is public information, but much of it is not. Making sense of this by translating the data into information that can be applied to improving performance is extremely complex.

All these sources of data are like listening posts. No single data source will provide you with precisely what you need. Collectively, however, if you filter out the noise, the various listening posts can be used to tell a story of what has happened, why it's happened and provide enough insight to develop a range of hypotheses and options about the future.

Any performance-tracking capability must:

1. Link what the team do on a day-to-day basis to the underlying strategy.
2. Link what each individual does to the overall performance of the team.
3. Make performance visible, current and actionable.

If you want to get Match Fit, you need to know what questions to ask, where to find the answers, how to present the information and what to watch out for.

What to ask

The first step is to understand what questions you need to ask as a Run Team leader. I've always found it useful to break this down into chunks and ask a series of questions. Taken together, you get a view of how the team operates overall and you can drill down on each chunk as you establish yourself on the team or as particular hot spots arise. The questions I ask are:

- **Corporate context** (largely covered in Chapter 2)
  - What is our purpose?
  - What are our goals and objectives?
  - What is our strategy?
  - What are our priorities?
- **Customer**
  - Who are our customers?
  - What products and services do we provide to these customers?

- ○ What are the customer journeys for each of these products and services?
- ○ What do they value about these products and services?
- **Process**
  - ○ What processes are required to deliver these customer journeys?
  - ○ What tools and technologies are required to execute these processes?
- **Ecosystems, networks and partners**
  - ○ Which partners help us deliver these processes?
  - ○ How do they add value?
- **Capacity**
  - ○ How many work requests do we get, and when do we get them?
  - ○ Do we have enough resources to fulfil these requests?
- **People**
  - ○ What type of skills do we need to fulfil these service requests?
  - ○ How are the people organised?
  - ○ How are they recognised and rewarded?
- **Performance**
  - ○ How is performance measured and reported?
- **Risk**
  - ○ What can go wrong?
  - ○ What plans are in place to prevent it going wrong?
  - ○ What plans are in place to recover if it does go wrong?
- **Innovation and improvement**
  - ○ How are new ideas generated, prioritised and implemented?
  - ○ How is change managed?

Your team operates in its own microclimate. Answering the questions above will help you understand that microclimate. As with any system, it is all connected; therefore, if the elements in the system are not perfectly aligned, then the system will produce different results. At the heart of customer satisfaction and operational excellence is stability and consistency of output. This means fulfilling the service request, precisely as specified, each time and on time, at a price that reflects value for money in the eyes of the customer.

To reduce variability and create consistency is very much the "Holy Grail" of operational excellence. A system that is not perfectly balanced will allow variation to creep in and create poor outcomes for customers. The chunks—or categories—identified above are a useful frame for all operational decision making. Doing this as a team exercise is a very good way of getting alignment and links into the context setting from Chapter 2.

Whenever you have an important business decision to make, you and your team can quickly scan each decision against the frame: "If we proceed with option A, is it on strategy? What will it mean for our customers? How will it impact our processes and technology? What will it mean for our ecosystem, network and partners? How will it affect our capacity? What will be the impact on our people? How will it impact performance? What will it do to our risk profile? How will it impact our innovation and change program?" Great leaders can do this naturally and in real time.

With a digital transformation, you will need to ask these questions repeatedly and for each component. The transformation will create substantial shocks to the system—the rate at which change will be introduced, the potential quality impact of a "minimum viable product" and "fail-fast" mind-set, parts of the organisation adopting different ways of working—all of these will disrupt the performance of the processes your team manage. The listening posts are the sensors that tell you whether your system is operating within specification.

Where to find the answers – critical listening posts

In a work context, I find it useful to think of the range of data sources that are available as listening posts to you as a team and as a leader. There are many different types: some subjective, some objective, some structured, some unstructured, some periodical, some in real time, some numerical, some text-based, some descriptive, some predictive and some prescriptive. All data types will give you some indication of how your team are performing; the trick is to interpret it and know what it's telling you.

Typical listening posts at work might include:

- Routine management reports (e.g., expense reports, sales reports, customer satisfaction reports and customer complaint reports).
- Dashboards and performance reports.
- Project portfolio and status reports.
- External reports such as analyst reviews, external audit reports, benchmarking reviews and consulting white papers.
- Strategic reviews: purpose, strategy on a page, operating model on a page, strategy maps, market research, analyst reports and consulting reports.
- Presentations on many different subjects (e.g., surveys, questionnaires and focus groups).
- Individual conversations across a range of stakeholders from your team, peers, customers, business partners, suppliers, regulators, etc.
- Finally, there are the reports you can commission yourself, from simple online surveys to more detailed consulting reports.

It would be nice if these reports all came neatly bound and consistently formatted in a single pack—filtered for just what you were looking for. Typically, you must hunt the relevant reports down and can expect inconsistent formats, time frames and structures, which will require some forensic activity to pull it all together into a cohesive whole. The levels and reporting periods will be inconsistent, and the comparators will be different. For example, some reports will be based on the calendar year, others on the financial year, the teams and business units referred to may no longer exist, or the numbers will not match between different reports. The time taken to gather data and the quality of what you get is a great indication of the maturity, complexity and culture of an organisation.

Building an analytics capability is frequently cited as one of the intended outcomes of a digital transformation—a capability to find patterns in big data, social media and transactional systems. Typically, this requires specialised software with complex algorithms, drawing heavily on statistics and operational research techniques to improve decision making.

You, like leaders in many organisations, may not have this type of analytics capability, but you must set up an interim performance tracking system. You simply cannot run your team without facts and data. While it may not be as sophisticated as is possible, you will be able to create something that is fit for purpose.

Despite the complications outlined above, I've rarely struggled to find the information I need to run a team. It may not be precisely what I'm looking for and may not be 100% complete, but it will be a reasonable proxy. More often than not, the problem is that there's just so much of it, so how do you amplify the signal and filter out the noise?

A word of caution: I've met many managers who, when asked for data, respond that it is not available. This is unlikely to be the case, and it's probably more a question of effort. For some managers, a lack of data is a positive—it makes it far harder to hold them accountable!

What to measure?

One obvious question is, "What to measure?" In any team, there are standard metrics that should always be there (e.g., volumes, service, quality, productivity and costs). But each team will have unique aspects that reflect the underlying strategy. I tend to think in terms of operational and strategic dashboards. The strategic dashboard communicates the story of the strategy and whether the various initiatives are having the intended effect. The operational dashboard is more focussed on the core metrics that tell the story of current performance.

Strategic metrics

Strategy maps are useful inputs to determining what strategic metrics you should track. A strategy map is great for showing the cause-and-effect relationships or logic chain that will lead to the overall desired outcome. Based on Kaplan & Norton's Balanced Scorecard (Figure 18), by clarifying how the organisation will be different in the future from four different perspectives (financial, customer, internal business processes, learning and growth), if it achieves its strategic ambitions, the organisation's goals and objectives become clearer. This in turn makes it easier to identify the right metrics to measure progress against the objectives. Essentially, each shape on the map represents an objective, and for each objective there must be a metric that highlights progress. Translating the metrics into a dashboard, an informed bystander should be able to look at the dashboard and describe the strategy.

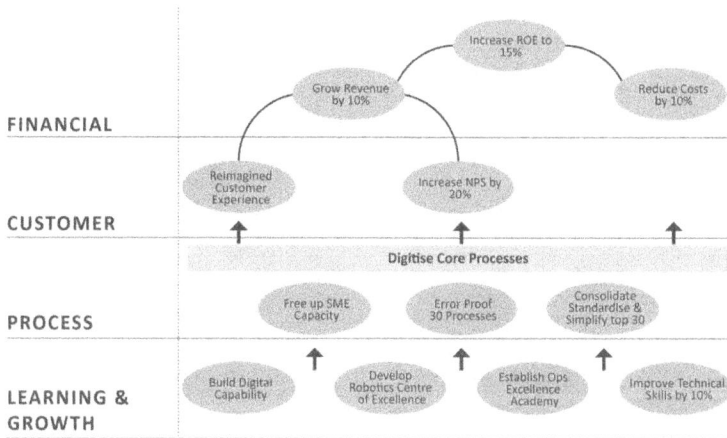

Figure 18 – Strategy map example.

Given that this is a strategic dashboard, besides the metrics, I also like to see the list of initiatives that are supposed to be driving the change in the metrics and the current status of the projects. This should include the current stage and typical project reporting data, such as timeliness, cost and scope. Then you have cause-and-effect line of sight. If the metric is not moving in the right direction, is that because the initiatives intended to "move the dial" are off track? If not, are the assumptions around cause and effect incorrect, or is another driver counterbalancing the effect?

Operational metrics

With operational metrics, the focus is on ensuring the system is in control and that everything is working the way it is intended to work. Unfortunately, it's not as simple as saying you just need one dashboard. The dashboard will vary depending on the time frame, and you need to cover real time, daily, weekly, monthly, quarterly and longer term. For each time period's dashboard, the metrics seen in Figure 19 are a good place to start and Appendix 5 provides a broader range to consider.

Core Metrics	Real Time	Intraday	Daily	Weekly	Monthly	Quarterly	Annually
Volumes (In/Out/WIP)	✓	✓	✓	✓	✓	✓	✓
Quality		✓	✓	✓	✓	✓	✓
Service		✓	✓	✓	✓	✓	✓
Productivity/efficiency[1]			✓	✓	✓	✓	✓
Utilisation			✓	✓	✓	✓	✓
# FTEs				✓	✓	✓	✓
Costs					✓	✓	✓
Risk	✓	✓	✓	✓	✓	✓	✓
Staff engagement[2]	✓	✓	✓	✓	✓	✓	✓

1. Technically two different metrics – the former measuring output relative to input and the latter output relative to a standard. The terms are sometimes used interchangeably.
2. This is typically measured in an annual survey, but it's important to find a proxy measure to track on a more regular basis. This can be a continuous pulse check survey or a simple daily check-in

Figure 19 – Core operational metrics.

The precise definition of each metric will vary by team. For example, quality may be measured as defects per million opportunities (DPMO) for one team and the number of items reworked for another. As long as the definition is understood by the team, is clearly relevant to the customer and is a reflection of how the customer perceives quality, the actual metric used doesn't really matter.

In terms of the reporting frequency, the following should be considered:

- **Real time** – This is usually reserved for things that go wrong: system fails, a large proportion of the team are absent, an unexpected influx of service requests, an environmental issue, a flood or storm preventing people from getting into work, a power outage, etc. When these events hit, every second counts; hence, the most important task is to make sure you have a clear line of sight of the work in progress and an escalation path to ensure the appropriate level of seniority is brought to bear. This means that everyone on the team knows what constitutes a critical event when they see it and who to tell. Ideally, this is picked up through digital monitoring from a command centre and escalated via push notifications, but if that's not in place, you must have a manual process to ensure the right people get to know. The exact path and how far up the hierarchy it is escalated will depend on the criticality of the processes impacted and the nature of the event. This must be pre-documented, with prearranged scenarios, as there is no time to argue about who to tell in what circumstances when an event hits!

- **Throughout the day** – On a daily basis, it is really a question of answering a single question: "Is my team in control?" This means that, at any point throughout the day, you are confident that you will get to the end of the day having fulfilled all your customer obligations. To do this, you should be able to answer the following questions within 30 seconds:
  - Are my volumes (volumes in and volumes out) in line with expectations?
  - Are my systems working as expected?
  - Is my quality as expected?
  - Are my team meeting service level expectations?
  - Are my team members available as expected?
  - Are my facilities operating in line with expectations?
  - Are my suppliers operating as expected?

  As you will no doubt have noticed, all the statements refer to being "aligned to expectations". Within the day, it's unrealistic to take a poorly performing system and expect it to achieve miracles. If everything is working as expected, then there's no need for a heroic, knee-jerk reaction. Just keep following your daily plan—the key to success is active management. If the systems are running at 95% when that is their level of availability most days, there's no need to panic or do anything unusual on any specific day—just execute the plan. If this level is unacceptable, then set up a project to address it. A control chart will guide you here (see Figure 20).

- **Daily** – The end of the day gives you a chance to reset. Reviewing performance and then feeding this into tomorrow's plan by communicating it in the daily morning huddle is critical to control output from the team.

  One of my favourite anecdotes when explaining what's required on a daily basis happened within a few days of taking over a new team. I asked the manager of the payments team how many payments the team had processed yesterday. The answer he gave was, "All of them!" Had he been right, I would possibly have been less exasperated. A question starting with "How many...?" must have a number in the answer!

- **Weekly** – Similarly, at the end of the week, it's time to reflect on what's gone well and what you must do better to prepare for the following week. It's also time to review metrics that are not as critical on a daily basis, such as Full Time Equivalents (FTE) counts.
- **Monthly** – The monthly report is typically a relatively comprehensive view that introduces data captured less frequently, such as financial information, and it provides more detailed customer and people information, as well as project reporting.
- **Other and ad hoc** – Reports tabled quarterly, biannually or annually tend to be an aggregate of the monthly report. There are occasional metrics added that are captured less frequently (e.g., the annual employee survey results). More and more organisations are recognising that key metrics such as employee engagement should be captured far more frequently, which obviously reduces the number of annual metrics. There are also ad hoc reports, such as reviews or assessments (e.g., operational audits that are tabled as one-off documents).

One point to bear in mind here concerns definitions. It should be clear that we are looking for:

- Something that gives an indication of how much we had to do and did do (e.g., volumes and throughput).
- The cost of doing that work (e.g., productivity).
- The customer impact (e.g., customer satisfaction and service levels).
- The quality of the work. This is called out separately to customer impact as it will impact both the customer and the amount of work and rework to do
- The staff available to do the work, as this will be a good proxy for the health of the team.

Getting the design right

Creating a good operational dashboard is very much a skill. Of the many hundreds of examples that I have seen, it is rare for them to hit the nail on the head. Some of the more common pitfalls are covered later in the chapter, but in the first instance it's important to understand what "good" looks like and what the dashboard should include.

Many large organisations have dedicated specialists to pull these together, but they tend to have lengthy backlogs of requests, and you may not always be high up the priority list, which may mean you need to build your own.

Before you start, it's a good idea to get to grips with some of the more common aspects. *The Multidimensional Manager* (Connelly, et al., 1999) is 20 years old, but it gives a very good explanation of some of the basics. It really helps to understand a little about the dashboard production process, data dimensions, hierarchies, data types, roll-ups, drill-down paths, etc., but it's probably beyond the scope of this book.

With that in mind, trying to monitor every element of the system every minute of the day would be a Herculean task. In a digital world, it is particularly tempting to want to have everything in real time. This creates clutter, but fortunately it's not required, as many aspects of the system don't change frequently (e.g., the strategy (hopefully!) and customer segments). However, there are some aspects that do change frequently and need to be monitored closely and in a timely manner.

The most important point to remember when designing a dashboard is that it is a communication and decision-making tool. It's not wallpaper, it's not a prop to stabilise a wobbly desk, it's not something to keep the new hire busy and it's not something to bring out for senior executive visits to highlight that your team are particularly important. A good dashboard should tell the story of your team: what's just happened, what's happening now and what's about to happen. It should inform the leaders of the team, help them make decisions and be visible to all, because if you hide your performance, don't expect the team to help you achieve your goals. It should be consistent, current and persistent. If you change the metrics every couple of months so that you only show, by chance, those metrics that cast the team in a good light, your chicanery will eventually be revealed to your team, your peers and ultimately, your managers.

With that said, the elements of good, basic dashboard design are fairly straightforward:

- Keep it simple.
- Trends matter.
- Less is more.
- Keep it current.
- Keep it visible.
- Focus on exception handling.
- Use targets and tolerances.
- Use performance icons.
- Think carefully about how to set targets.
- Use standard definitions.
- Make sure the metrics are actionable.

These are all covered in more detail in Appendix 4. The acid test is the team using the dashboard for decision making, and to do this they need to be involved in the design process.

Building the baseline

It would be nice if all of this was available on your smartphone and desktop in real time and you could collaborate dynamically by sharing dashboards and commenting on them with your team. Organisations have made great inroads in terms of developing performance management systems. Building an analytics capability is seen as a critical goal for the digital transformation. Unfortunately, many service organisations have a long way to go with regards to operational dashboards. This doesn't let you off the hook. You must have a performance management system, and if you must build one in Excel and have team members populate it manually, so be it. It's too critical to put it in the too-hard basket.

The most critical aspect is how you present the data. This is very much a case of "less is more". Your team operates as a system; its performance will vary every day. What we are interested in is if the degree of variation is relatively normal or unusual. Have we done something either consciously (e.g., an outcome for a project), or has something else happened (e.g., an influx of new hires to change the performance of the system)?

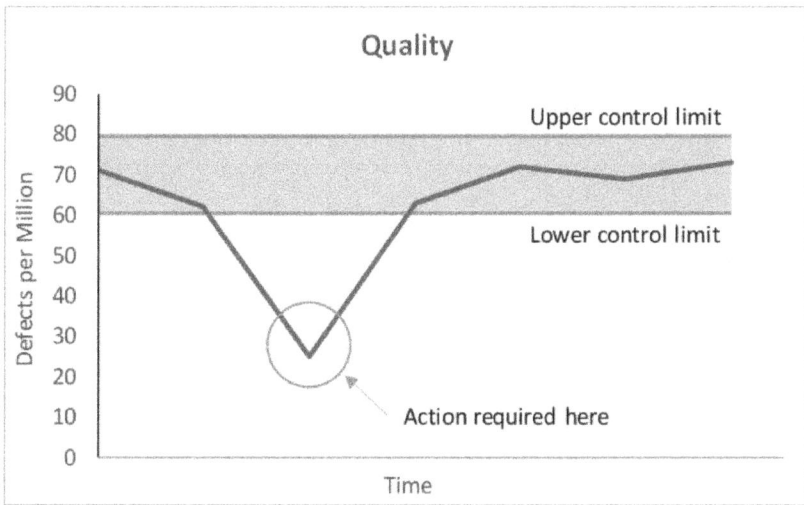

Figure 20 – Control charts example.

We need to measure the performance over time. Charting the performance of any process will "wobble around" over time. This is normal and not a reason to worry or chase rabbits down the rabbit hole. It's only when it's an unusually large "wobble" that we need to act. Plotting the performance on a line chart with a +/– tolerance range, an appropriate label and a scale is all we need (Figure 20). If the line wobbles around within the control limits, no action is required. If it spikes above the upper control limit or drops below the lower control limit, you must act. Over time, reducing the spread between the upper and lower control limits is a task for ongoing improvement efforts and an indication of process that is more tightly controlled. Where metrics have targets, the target should also be plotted.

It can be a difficult, trying and time-consuming process to source data, arrange data extracts, and scrub and filter the data. If you must develop a dashboard from scratch, don't wait until you have gathered all the data elements. Source what you can quickly and start using it immediately with gaps tagged as "Under Construction" for missing charts and data. Put someone's name to it and a target date for completion, and you will have your dashboard built in no time. The effort is worth it. Without a scorecard and dashboard, you will have no idea whether you are on track to deliver your objectives. A well-designed dashboard should make this patently obvious (Figure 21).

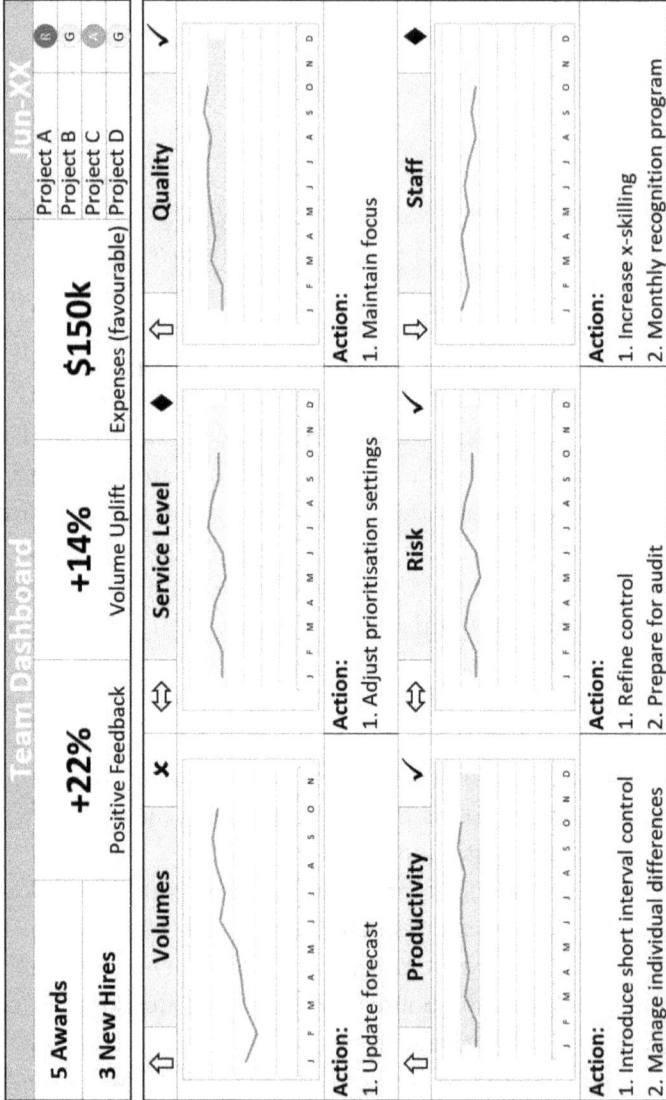

Figure 21 – Sample dashboard.

Individual performance metrics

Having figured out what you need to measure at a team level, you must cascade the relevant metrics down to each individual team member. These key performance indicators (KPIs) substantiate what is expected of the team. If each team member meets their targets, then the team should achieve its targets. There is no point in setting a quality improvement objective of 10% at a team level and 5% at a team member level unless you have some other intervention planned that will make up the difference.

Measuring and managing individual performance is quite a contentious topic. Many organisations have tried a balanced scorecard approach, some have tried the forced ranking approach, some have applied the "bell" curve, some try "league ladders", some assess both the "what" and the "how", and others have done away with measuring individual performance at the frontline. For some organisations, it is a continuous process; for others, it's an annual event. The relative success will depend on how the approach is implemented. I've seen leaders implement "league ladders" and face a staff revolt because they saw it as a means to "name and shame". I've seen team members in supportive cultures ask for "league ladders" to be implemented because they saw it as a way of getting help when they were struggling. So there is no perfect solution. What's more, it's highly likely that the methodology will be set by human resources, so it may not be possible to change the overall approach. However, in my opinion, these are the key factors to consider:

- Individual KPIs must reflect the team's goals, both in definition and relative to the target.
- Less is more: for more junior staff, no more than 4–6 KPIs.
- KPIs should be balanced (e.g., financial, customer, process and learning, and growth).
- Equal weight should be given to individual and team performance (e.g., half of the assessment is based on how the team performed and half on how the individual performed to drive collaborative behaviour).
- Peers should be able to provide input into who they think is the "Most Valuable Player" on the team. It is not always the same player as the one the leader picks.

- Targets should be discussed in detail with the team prior to committing.
- Team members must understand how the KPIs will be calculated and be able to track their own progress.
- If there are categories of performance—for example, "poor", "good", "strong", "outstanding"—the thresholds for each must be objective and clear.
- The "how" is just as important as the "what", so examples of what constitutes "good" in terms of how someone has gone about their performance should be shared to help understanding.
- Fact-based performance conversations are more likely to impact performance than simply setting a target in a scorecard.
- Performance management is a continuous process—the team member should not be surprised by the outcome at the end of the year.

One final word on individual metrics for leaders: don't move the goal posts. Agreeing with a team member that they must get 8 out of 10 to get a bonus and then halfway through the year changing the target to 9 out of 10 is a fundamental breach of trust.

Tips, tricks and red flags

The quote popularised by Mark Twain, "Facts are stubborn things, but statistics are pliable," should serve as a warning. The objective of any dashboard or performance management system is to provide the facts and data to help you make decisions. Given the sheer volume of data, filtering the data and then presenting it to focus on the most salient aspects of the system is critical.

In doing so, it is very easy to manipulate the story and, as the primary owner or user of the performance management system, there are a few things you need to watch out for (see Appendix 6 for more detail and examples):

- Is it a credible data source?
- One period of data does not constitute a trend.

- Are your metrics watermelons (red on the inside, green on the outside) or avocados (green all the way through)?
- Have you read the scale on the chart?
- Beware messy charts—what are they trying to hide?
- Is there evidence of bias (e.g., only reporting the better performing teams)?
- What's been omitted?
- Be careful how you interpret percentages.
- Are you comparing apples with oranges?
- Is it tracking green because it's just been re-baselined?
- Do the metrics reflect what needs to be measured or what can be measured?

Assuming you've avoided these traps, the most important tips are consistency, transparency, credibility and currency. Don't change the metrics willy-nilly; make sure they are available for all to see, are taken from a credible source and are up to date. They should reflect your operating reality, and if you don't like the story they are telling, at least you can find the root cause and take corrective action. But don't hide from poor performance. One hallmark of an authentic leader for me is someone who can stand up in front of the team and acknowledge that things aren't going the way they had hoped, but this is what they are going to do about it.

Being able to compare performance with others is always useful, and benchmarking exercises make sense if comparing apples with apples. However, I've found that in practical terms, it is very hard to benchmark with peers. Invariably, processes and teams are organised differently and it's very difficult to get the right level of alignment other than at a very high level. What is more practical is to compare similar teams within the same organisation (e.g., comparing the organisation's service team in one country with that of another). This is a great way to find improvement opportunities.

Given the breadth of the topic, it's hard to provide a comprehensive summary of what to watch out for when you lead a team, but there are some useful indicators I've seen that warrant further investigation. Some of these are metrics derived from reports and some from events. It's important to remember it is a relative term, so you will need to find another team or area to compare your team to. For example, a 15% staff turnover rate may be low in a contact centre in the Philippines, but it is excessively high for a regional centre in the north of England, so make sure you're comparing apples with apples. Your peers are probably the best reference point. So, in no particular order, here are red flags that you can spot in your metrics and management reports:

- **Absenteeism** – Is it high relative to peer groups?
- **Staff turnover** – Is it high relative to peer groups?
- **Overtime** – Is it over budget?
- **Budget shortfall** – Is it significantly greater than that of your peers?
- **Poor service levels and backlogs** – Is this just a point in time or a deteriorating trend?
- **Complaints** – Are they above normal levels and deteriorating?
- **Customer defections** – Is there clear evidence of this, and if so, is the situation deteriorating?
- **Operational losses** – Are they significantly above budget?
- **System stability** – Is the system stability/availability markedly lower than other systems?
- **Rework and poor quality** – Are there dedicated teams to address rework (e.g., remediation teams and fix-up teams)?
- **No metrics** – If there are no operational metrics, poor performance will almost be guaranteed.
- **Span of control** – Are there leaders with more than 15–20 direct reports?
- **Adverse audit findings** – Are internal audit ratings worse than those of your peers?
- **People issues** (e.g., bullying and harassment) – Are there any human resources cases under investigation? Is it a one-off or is there a history?
- **Outside intervention** – Has there been a whistle-blower event? Are regulators or emergency services engaged with the team?
- **Projects** – Are there any off-track projects where the benefits have been "locked in" for your team?
- **Your diary** – Who's requesting your time? Is it frontline staff raising concerns over performance?
- **Policy changes** – Have there been sudden budget cuts, travel bans, etc.?

- **Authority events** – Are you "caught in the middle" between senior stakeholders with conflicting priorities?

Unfortunately, these red flags tend to sneak up on you and rarely appear in isolation. To paraphrase the work by Heskett, et al., 2008 in *The Service Profit Chain*: "Happy staff equals happy customers equals happy shareholders", and if you want happy staff, then you must focus on quality.

A typical scenario would be a poor work environment (it may be driven by systems instability, poor leadership or a poor culture, not enough staff, poor resources, etc.), which leads to high absenteeism and staff turnover. This in turn leads to work not getting completed on time and backlogs.

Customers then complain and staff are expected to work overtime to address the complaints and reduce the backlogs. This places further stress on the system, impacting staff morale, which leads to errors and operational losses, more complaints, customer defections, higher absenteeism and staff turnover. It is a veritable vicious cycle.

Another example is where you have two line managers and one of them wants you to enforce one policy and the other wants you to enforce a contradictory policy. Or a powerful project sponsor is determined the project will go live on schedule, even though it is still riddled with defects that will impact the customer and the workload of your team. The minute you recognise these issues you must address them immediately. They rarely go away of their own accord.

Chapter summary

This chapter introduced the need to establish a performance monitoring system and the importance of listening posts. Covering the questions to ask, what to prioritise and where to get the data; the topic is broader than just a dashboard.

Given the volume of data, you need to be clear about what questions you want to answer and what you need to know and when. You also need to recognise that some performance indicators are operational in nature and will always be required, irrespective of the environment. Others are change-related and only have value for as long as it takes to implement the change and see the benefits materialise as expected. Understanding the basic process of how analysis works will help you to figure out how to set up your system.

Designing a performance management system is full of traps for new players, but by following some basic principles, you can be up and running relatively quickly; however, it may take a while to fully populate your dashboards.

Your performance monitoring system is there to help you make decisions. Unfortunately, it's very easy to manipulate the data and present a story that reflects an alternate reality. Being aware of these tricks will help avoid being misguided.

For the team to perform, the team members must perform. Developing individual KPIs can be contentious, but done well, they play a critical role in driving team performance.

Finally, there are also many red flag events that can spiral out of control quickly. These events are significant stress inducers and must be dealt with as a matter of urgency. It doesn't matter how well your team has performed to date, the overall performance will be characterised by either an avoidance of red flag events or how well you manage them.

Checklist:

Checklist Item	Status
Do your team know the key questions to ask to help them understand what's important?	❑
Do your team know the listening posts and data sources that will help them find the answers?	❑
Do your team know the specific strategic and operational metrics required to manage their performance?	❑
Do your team understand the design of each dashboard in use for the different periods of time?	❑
Do your team know the baseline for each of the metrics?	❑
Do your team know which metrics are cascaded down to each individual?	❑
Have you checked the reporting for any design flaws that may impact interpretation of your team's performance and for any red flag indicators present?	❑

Chapter 5

Know the Rules. Read the Game – Understanding Customer Quality

"It is not enough to do your best; you must know what to do, and then do your best." — *W. Edwards Deming*

One critical task during the pre-season is to work through the rule changes. Throughout the season, governing bodies are looking at ways to make the game safer, more entertaining for fans and easier to referee. Knowing how the changes will affect the flow of the game, how the rules will be interpreted by the opposition, umpires and referees, and learning how to adapt is critical to gaining a performance edge.

Listening to the commentary of any major team-based sport, you will invariably hear the commentator mention a player who "reads the game so well". This is someone who can anticipate what will happen next, where he/she needs to be positioned, how to be at the right place at the right time and conserve energy getting there. This is someone who seems to know what the opposition will do even before they do.

It is the same with service. Understanding how services work, how customers define and perceive quality in advance and the options available to leverage this is critical to becoming Match Fit.

The ubiquity of process

Everything we do is a process. From getting up in the morning, showering, having breakfast, brushing our teeth and getting to work, let alone everything we do at work. In simple terms, a process is a series of actions and steps that transform inputs into outputs. To deliver consistency for the customer, we need to design a process in such a way that if we always use the same inputs and follow the same steps, the output will be identical.

If you think about baking a cake, the inputs are the ingredients and the other resources, such as an oven, utensils, bowls, etc. The process is the method: mix the butter and sugar; add the eggs, flour and fruit; scoop the mixture into the baking tin and place in an oven set to 160° C for four hours, remove and allow to cool. If you use the same ingredients, the same equipment/utensils and the same oven set at the same temperature for the same time, the cake should turn out identical every time.

We may expect some variation the next time—maybe the eggs are a little fresher, the ambient temperature at which you mixed the ingredients was slightly higher, you didn't cream the butter for quite as long, or you got caught on the phone and left it five minutes longer than usual. So at a high level, the output is identical, but when you dig into the detail, there will be small variations—every time! That's normal. What's not normal is if you forget an ingredient, add two cups of flour instead of one, or fall asleep and leave the cake in for an extra hour. Then the result will be very different!

And so it is with business processes. Every time a process runs, if you use the same inputs and follow the same steps, the output will be basically the same with minor variations. Change the inputs or the steps, and who knows what you will get. Throughout the book so far, I have stated that if our objective is to satisfy customers, then this needs to be underpinned by consistency. There's no point in delighting a customer one day and then utterly failing to deliver the same service the next day.

This is what makes services so hard—there is inherent variability in the inputs and a degree of variation in the steps. It's not like in a manufacturing business where the specification of inputs and the calibration of machines make it far easier to get a standard output. For the most part, in services you are dealing with people—both your own team and the customer—and they all play a critical role in the delivery process. It may be tricky, but the more consistent you are at meeting customer expectations, the more satisfied your customers will be.

Easier said than done. Unfortunately, there are lots of things that get in the way of delivering services consistently:

- Trying to understand what "good" looks like, and then to measure it, is a challenge.
- Making sure you have the same inputs and that everyone follows the same steps is practically impossible when there are so many steps, systems, handoffs, decisions to make and variants of the process.
- If this isn't hard enough, we're not trying to solve this for just one process; in most mature organisations, there are tens, if not hundreds of thousands of processes.

The problem with service quality

If your objective is to meet customer expectations consistently, then you need to define those expectations—that is, define what "good" looks like and create a specification for your team to follow. Customers are typically satisfied when their perception of the service they've received matches or exceeds their expectations of the service. Knowing this is important, as it creates options to manage customer expectations and adapt delivery of the service in a way that keeps both aligned. But one of the challenges with quality, particularly in a service context, is defining it. Beauty really is in the eye of the beholder, and every customer will define it differently. What's worse is those expectations will change based on their prior experience of the service, their current mood and what they've heard about your organisation. For example, if a customer submits a service request during a very busy period, it may take four days to get a response. Their expectation the next time they submit a service request is that it will probably take four days, even though the team's objective is to resolve the request the same day, and most of the time that is what they do.

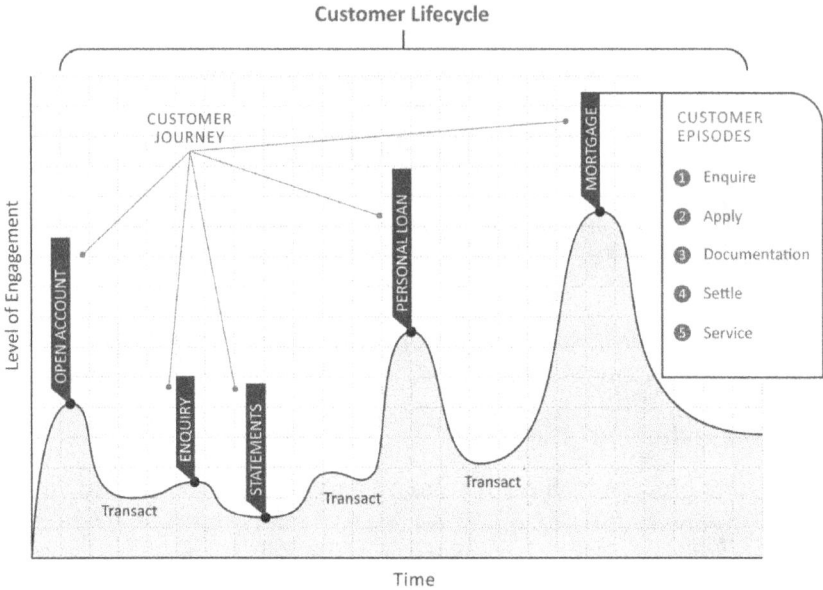

Figure 22 –Customer lifecycle, journey and episode example.

To understand this further, it's useful to recognise three points:

- Customers may stay with the same service provider for many years. Their level of activity will ebb and flow. For example, a bank customer may open their first savings account as a teenager and transact. They may go overseas, and the account lies dormant. When they return, they may take out a personal loan to buy a car and a few years later look to secure a mortgage for a house. The customer's perception of the bank is constantly adjusting. During the more intense episodes (e.g., taking out the personal loan and the mortgage), the level of engagement is far higher, but that doesn't mean that during the more subdued times the customer is immune to changes in satisfaction (e.g., a payment systems outage resulting in the customer being stranded in the supermarket unable to pay for groceries will have a major impact on their satisfaction—particularly if it is a relatively frequent event). This is where customer lifecycles, journeys and episodes are useful (Figure 22).
- The service quality that the customer perceives is typically a function of the service outcome received and the experience the

customer went through to get that outcome. If both the outcome and the experience are in line with the customer's expectations, then you will typically have a satisfied customer.

• Customers are constantly evaluating the reality of what they are experiencing and what they expected to experience. Prior experience informs current expectations (Figure 23). If their perception of the service is greater than expected, they will be delighted, and vice versa. When the next interaction occurs, their prior experience will play a major role in setting their expectations for what's to come.

Figure 23 – Customer expectations v perception over the customer lifecycle (Johnston et al., 2012).

As an example, many years ago I took my car for a routine service. The garage informed me they would call if there were any major issues, otherwise it would be ready for collection at 4:30 p.m. and the cost would be $200. I arrived at 4:30 p.m., the car had been serviced according to the service handbook and they charged me $200. Was I a happy customer? No, because when I arrived at 4:30 p.m., there was no one at reception and the radio was on so loud in the garage that they couldn't hear me. It was a 40° C day, there was no water in the water cooler and when I sat down on the sofa, I got oil on my suit. So while the outcome was precisely what I expected, the experience I went through to get the outcome was dreadful; hence, one unhappy customer.

The outcomes tend to be somewhat easier to measure, with most service businesses focussing on defects/errors and timeliness (i.e., was your service request fulfilled correctly within the time specified). The problem is with the experience part. Some customers may want to engage in small talk, while for others this is an irritant. Some customers may like the temperature to be warm, but others perhaps prefer it to be cool. Some customers may like to be walked through the process step by step, while others just want to get on with it. When the customer calls, walks in through the door or submits their request, how do you know what good service looks like for them?

Another issue that makes quality in services so difficult to manage is process complexity and the variations it creates. For a mature organisation, the processes tend to have evolved over time with no underlying design intent. A new system may be introduced that changes one part of the process, while another system changes a different part, but neither system talks to the other. The team doing the work is restructured and part of the work is outsourced, part is offshored, and the balance is split across multiple onshore centres.

New regulatory requirements must be designed into the process quickly to be compliant. New forms are introduced to capture more customer data for marketing. New clients want enhancements, new features are added, different pricing and fee structures are introduced that need to be accommodated, and team members with specialised knowledge leave. Every time this happens, the process is changed and evolves into something far more complex and fragmented. Under time pressure, it's nearly always quicker and cheaper to introduce a process variant, a work-around or a completely new process, even though 90% of it is the same as the parent process.

Let's go back to our cake example. Making sure the cake always tasted the same required us to have the same ingredients and equipment, plus we had to follow the same recipe. For a service process, this is very hard. In terms of the inputs: system latency may change the processing time, system outages create rework, staff experience and expertise vary, printers run low on toner, couriers get stuck in traffic, inaccurate and incomplete forms increase the chance of getting it wrong, and inadequately trained staff make mistakes. Just like with a recipe, the underlying complexity created by the number of steps, number of decisions, number of handoffs and number of systems virtually guarantees that a process will fail. It is miraculous that so many of them succeed at all. Watching a team member navigate multiple screens, cutting and pasting 10–15 applications, is a thing of wonder. Add to this the fact that it's highly unlikely that the processes are adequately documented, and if everyone follows their own process, with their own checklists, top tips and shortcuts, it is hardly surprising that the output is different every time.

Specifying outcomes and managing expectations

If satisfying customers is all about meeting expectations, then one way to meet them more consistently is to manage those expectations. We've already seen that complexity and variation in services make it very difficult to guarantee a consistent output, and customers' expectations will be different with every interaction, so being able to adjust expectations is a powerful way to keep customers satisfied. Customers expect services to fail now and again (not repeatedly!) Managing a service failure well has been shown to enhance customer loyalty. If there are backlogs, delays or any other service-related issues, communicating these to the customer is always a good thing. We've all experienced service staff wearing a badge with "Trainee" written on it to encourage customers to go easy with the new hire, or web banners that apologise for an outage and informing the customer when they should be able to log on again, or call centre recordings that let you know there is a queue but offering to call you back at a time of your choosing. This approach hands back control to the customer, and they are grateful for it—they can get on with their day. But it must be clear! If you are standing on a platform, waiting for a train that is running very late, there is nothing more frustrating than hearing an announcement about the service, but the actual message is inaudible.

The key to managing expectations is to know what your processes are capable of and being able to communicate these appropriately.

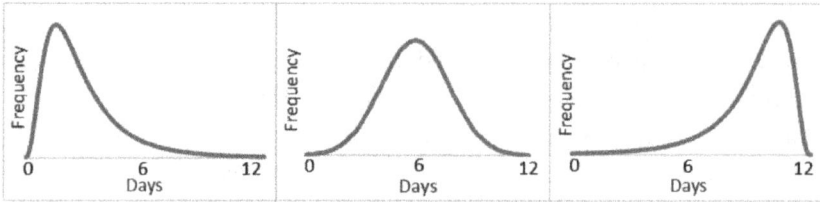

Figure 24 – What do you tell your customers?

To know what your process is capable of, you need to understand the range of outputs it delivers and the frequency for each output. If you put this on a chart, you will usually end up with something that looks like a bell curve or one of the other charts in Figure 24. The range between the two tails in the charts—anywhere between zero and eleven days—is what your customers should expect and what you should communicate to customers—you can chop off the end points, as these are unlikely. If you look at the range of possible times to complete a service in your system, you might be alarmed at the impact of variation. The greater your control of the inputs and the process, the narrower the range and the easier it is to explain to the customer.

One example I experienced is where a corporate client sent a file at the same time every day, early in the morning. Fulfilling the client request was dependent on an upstream process completing on time. Unfortunately, there was so much variability in the upstream processing time, the client's file frequently missed its deadline. Essentially, the business committed to deliver something that the process was never going to be able to deliver with confidence!

Some service organisations rely on service guarantees or customer charters to help manage customer expectations. They are useful to the extent that they reflect a clear commitment to the customer and help ensure staff know what they are accountable for, but they must be meaningful, easy to understand, unambiguous, explicit and unconditional, and they must set a clear payout expectation if the guarantee is invoked (Johnston, et al., 2012). Before embarking on a path of publishing service guarantees, it pays to understand what your processes are capable of and the cost of providing the guarantee.

Far more service businesses rely on an internal mechanism—service-level agreements (SLAs)—to specify what customers should expect, but in my experience, they are rarely based on the actual capability of the process. They tend to be either aspirational (e.g., zero defects) or low balling to ensure the team meet their targets. In fact, all SLAs are the "least acceptable" level of performance. They are designed as much to help the capacity management challenge that most service businesses face (more of this in Chapter 7) as they are to work to customer expectations. That doesn't mean they shouldn't be used. They are very important to set performance expectations of the team that can be communicated to customers, but you must be very careful about how the performance of the process is translated into something the customer can understand and will accept.

One other observation on SLAs is that teams often see them as an asymmetric target: if performance is within the SLA and is not breached, then performance is good. That is not always the case. Many years ago, I worked with a team responsible for installing merchant terminals, and they improved their installation time so dramatically that, in some cases, they could install the same day. However, in many cases, this was ahead of the customer—the customer may not have taken possession of the shop. A quality outcome is where you clearly specify the service expectation and stick to it. If you say you will respond within two hours, respond within two hours. If you try to respond in 30 minutes, it may be inconvenient for the customer.

Remember also that for most customers, their understanding of the service expectation will be based on prior experience. If you took two days last time, that is what they will expect this time. This is a particular problem where demand is very seasonal. The team will deliver service in a shorter time frame during the quiet periods and a longer time frame at peak periods. This is confusing and unacceptable. The team must learn to manage capacity to deliver service consistently (see Chapter 7).

All this is fine for the more tangible measures, such as outcomes, but it is more difficult for the experience component. Many service teams are quite removed from the customer, especially if they operate from offshore service centres. It is often difficult for the team to empathise with the customer. They may not have used the service themselves and, in their culture, the expected experience is completely different. This can lead to tense exchanges between onshore and offshore teams. Uplifting technical skills should be quite straightforward, but building the soft skills to enable empathy and bringing the customer experience to life for the service teams is far more difficult. Customer journeys, with their focus on the emotional expectations of the individual, are one way to do this. Regular focus groups to review customer calls, reviewing complaints, briefing sessions by account managers on larger corporate clients, and personas and avatars that bring the customer to life are all valid ways of helping the service teams understand the customer in more depth. One senior leader responsible for running a Bengaluru-based service centre filmed a property auction in Australia so that the team handling the processing of mortgage documents had a much better understanding of what customers were going through. I've even seen teams bring in mannequins dressed up to look like the type of customer using the service. If they needed to change something, they would walk over to the mannequins and ask, "What would Priya think?" (Priya was the name given to the mannequin.)

The other part to this is where staff are managing expectations with customers "in the moment". For service experience expectations, this can be very challenging. Training staff to actively listen with empathy, reassure the customer and deal effectively with the customer's concern requires skill. This is particularly the case when, behind the scenes, the staff member is trying to navigate many different systems to find the relevant customer details.

A great example I have of this was when dealing with a utility company. They had sent me two bills for different amounts. It was a Friday, and I'd had a bad day at work. When I went home, I decided to ring the contact centre to confront them about the organisation's incompetence and leave them in no doubt about how disappointed I was. The contact centre agent was so good at listening to my problem, diagnosing the situation, empathising with me, reassuring me that it wouldn't happen again (this was a big call and probably unachievable) and clarifying the steps they would take to address the situation, including giving me a discount, that it was impossible to express my dissatisfaction. Amazing service!

Measuring this emotional and experiential aspect of a service at a granular level is difficult. More to the point, customers do not dissect the service in this way; hence, many organisations have turned to the Net Promoter Score (NPS) system. By asking customers how likely, on a scale of 0–10, they are to recommend the organisation to others, and then subtracting the percentage of detractors (those rating the organisation between 0 and 6) from the promoters (those rating it between 9 and 10), they get a Net Promoter Score. A positive score is obviously a good thing. It also asks customers to elaborate on why they scored the way they did. This provides a clear feedback loop. The measurement system is simple for customers, and the feedback loop, when implemented well, is tight and allows issues identified by customers to be acted on quickly. While doing the detailed analysis is useful on an ad hoc basis (e.g., when designing a customer journey), in terms of providing continuous customer insight, the NPS approach is far more practical.

The cost of poor quality

As you can see from the preceding section, the complexity and variation make it extraordinarily hard to deliver consistency, and this lack of consistency translates directly into a cost of poor quality. This is a significant cost for an organisation. To figure out how you can tackle the cost of poor quality, it's important to understand what makes up those costs (Figure 25). They are typically broken down into four categories:

- **Prevention costs** – Process governance, simplification, managing expectations, process documentation, quality training, preventative maintenance, error proofing and effective risk management.
- **Appraisal costs** – Checking, quality control, sampling and audits.
- **Internal error costs** – Rework, backlogs, system downtime and system latency.
- **External error costs** – Complaints, remediation costs, operational losses and revenue leakage.

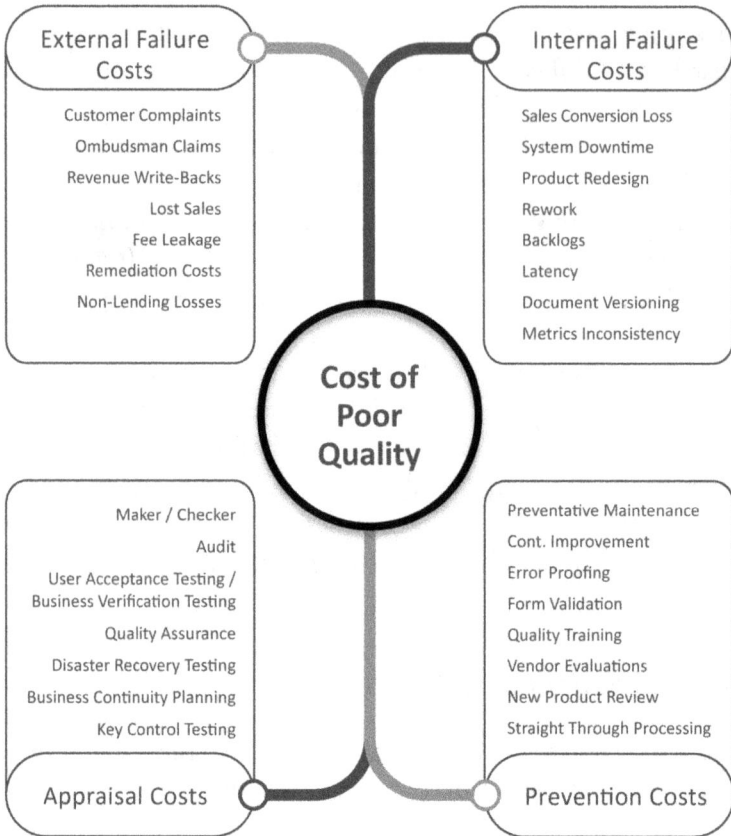

External Failure Costs

Customer Complaints
Ombudsman Claims
Revenue Write-Backs
Lost Sales
Fee Leakage
Remediation Costs
Non-Lending Losses

Internal Failure Costs

Sales Conversion Loss
System Downtime
Product Redesign
Rework
Backlogs
Latency
Document Versioning
Metrics Inconsistency

Cost of Poor Quality

Maker / Checker
Audit
User Acceptance Testing / Business Verification Testing
Quality Assurance
Disaster Recovery Testing
Business Continuity Planning
Key Control Testing

Preventative Maintenance
Cont. Improvement
Error Proofing
Form Validation
Quality Training
Vendor Evaluations
New Product Review
Straight Through Processing

Appraisal Costs

Prevention Costs

Figure 25 – The cost of poor quality categories and examples.

These are all costs borne directly by the organisation. There are also additional indirect costs, such as those borne by the customer, investors, suppliers and regulators.

Many organisations don't capture costs in this way and, even if they do, they do not connect them to the same root cause. Quantifying the costs in this way soon casts the problem in a whole new light. A typical organisation spends the most in appraisal costs and internal error costs. The natural tendency when something goes wrong is to introduce more controls, adding checkers to the checkers. What's worse, they tend to buffer up at the end of the process. This is typically a false economy. Processes with a "six-eye" or "eight-eye" check still fail. The more signatories a document requires, the more likely people are to rely on safety in numbers and not review the document thoroughly.

This paints an unattractive picture for a single process. For large, mature organisations, as they have evolved through mergers and acquisitions, product, channel and market expansion, technology change, and restructures, the number of processes has exploded. The quest for digital transformation and agility will be stymied by this process proliferation. The difficulty of controlling a process rises exponentially with the number of process inputs and steps to be controlled.

It is very hard to quantify the cost of this complexity and variation, but I feel confident that I could gather enough evidence and mount a credible claim in most mature organisations that it is at least 30–50% of the cost base.

Why is the cost so high? Every variant of a process must be documented, operationalised, coded in a system, tested, audited, reviewed, improved, learned and set up with a business continuity plan. The compounding effect is that the more variants there are, the longer the time to competency, and the more likely it is that team members will get confused and make mistakes. Process variants that are called on infrequently will be slow to execute, as the team try to remember how to operate the process and will undoubtedly make mistakes. How we deal with variation will be covered in subsequent chapters, but at this point it is enough to know you must root it out and eliminate it.

Cost of Poor Quality

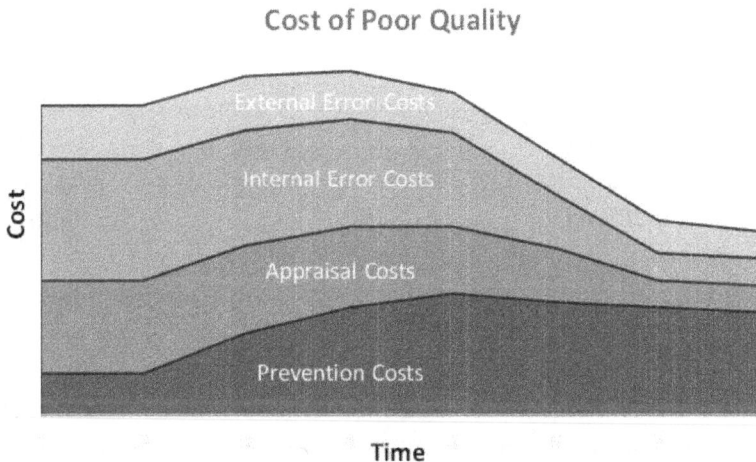

Figure 26 –Total cost of quality reduces when greater weight is given to preventative costs.

It's highly unlikely you will be able to make these costs go away, but the important point is to reweight the cost. Focussing more on prevention costs will lead to an overall reduction in the total cost of poor quality (Figure 26). It will also help drive consistency and improve customer satisfaction and employee engagement. The start point for the Service Profit Chain is a focus on internal quality.

The more effort you put into preventing the process from failing and designing out failure points, the better. Chapter 6 will focus on what you can do to reweigh your cost allocation towards preventative costs.

Chapter summary

To deliver consistent quality requires the skill of an orchestra conductor. There are so many elements that need to work in harmony, it's a wonder that the system works at all. The cost of poor quality in any large, mature organisation is significant but rarely calculated. Most of the effort goes into checking and fixing the mistakes. If more time and resources were spent on preventing failure, the total cost of quality would reduce substantially.

At the same time, this suggests that quality is an absolute, whereas in a service environment, there are both objective and subjective elements. Measuring the outcomes such as defects and timeliness is relatively straightforward. Measuring the experience element is very difficult, and the perception of quality in the eyes of the customer can be dependent on their mood and other aspects in their life, which have nothing to do with you or your organisation. Attempt to measure it we must, and in recent years, programs such as the Net Promoter Score have tried to synthesise all aspects of the service into a single metric. This, along with some additional digging, can provide the necessary insights for improvement.

The level of complexity introduced through natural evolution of a mature organisation, both at a process level and an organisation level, makes quality control a Herculean task. Delivering quality consistently may feel like an impossible task—an eminently visible but highly elusive goal. However, without quality, your customers will abandon you. In all but the most monopolistic of industries, there are now simply too many alternatives.

The cost of poor quality is significant. Reweighting spending towards preventing poor quality will, in the long term, reduce the overall cost of poor quality. As we will see in the next chapter, preventative techniques (organisational simplification excepted) are, for the most part, low cost, relatively quick to implement and can be managed with the resources to hand—your team.

Checklist:

Checklist Item	Status
Do your team understand that processes underpin everything they do and that customers expect consistency?	❏
Do your team know the customer journeys they support and how customers evaluate quality?	❏
Do your team know what outcomes and emotional experience your customers expect, how what they do affects the customer experience, and the impact of variability and how SLAs work to manage this?	❏
Do your team understand the cost of poor quality for the work they do?	❏

Chapter 6
Skills Clinic – Quality Essentials

"Quality is not an act, it is a habit." — Aristotle

A significant proportion of pre-season training is spent on basic skills training. Even elite athletes constantly repeat basic training—practicing and honing core skills until they are absolutely second nature. Visit any sports ground to watch a team in pre-season training, and you will witness the players repeating simple drills that they would have practiced since they were schoolchildren. Yes, they do more complex drills as well, but they still dedicate significant amounts of time to getting the basics right: passing, throwing, stopping, running and catching a ball, tackling and set plays to restart the game.

Day in and day out, they practice. The coaches will introduce variation to avoid boredom, they will provide formal training using whiteboards and pictures in a classroom, they will watch how other players perform the various skills and they will buddy up and practice with their teammates. They will find subtle nuances about how a ball moves in certain weather conditions, how pace changes based on the condition of the pitch and how the skill needs to be adapted reflecting the equipment of the day—for example, where to strike a ball to set it on the right trajectory depends on the make and model of the ball, etc.

This repetition—constantly challenging and experimenting with the technique under different conditions—is what will build subject matter expertise, quality and excellence. This level of training builds trust. When you know your peers know exactly what to do and how to do it, and they know you know what to do and how to do it, there is a solid foundation of trust. A chain is only as strong as its weakest link. Every member on the team needs to command the basics.

A relentless focus on quality, from front to back and top to bottom, is a hallmark of any world-class team. Why? Simply because the cost of poor quality is so great. In most organisations, it is hard to calculate it precisely. In world-class organisations, less than 15% of the time in system for a process is adding value to the customer—85% is an awful lot of waste! And that's for world-class organisations—I've seen processes where over 99.99% of the time in system is not adding value to the customer.

We know that an organisation undergoing a digital transformation will be stripped of resources, but the bar will be raised in terms of expectations. The Run Team will feel that they are up against the odds, uncertain of the future and under pressure to complete seemingly unrealistic workloads. Finding capacity is therefore critical for a Run Team to survive and thrive in this type of environment. The preceding chapters have covered what you need to do to get the foundations in place. Now it's time to find capacity. The first step to free up capacity is to focus on the preventative costs of poor quality. It requires an investment in governance, documentation, simplification, quality training and preventative maintenance. This will typically free up between 15 to 25% capacity, and quickly—within three to six months.

The need for governance

The first question to resolve is, "What do we want the team to do?" The preceding chapters will have given you a high-level answer. You'll know what your team's purpose is, you'll know broadly what the organisation expects of your team, the services they provide and the key processes the team are responsible for that will deliver these services (some services may only require a single process; others will require multiple processes to be aligned seamlessly to deliver the service). But this is high level. Processes never fail at the high level. It's the detail that matters.

Given the criticality of processes in satisfying customers, the demands they place on the resource and cost base of the organisation, and the frequency with which they fail, it's important to know who "owns" each process and what it means to own a process. For example, what decisions can the process owner make, who specifies what outputs are required or how the process should be designed, who sets the targets, who provides and funds the resources, who can change the process and who is accountable if things go wrong? For many service organisations, this is one of the most vexing issues. Customer journeys typically span multiple departments. Coordinating all processes required to deliver a single journey can be politically challenging. Success may have many fathers, but there are not as many for a process where investment funds are up for grabs or as few when a process fails and there is substantial financial and reputational damage to be covered.

What is required is clarity on what needs to get done and by whom. It doesn't mean you have to have a single point of accountability. Having more than one owner of a process is fine if there is a clear understanding of roles and responsibilities, the decision rights that flow from these responsibilities and how conflict will be resolved.

One other aspect of governance that is critical is for the process owner and senior leaders to go and see the process in action. In Lean terminology, this means going to "Gemba". As John Le Carré said, "A desk is a dangerous place from which to view the world." It doesn't matter how detailed and accurate the mapping and reporting, you must go and see it for yourself and talk to the people running it.

Establishing a robust process governance framework across a large, mature organisation can be a thankless task. Establishing the policies, guidelines and standards for how processes should be managed and changed across so many stakeholders can be very challenging. It can seem to be an exercise in senseless bureaucracy, interminable meetings and political infighting with all the usual organisational projections of power on display. This doesn't excuse you from making sure there is a named owner of the process your team manages. You don't have to fix this for the organisation, but you can't get Match Fit without at least clarifying ownership for the area of your responsibility.

Documentation

The start point for good documentation is to have a master list of the services offered and a list of the processes required to deliver the services. Once you know what processes your team needs to run, what outcomes are expected from them and who owns them, if we go back to our cake-baking analogy, the next step is to figure out what you need to do to make sure the cake comes out of the oven looking and tasting the same every time. As with baking, the first thing to do is to write down the ingredients (inputs) and the method (procedures/work instructions)—that is, document the process.

To some, documenting processes is seen as an organisational curse that is only good for cluttering up filing cabinets or acting as temporary doorstops. In an organisation with tens of thousands of processes, this may be like a Sisyphean task.

Good process documentation is not a set-and-forget exercise. If your objective is to provide consistent outcomes, then you must ensure that everyone follows the same process. Good documentation sets the standard for how everyone must perform the task at hand—one way, the same way. To do this, write down what you want your people to do and find a way to get your team to follow the guidelines. Getting the team to do this is usually an eye-opening experience. Team members may have been doing the same job for years, but it is highly unlikely each of them will do it the same way. They will have their own little shortcuts, checklists and knowledge blind spots. The mere act of bringing them together and getting them to work through the exercise will uplift quality.

This presents issues in both documenting the processes and getting people to follow the documentation. Many see process documentation as a disempowering inhibitor to their creative muse. Others recognise that it makes life far easier.

To understand the issue, it's important to know what process documentation entails. In its simplest form, all we are trying to do is communicate what needs to happen. There are different tools depending on what you are trying to communicate:

- **Customer journey maps** – These call out specific customer types and what they expect to happen for the service provided to be deemed a success. They are high level and refer to the range of processes required to deliver the service, but more importantly, they also refer to the emotion customers are expected to experience.
- **Process maps** – These are simple flowcharts showing the major steps and decision points in a process and who performs them.

They are great for providing a high-level overview of what the process is trying to achieve.

- **Value stream maps** – They are like process maps but with a focus on information, material flows and understanding the time in process and the waste in the system. They are a critical part of the Lean toolkit.
- **SIPOC diagrams** – SIPOC stands for Supplier-Input-Process-Output-Customer. The diagrams are intended to show what happens upstream and downstream of a process, what inputs the process requires for completion and what outputs it will deliver. They are perfect for providing a high-level view and summarising all the relevant elements of a process.
- **Work instructions** – These tend to be very detailed, step-by-step guides depicting how to complete a process.

All of these are relevant and have a place to give a new hire an overview of what the team do. However, a customer journey map, a SIPOC (which is typically a single page) and a process map are a good combination. The customer journey map highlights what the customer expects to experience. The SIPOC covers what inputs you get, from where, what you need to output and to whom. The process map shows how these inputs flow and convert into outputs across the various teams.

A good process map, with 6–10 boxes on a single page showing the order of the steps and who does them, is a very quick way of getting to grips with the work to be done. In short, it is a simple communication tool. Unfortunately, many people go down to such a level of detail that, even with 3-point font, it's impossible to get all the boxes on one page. Then there is the problem that the processes have so many variants that the team create a new map for each variant (i.e., creating hundreds of documents with 90% overlapping content).

The way round this is to use process maps as a high-level communication tool and then, depending on the nature of the task, draft appropriate work instructions to specify how the process needs to be performed. Some tasks in clerical/administrative teams will need detailed work instructions, and in some cases, at keystroke level (e.g., "Now press F9"). In that case, there is very limited discretion for the operator, and it is critical to quality that everyone follows precisely the same instructions. For other tasks that require more individual judgement (e.g., drafting a proposal, analysis of a new solution or developing an operating model), there still needs to be an agreed way to run the process. This may be something as simple as a style guideline and a template. You must document what needs to be done by the staff member in such a way that they will be able to perform the process and deliver consistent outcomes, assuming they follow the process.

If your team has hundreds or thousands of process variants, you need to document all that you perceive to have a material impact on your performance. If ever there was a case for process consolidation, this is it. We will discuss this in Chapter 10. In the meantime, if you don't write it down, share it with the team and explain why it is so important to follow the same process, it won't get done the way you want it to. It will lead to poor customer outcomes, expose you to unnecessary risk and your ability to improve will be impaired. It's far easier to improve one process than it is hundreds of processes.

One of the issues with process documentation is how to get an accurate view of the process. Ask the process owner to document it, and you will get one view. Ask the team that perform the process to document it, and you will get a different view. Ask different members of the team to document it independently, and you will get as many versions of the process as there are team members. It can be a significant workload, so judgement needs to be exercised about where you start and stop. Bringing the team together to agree on the best way to run a process is both great for team building and indispensable from a quality perspective.

Unfortunately, it's not a foolproof process. What people say they do in a classroom environment and what they actually do in the workplace can be two very different things. In recent years, addressing this issue with process mining software has taken off. Its unique proposition is that by extracting a subset of event time stamps and their identifiers from the systems used to manage a process, the software can essentially document the actual process followed by team members. It will show you what really happens—not what the team tell you they do. It will generate reports that allow you to follow individual cases and transactions through the process. It will highlight the rework loops, orphaned cases, bottlenecks, queues and time to complete. It can be quite a harrowing picture and a revelation for the team responsible.

Simplification

It should go without saying that a simple process is far less likely to fail than a complex one. In the preceding section on complexity, I stated that the five drivers of process complexity are the number of steps, handoffs, decisions, systems or applications required to run the process and variants of the main or parent process (Figure 27).

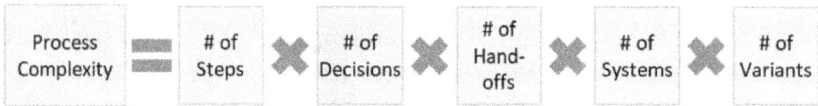

Figure 27 – Process complexity calculation.

By using a simple process map, you can put a number to this degree of complexity. Count the number of rectangles (the steps), the number of decisions (the diamonds), the handoffs (every time the flow crosses a "swim lane" from one person or team to another), how many different systems are required and how many variants of the parent process there are. Multiply these five numbers together to get a process complexity score. Intuitively, reducing the number of each of these factors makes the process less complex and less likely to fail. By working progressively through the process, trying to reduce each of the five factors, you can come up with a target level of complexity and the corresponding degree of simplification.

For example, if a process has ten steps, three decisions, four handoffs, requires knowledge of five systems and has three variants, then the complexity score is 1,800. If you could consolidate the variants to a single process, reduce the number of decisions to two with two handoffs and only eight steps, the revised complexity score is 160—a 90% reduction in complexity without changing the technology! This may sound incredible but take the example of the variants. In most cases, a variant is different by less than 10% from the parent process, so design the parent process to accommodate the variant (if you can't get rid of it altogether, which is quite possible when people understand the impact). You need to document fewer processes, your team need to learn fewer processes and there are fewer processes to audit.

Simplification is well within the capability of your team's own resources. Start with the list of services you provide and a customer journey map for each service. The customer journey will help you identify what customers value about the service; in short, what are they prepared to pay for? Once again, you will be surprised about how little of what you do is valued by the customer.

Once you know what the customer values, you create value stream maps of the processes required to deliver the service. As mentioned earlier, a value stream map is like a process map, but it is more detailed and has a specific focus on the information flows and the time to get the request through the system, backlogs and bottlenecks, and any constraints. For each step in the value stream map, you tag the step as either "customer value adding" (CVA), "business value adding" (BVA) or "non-value adding" (NVA). NVA steps are waste and can be eliminated. BVA steps are those required by some other function within the organisation (e.g., a compliance step). These should be challenged to verify they are really required. The objective of value stream mapping is to speed up the process by removing waste from the system.

Facilitating a value stream mapping session does require some specialist Lean expertise, but there are many practitioners available to help you get started, and it is a relatively quick and inexpensive exercise. A good, focussed session can typically be completed within a week on an end-to-end process, generating a raft of improvements that can be executed within a 30/60/90-day time frame or broken down into Agile sprints.

Given the amount of waste in the system, a series of these sessions will dramatically simplify what your team do and free up capacity. However, there is an even easier way to free up capacity, and that is to create a "stop doing" list. Ask the team to brainstorm and write down everything they do, and then go through the list and ask whether they really need to do those things. Is that report really required? Does that leader really need a hard-copy briefing pack and another member of the team to accompany them to the presentation? Do you really need two people checking?

One of my favourite examples was when a supplier was bundling and stapling documents before sending them to our team. The first task for our team was to remove the staples and then separate the bundles! There were thousands of original documents per day. Asking the supplier to stop stapling saved both parties a considerable sum of money.

At an organisational level, simplification follows a similar approach. Anything that reduces the number of channels, products, geographies, systems and divisions will make the business far simpler to run. These decisions are obviously far more structural and will require senior executive sponsorship.

All organisational dimensions play a major role in complexity. One worthy of note is the product dimension. "Products" in a service environment are very different to those that roll off a manufacturing production line. They are predominantly intangible. One of the consequences is that it is easy to create variants of them, which in turn leads to the design of a new process—for example, an insurance product that is only available through a mobile device. This may be thought of as a brand new product with unique terms and conditions, unique processes, unique documentation, etc., where the underlying product is practically identical to those sold through other channels. The issue here is more one of perceived complexity than real complexity. From a marketing perspective, when creating offers that are attractive to specific segments and subsegments, targeting ever-smaller slices of the market is critical. That doesn't mean to say the production process needs to be new. One way to radically simplify the number of products on offer is to think of them in a modular way—the way that manufacturers do. For example, when you buy a car, you are offered a limited range of options and extras. For each option there is a limited number of choices, e.g., two engine sizes, five colour options, two interior finishes. In this way you can design a small number of processes capable of handling the many and varied needs of customers.

This approach doesn't mean we're heading down an "any colour you like as long as its black" path. The key point is to understand what value customers place on variation and then to design the processes in such a way that they allow for value-adding variation for most customers. Every car that comes off a modern production line is different—the

MATCH FIT FOR TRANSFORMATION

accessories, upholstery, colour, engine size and transmission will be different. But no one asks for a chassis to be three centimetres longer or a change in the rubber compound used in engine hoses. If you ask for alternatives that are not on the brochure, the answer will almost certainly be "No", unless you are prepared to pay considerably more for the car.

Quality training

It's one thing to document and simplify processes; it's quite another to make sure the team know, understand and have the right competencies and aptitude to execute and adhere to them. Several years ago, as part of a study tour, I visited Disney University. There were many memorable moments, but one quote really stuck with me: "What's worse, train someone and they leave or not train someone and they stay?" There really is no excuse for not training your people. The start point is to make sure you have the work instructions documented. There are then two parallel activities:

1. Assess the current team's ability to perform the processes, tasks and their bench strength.
2. Put a plan in place to build bench strength.

The first activity has to do with the here and now. Are your current team fully trained? Do they have the required competencies? Where are the gaps? How critical are the gaps? How much risk are you carrying? What happens if a bout of illness or a flood of resignations flow through—can you cope? I have heard many senior executives say recruit for potential, attitude and fit; train the technical skills. In the short term, you will need to focus on the technical and skills training. Building bench strength, nurturing the talent you have and recruiting to lift the bar takes time, and we will cover that component in Part 3. In the meantime, you need to make sure you have a team in place that can get you to Part 3.

In Chapter 3, we covered the drivers of individual productivity. With aptitude, the responsibility of the leader is to ensure that every team member is trained to do their job. There are no excuses. The specific training can take many forms depending on the underlying culture. Using the skills matrix as the primary assessment tool, you can design a program that will address the gaps, both across the team and for each individual. A structured 70:20:10 approach may work well. For example, 10% classroom training, 20% coaching and then 70% on-the-job training with a buddy—a willing buddy who will be available to answer questions. Alternatively, business process guidance software that provides immediate answers to process-related questions with context-sensitive help is another approach. One team I knew had learning passports and received a stamp every time they mastered a new task. I've seen teams use daily quizzes in their morning huddles or vlogs and podcasts recorded by SMEs. Which method you choose is not really that important, just pick one the team are happy to support and work with and make sure you allocate time for them to develop their skills.

For anyone who has run a team suffering a high degree of staff attrition, they will know the impact staff turnover has on the team's performance: more mistakes, more errors, more rework, more complaints and lower productivity as new members work their way up the "experience curve". An experienced team that is motivated, enthusiastic and willing to learn is a great start for those leaders trying to build a champion team.

Effective risk management

The more observant of you will have noticed that many of the traditional techniques associated with risk management form part of the Appraisal Cost category (e.g., inspection, checking, audits, etc.). For me, operational excellence demands a more pro-active approach to risk management, which means rather than piling up control after control, checker after checker, processes are designed so that they cannot fail. What I would like is the maximum amount of control with the minimum number of controls. This is a very fundamental mind-set shift. Every control costs money to implement, operate and maintain, so creating the appropriate level of control within the team's risk appetite with the fewest controls makes perfect sense.

We'll cover the techniques to reduce the risk of failure in the next section. The start point, however, is to understand the key risks your processes pose in the first place and the underlying risk appetite for your team (this will usually be set for you at an organisational level). These are some of the more important points to bear in mind:

1. Understand how the processes can fail. The first step is identifying all the ways the processes you are responsible for can fail. For example, there may be environmental disruption, such as adverse weather events or natural disasters, strikes, economic shocks or electrical/facility outages. There may be technology issues—such as systems outages, denial of service (DOS) attacks, latency or product/service design flaws—and these can be particularly insidious in service businesses, as they may not be readily apparent. Other potential issues may impact suppliers, customers may make mistakes or your team members may make mistakes. This can be done at a business or team level, but for the most critical processes, you must complete a failure modes and effects analysis (FMEA).

2. Despite its grand title, an FMEA is relatively straightforward to do. It is, however, one of those things that when someone asks you to do it, you wonder what you did to upset them. It's a painful exercise to go through, but once you've completed it, you'll wonder why you had never done it before.

   For each step in the process, identify all possible ways that each step can fail— the failure mode. If this is not a very long list, send the team back to think again. Then for each failure mode allocate three scores (typically a 10-point scale). The first score is how likely the failure mode is to happen. The second score is the impact on the customer or business if it does. The third score is how likely the failure mode is to be detected— the less likely, the higher the score. You then multiply the three numbers together to get a risk priority number (RPN) and rank them from highest to lowest (i.e., the most concerning failure mode is at the top of the list with the highest RPN). For the most critical failure modes, you must then specify what you're going to do about it: design it out, mitigate it (contain the effect if it does fail) or accept it. Once completed, rescore based on the treatments identified and compare the two.

To do this well takes time, and you need the SMEs in the room, but you will benefit from materially de-risking your processes and gain significant insight into how those processes operate.

3. Armed with an FMEA and an understanding of the possible failure points, the next step is to design out the failure points where possible. There are a range of techniques under the headings of preventative maintenance, redundancy and error proofing in the next section.

4. There will be failure modes that cannot be designed out, and for these, the next step is to identify how the risk can be mitigated. There are a number of possible techniques, including prior event analysis in comparable teams or organisations, insurance, hedging, containment (where you stop the risk spreading by ring-fencing) or loss minimisation (where you close down a service as soon as an anomaly is spotted).

5. The final step is to ensure there are adequate recovery plans in place including a clear process and appropriate levels of governance (e.g., crisis committees to manage an event). The process must ensure an adequate scenario plan, a triage approach to identify the root cause of the problem as quickly as possible, a playbook of actions based on the nature of the scenario and a review and reflection step to update the plan for next time. Mean time to fail and mean time to recover are the critical metrics for determining how good the team are at managing these events.

It should come as no surprise that preventing the processes from failing in the first place is the preferred outcome. The next section covers the principal techniques to achieve this objective.

Preventative maintenance, redundancy and error proofing

Despite the challenges, there are many aspects of poor quality that you can address and address quickly with the resources to hand. We've already covered the importance of governance, simplification, documentation and training. Another approach is preventative maintenance.

This can include obvious things like making sure you stock a printer with paper every day, changing the toner once a week, etc., so that it doesn't fail at the critical deadline. Other examples include making sure you have service contracts in place for machinery or equipment, making sure the stationery cupboard is stocked, implementing Lean programs like 5S—everything in its place and a place for everything—so you don't lose things, setting a standard naming convention for files and folders, scheduling the renewal of digital certificates, backing up data, using share folders, keeping licences and software versions up to date, etc.

A second option is to create redundancy. This means there is a back-up capability in case the primary capability fails. For example, many service teams operate out of multiple sites in case one of them goes offline due to an adverse weather event, facilities outage, traffic disruption, etc. Many technology services have multiple communications lines in and out of data centres in case one gets accidently cut. The aim is to avoid a single point of failure. It is expensive, but for critical services, it is an important part of the overall design.

This means that processes must be capable of operating in both BAU and business continuity planning (BCP) mode. How they operate in each mode will be different. As part of your planning, you must create scenarios that identify the possible failure points that will trigger a BCP event and document how your processes will continue to operate. For each scenario, you must have a plan of what you will do, who will be responsible for doing it, how you will trigger the plan and how you will communicate. Most importantly, you must rehearse the plan on a regular basis.

Another option is error proofing. These techniques are simple ways to prevent a process from failing. They are relatively common in everyday life, from speed bumps on a road that force cars to slow down, to lights in airplane toilets that only come on when the door is locked to protect privacy.

It is an extraordinarily powerful way—and in most cases, a low-cost way—to improve quality. It can, however, be quite tricky to implement in a service environment. I tend to break the techniques down into four categories with detailed examples provided in Appendix 7:

1. **Desktop techniques** – Form validation, drop-down boxes, templates, spelling and grammar checks, dual-blind keying, structured forms, generic mailboxes and user access management.
2. **Documentation** – One-point lessons, tags, checklists and documentation types covered earlier in the chapter.
3. **Flow and queue management** – Colour coding, prioritisation, WIP windows, "pull" systems, short-interval control, visual control and single point of entry.
4. **Quality culture and other** – Ensuring everyone knows that quality is everyone's job, not passing on defective work, providing space, reducing clutter, clean and organised workplace, multisite operations and inbuilt redundancy.

All these techniques will help improve quality. However, there is one that is of particular importance in a service environment, and that is the use of checklists. The impact that checklists have had on both aviation and medical safety is extraordinary for something so simple (Gawande, 2010). While they are in common use in the service teams that I have been a part of, one observation is that individual team members have often had their own. This means people responsible for the same process have different checklists. This is both an opportunity to share best practice and an obvious risk that different team members are operating the same process in different ways.

One particularly powerful application of checklists is a daily control list—a simple list of all the tasks required and deadlines as part of the start-of-day, through-the-day and end-of-day procedures. The best example I've seen was a magnetic whiteboard with all the tasks listed in chronological order with a red button magnet placed next to each task. As the task was completed, the red magnet was swapped for a green one. Every hour a magnetic strip that acted as a ruler was moved down. The whiteboard was in the middle of the room and visible to everyone on the team. Any task above the ruler with a red button was a call to action—something had been missed.

The main point here is that prevention is better than cure. When a process fails, it is very, very rarely the fault of the individual operator. The design of the process is the real culprit. The people working in the process are the real knowledge workers; they have the imagination and the process understanding of what to fix and how to fix it. Management's role is to empower them to do so, create a safe environment for them to succeed and then get out of the way.

Chapter summary

Nothing bad will happen if you focus on quality. It is a virtuous circle. Good quality starts with good governance. This means that every process must have an owner and there must be an agreed approach to manage and maintain it.

At the heart of good process governance is documentation. There are a range of tools that can be applied to document processes depending on the circumstances. While it may seem quite bureaucratic, process documentation is not a compliance task. Good process documentation enables standardisation and drives process conformance. Without these two attributes, it is very hard to improve processes. The reason documentation may appear onerous is more due to process fragmentation. Consolidating and standardising process greatly reduces the documentation burden.

Good documentation establishes a platform for simplification. Process complexity is driven by the number of steps, number of handoffs, number of decisions, number of applications and number of variants of the process. Reducing these factors will simplify the relevant processes. This will lead to a reduction in risk, fewer errors, less rework and improved customer and staff satisfaction.

Needless to say, without training, any efforts at improving quality will likely fail. It is far easier to build skills and capability on simplified processes that are well-documented than thousands of poorly documented process fragments.

It should be clear by now that quality and effective risk management go hand in hand. Following on from the Cost of Poor Quality in the previous chapter, this chapter introduced a range of techniques to increase the focus on the Prevention Cost category. By using tools and techniques like FMEA, preventative maintenance, redundancy and error proofing, the Run Team will see a significant improvement in quality.

Checklist:

Checklist Item	Status
Do your team know which processes they are responsible for and who owns them?	❑
Do your team have access to adequate process documentation (SIPOC, process map and work instructions)?	❑
Have your team removed excess steps, decisions, handoffs, systems and process variants from your processes?	❑
Do your team have a skills matrix and a training plan for each individual in place?	❑
Do your team understand the key risks associated with the processes they are responsible for, have they completed an FMEA for each major process and have they developed a treatment plan for prioritised failure points?	❑
Have your team identified and implemented preventative maintenance and error-proofing options across major processes?	❑

Chapter 7
Picking the Team – Managing Capacity

"The future is already here—it's just not evenly distributed."
— *William Gibson*

A coach will say that the team comprise not just the players on the field but a whole squad. The depth of talent available is generally referred to as bench strength. Developing a strong bench is all about having the flexibility to pick the right team for the right match. Over the long term, it includes setting up schools' programs, supporting amateur clubs, establishing academies and scholarships. In the short term, it's about getting the right mix of specialists and utility players, buying new talent and strengthening the basics.

The reason for building this depth is the heavy toll that the physical demands of the season can take on your team. There will be periods when the team play twice in a week and other periods when they may not play for several weeks. Each competitor will be evaluated on their merits, and the team will be picked for the task at hand—the players best able to counter the competitor's strengths will be selected. This will change from game to game. The club also must deal with injuries and other absences. Some positions on the field are specialist positions, such as a goalkeeper in soccer or a prop in rugby, while others are more generalist in nature. Deciding how many goalkeepers or props to have, how to build flexibility amongst the generalists, identifying gaps and deciding whether to test other players or buy new talent are all part of the decision-making process. It's a process that is worked out in the off-season and pre-season and refined mid-season.

The skills matrix, which was discussed earlier, identified the skills required to run the processes that deliver the services that your customers request. It provided an assessment of the skills available on your team and revealed any gaps. This chapter focusses on making sure you have the right number of resources, with the right skills at the right time, to meet the demands of the day and deliver your services on time, every time. For a digital transformation, this is critical. You will have fewer resources but still be expected to deliver the same, if not higher, levels of service. It's highly likely that your most talented people will have been seconded on to the project, which then leaves you with skill gaps. Your team will feel under pressure with the potential threat of not having a role in the future, so you will need to create the time and space to reskill them.

Taking control

Most people have worked in a chaotic environment at some stage and will recognise how stressful it is. For a firefighter-turned-arsonist type of leader, this is perceived as an opportunity to shine. They imagine themselves as the heroic leader who arrives at the last minute to put out the fire, but this is not what great operational leadership looks like. Being in control reduces the stress on the team and ensures customers receive the service they expect, when they expect it.

What's required to get in control? You need to know how much work there is to do, when it needs to be done and then plan to have the right resources, with the right skills available, at the right time to do the work. If you can do that every day, every week and every month, you will not have backlogs, you will not miss your service levels, you will not have overtime and you will deliver your sales pipeline. However, this is another example of something that is far easier said than done. I frequently hear leaders ask:

1. My team do a variety of things, and they're all so specialised. How do I know how many people I need and how to fill the gaps?
2. Finance keep telling me I need to reduce my workforce, but I'm sure it will impact service levels if I do. How much capacity do I really need?
3. I don't see the point in forecasting; we never seem to get it right.

Why should I spend precious time trying to guess something I know won't be right?

4. Why is it that some days the team knocks their productivity targets out of the park and other days the game seems to be over almost before the day has started?

5. I was so sure we had enough hands on deck. Why do we still have a backlog?

6. Why can't I predict individual performance? Yesterday, Suzie and Karl beat the all-time productivity record, but today, they were my worst performers.

7. The team are now more efficient than ever, but for some reason we've got more people answering the same number of enquiries. How can that be?

Figuring out how to answer these questions will help you to free up the capacity you need so your team survives and thrives in a digital transformation. When your team are stressed and overworked, the last thing they need is to be given another task to do, but they need to get to grips with capacity management. It will free up capacity at a more material and faster rate than almost anything else the team can do.

In simple terms, capacity is how much work your team can do in normal operating conditions. Capacity management is about trying to balance how much work there is to do (demand) with how much work the team can do (capacity) and what to do when they don't balance. It's about planning for what you expect to happen and controlling what you do when the planning assumptions turn out to be wrong. For all its simplicity, there are several issues that make implementing effective capacity management tricky:

1. How you define and measure capacity is not always easy (e.g., if your team only handles enquiries, you could measure it as enquiries per day). But what do you do if the team handles enquiries and also assesses claims?

2. Measurement units for demand and capacity can be different (e.g., a sales forecast in dollars does not translate easily into how many people you need).

3. The levers you can pull for managing capacity will vary

depending on whether you're looking at the short, medium or long term.

4. There may be multiple resources that constrain your ability to do your job (e.g., you may have enough people but not enough desks for them).

5. Head count does not equal availability to handle customers' requests. There is also leakage (e.g., a person may be at work for eight hours, but after allowing for training, meetings, coaching, etc., they may only have time for six hours for customer work).

6. Capacity is really about output, but people are not machines. The output from an individual will vary depending on many factors, including the nature of the work for the day and their mood.

7. In services, we sometimes bend the rules when we're under pressure (e.g., it's more important to get the work out than doing all the checks).

8. At the heart of capacity management is an ability to predict future demand, and there are only two types of forecasts: lucky and wrong! These are covered in more detail in Appendix 8.

This may appear as challenging as trying to catch smoke, but I can say for certain you have more capacity than you think you have!

Capacity management approach

While the capacity management equation is relatively simple, coming up with the numbers is anything but because of the inherent variation on both sides. Trying to smooth out the peaks and troughs will make life a lot easier.

Some may struggle with this idea, but management accountants are truly blessed. One of their major tasks is month-end reporting, where there is a spike in workload around the end of the month and the first few days of the following month. The good news for these accountants is not only do they know it's coming, they know when it's coming—it happens every month, and funnily enough, at the same time every month. They may not be able to predict when the CFO will decide to change the format of the reports or embark on a restructure that requires a realignment of cost centres, but these are relatively rare events. Hence the demand pattern is well known, which makes the task of managing capacity relatively straightforward.

At the other end of the scale, consider those teams involved in settling foreign currency trades. Trying to forecast foreign currency movements and the impact on demand is practically impossible given how unpredictable financial markets are.

The degree of difficulty of the task at hand is driven by the relative mix of predictable and unpredictable variation in the workload. Those functions whose work is highly predictable, even if the swing from peak to trough is large, have a far easier job of planning capacity than those where there is a significant random element at work.

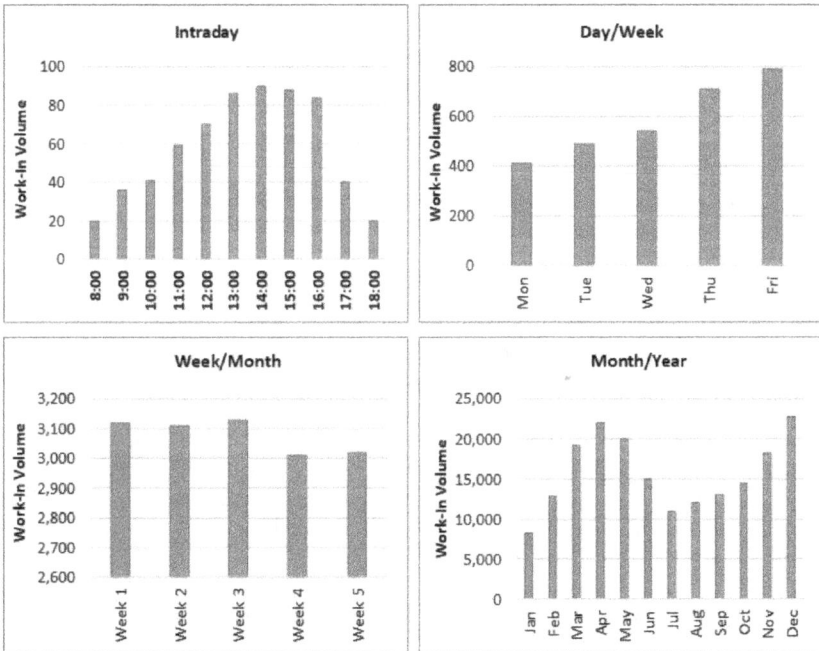

Figure 28 – Demand profiles.

A useful place to start is to visualise demand patterns of how work comes into the team (Figure 28). Once you understand the demand profile, you then think through the strategies you can apply to handle it—and the good news is there are only three strategies.

Assuming you have the relevant historical data, creating the profile charts is straightforward. It's important to look at the patterns over a range of time frames— hour/day, day/week, week/month or day/month (depends on the operating rhythm of the business) and month/year— as each will present a different challenge, with different treatments available to help solve the problem.

The charts in Figure 28 all represent "expected work in"—the volume of work requests that the team expect to receive. As you can see, all the charts display more than a modicum of variability, but if you have a known pattern, then you have a base from which to work.

A word of caution: be careful to read the scale—the week/month chart makes it look like weeks four and five are significantly quieter, where the volumes are only 3% lower. This is enough to make it worth acting on, but it is certainly not alarming.

Once you've created charts like this for your teams, the scale of the problem becomes apparent. Compare with the charts for the month-end reporting team (Figure 29).

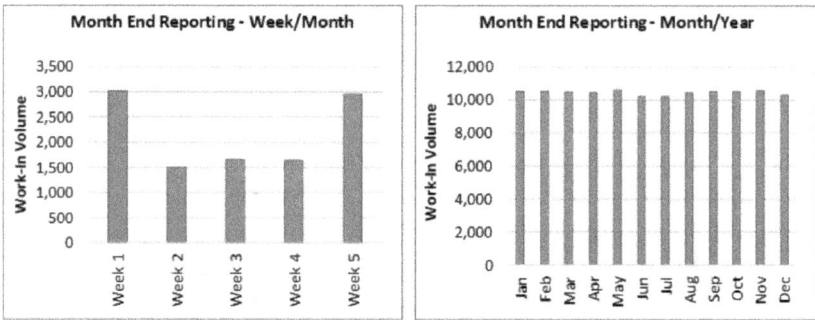

Figure 29 – Month-end reporting team demand profiles.

The week/month profile poses a challenge, though once you've figured out how to manage this period, it's relatively easy to apply this approach equally across the year given how smooth the month/year profile is.

The shape of the charts helps you set your base capacity profile— how many people you will have each day, the mix of full-time and part-time resources and the shift patterns they will adopt. The smoother the chart, the easier it is to manage. If you don't have a smooth chart, then the fun begins. Try overlaying how many people you have on the charts, and you will quickly see the size of the challenge. The hour/day chart is usually a great place to start. Many teams apply the same shift pattern (e.g., everybody works the same hours), but this is rarely how work comes in. By changing the shift patterns for a couple of resources, you immediately free up capacity and typically reduce overtime (Figure 30).

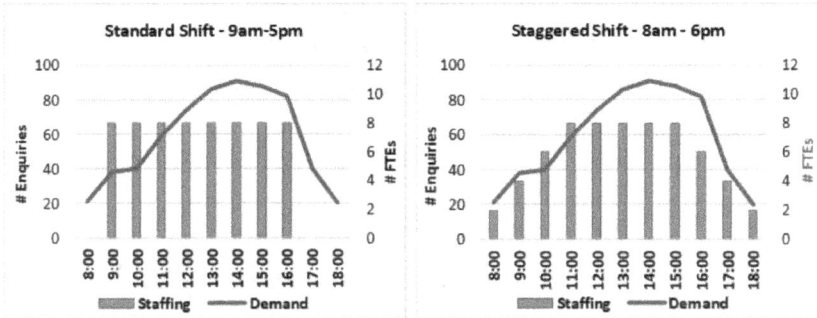

Figure 30 – Standard shift v staggered shift.

This simple exercise should raise questions:

1. Can you change the shape of the demand profile?
2. How do you adjust your capacity to meet this pattern?
3. Do you hire enough people to meet the peak and have them check out YouTube videos during the quiet periods?
4. Do you only hire enough people to meet the minimum and hope customers will forgive you?
5. Do you hire and fire with alarming regularity?

(NB For those functions where there is a significant amount of unpredictable variation, it still makes sense to strip out the one-off events to see the underlying demand profile. We'll deal with the random spikes later.)

The next step is to review how well your team are currently managing capacity. The way to do this is to use an In-Out-WIP chart. WIP stands for work in progress, which is the work that you have started but not finished. You may refer to it as a backlog or a queue. If you track the amount of work in, work out and how much work you have in WIP over a period (try for at least 30 data points), you will get a good idea of how well you are managing your work. In an ideal situation, the amount of work in and the amount of work out should be relatively closely matched. A sign that they are not is if the WIP figure is trending up or down. A WIP figure trending up will typically indicate a team that are under pressure and are at risk of missing their customer targets. A WIP figure that is trending down is a team that are at risk of running out of work and their productivity will be falling. Small movements in WIP can, however, be a sign of a team that are managing

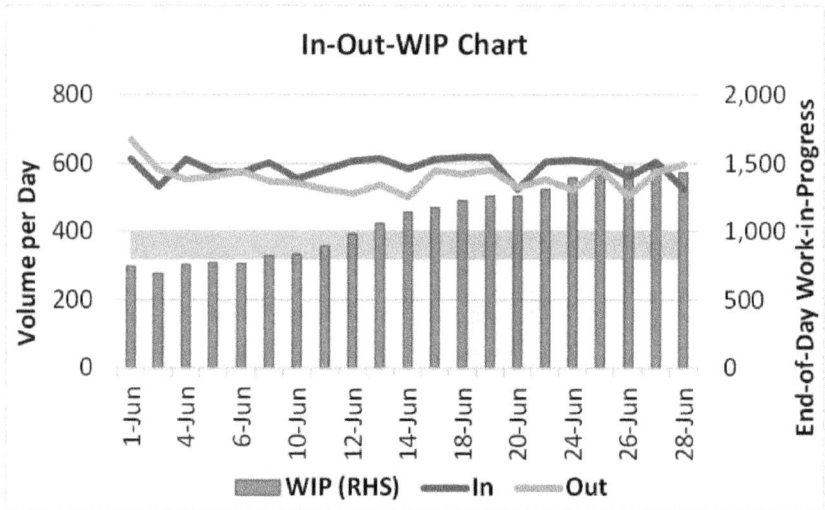

Figure 31 – In-Out-WIP chart showing WIP window.

their capacity very well. Allowing WIP to rise in busier periods and fall in quieter periods is fine if it doesn't impact the customer.

As mentioned in the section on quality and SLAs, your ability to deliver work consistently in line with customer expectations is critical, so highlighting the "safe" level of WIP to carry on the In-Out-WIP chart is a good idea. This is called a WIP window and is the shaded rectangle between 800 and 1,000 on the right-hand scale in Figure 31. How do you determine range for the WIP window? It's essentially a range of 75–90% of the amount of work you can typically handle within your SLA. If you can typically handle 550 enquiries per day and you have a two-day SLA, then the upper range is 90% and the lower range is 75% (of 2 × 550). This gives you enough buffer to allow for unexpected peaks. It's rough, but it's good enough for a visual control. If your WIP is within this range, you should be able to meet your turnaround time commitments. If you have a very volatile demand profile, deliver a service with significant negative consequences if the service level is missed, or have limited resources capable of handling a sudden spike, you may need to extend the buffer.

Once you know your profile and the size of the challenge you have ahead of you, it's time to think through the following options:

1. Level scheduling.
2. Manage demand.
3. Flex resources and "chase" demand.

Level scheduling is where you produce the same amount of work every day. It works well in a manufacturing environment, where the plant can build to stock during the quiet periods and draw down from stock in busier periods. This is one of the central principles of the Toyota Production System referred to as Heijunka.

It's hard to make it work in a service environment, as you can't make services to stock. You can't prepare a set of mortgage documents on the off chance a customer will buy a house next month or ask a customer with an urgent payment request to submit next week when you won't be as busy. Paradoxically, the way most service teams are set up assumes a level-scheduling approach. A team leader is usually told that they have a complement of X FTEs, and this is the same number throughout the year. It's probably fewer than the previous year, but it's still flat across the year. Logically this would suggest the team will produce the same amount of work each day. In reality, what happens is sometimes they don't have enough work and "idle", and sometimes there is way too much. They get backlogs and then do overtime.

One of the issues here is caused by a lack of trust between the service teams and the finance function. "What capacity management giveth, finance taketh away." In other words, the manager doing the right thing and releasing excess capacity soon learns a very harsh lesson when they try to add capacity to meet a demand spike and approvals are blocked. If the manager raises concerns about the level of resources, it's not uncommon to hear something along the lines of, "You'll just have to make do!" It's hard to imagine a production manager in manufacturing saying that there is only enough budget for 100 engines but build 120 cars today and send out 20 without engines. As a colleague once said, "Every three or four years, you just need to blow your plan so you are allowed to re-baseline."

If you do go down this path, where you set the "complement" level depends on a number of factors, but the key question is, "How often and for how long are you prepared to make your customers wait?" In a high-end service business, the answer may be, "Rarely and only for a minute or two at most!" In this case, you would staff towards the peak. In monopolistic services, customers haven't got a choice, so these businesses can staff closer to the 65–75th percentile if they choose. The assumption is that with a bit of careful leave planning and asking the team to work a bit harder during busy periods, they can mitigate the worst of the effects.

In my experience, this approach is usually wasting a 15–25% opportunity.

Manage demand is where you try to change the shape of the demand profile to smooth it out and make it easier to resource. There are several options here, but typically it is hard to have a material impact in a service environment, to say the least. It's very difficult to try and persuade customers, for example, to send in their tax assessments before the end of the financial year, and it's unlikely to be the only way you solve the problem. There are a few options:

1. Adjust pricing (e.g., the "happy hour" scenario).
2. Run promotions to lift demand in the off-season.
3. Change your service level in busy periods.
4. Use a reservation or a booking system.

5. Negotiate with individual, large customers to deliver work at a mutually beneficial time.
6. Find complementary services that will help smooth out demand.

Chase demand is the most practical approach in a service environment to "balance the books", where you adjust capacity to try to meet demand. There are several levers you can pull to flex the resource base (i.e., how much capacity you have available to ebb and flow in line with the peaks and troughs of demand). In simple terms, the basic building blocks for flexible capacity are driven by the resource choices you make. Typically, your options are to get the right mix of full-time, part-time and temporary resources, add a dash of flexitime, overtime, shift scheduling, leave management, loaning and borrowing and inevitably, but certainly not preferably, the occasional exhortation to "crank it up a bit" (i.e., work harder/faster). These are the basic resource management levers. Add to this the following and you will be set up for success:

1. Set the target productivity level at the 85th percentile to reduce the chance of pacing.
2. Actively manage the team and allow for individual differences.
3. Build bench strength through cross-skilling.
4. Create a small pool of highly motivated, cross-skilled resources, that can be deployed at short notice across a range of functions.
5. Adjust the overall workload by rescheduling non-core activities like team meetings, one-on-one conversations, training, etc.
6. Adjust the workload by managing WIP up or down, as previously discussed.

These are covered in more detail in Appendix 9.

In the longer term, there are other levers available to senior managers and executives— for example, process improvement to reduce the workload (either through customer self-service or process automation), outsourcing and offshoring. However, in the short to medium term, the list in Figure 32 is more than adequate to meet the most challenging of service environments.

Element	Hour/Day	Day/Week	Week/Month	Month/Year	Qtr/Year
Horizon	1 day	1 week	3 months	1 year	1-3 years
Forecast Level	Team	Team	Department	Function	Line of Business
Variables	Core Task Level	Core Task Level	Core Task Level	3-5	2-3
Team Leader	✓	✓			
Manager		✓	✓		
Senior Manager			✓	✓	
Executive				✓	✓
Decisions	• Work allocation • Prioritisation & sequencing • Ad hoc diverted • Demand management	• Leave management • Diverted time scheduling • Lend/borrow • WIP (up or down) • Overtime • Demand management	• Temporary staff • Diverted time • Skills flexibility – x-skill and up-skill • Leave management • WIP (up or down) • Shift patterns • Role grading	• Hire staff • Release staff • Skills flexibility – x-skill and up-skill • Simple outsource/offshore • Simple automation • Role grading • Line balancing	• Capital expenditure • Major outsourcing/offshoring • Platform upgrade • Facilities upgrade • Self-service

Figure 32 – Planning and control decision matrix levers.

Planning cycle

Now that you have the strategy in place and you know the levers that you can pull, the next step is to make it real. This means you must develop a planning and control cycle that becomes part of your team's standard operating rhythm. The cycle comprises four steps:

1. **Forecast** – Determine how much work there is to do going forward.
2. **Plan** – Identify the resources that will be required to do the forecast workload.
3. **Control** – Confirm that the plan holds true on the day and, if not, respond accordingly.
4. **Review** – Learn from the most recent cycle what went well and what you can do better next time, then implement those improvements.

You use this cycle for different time frames. At more junior levels, teams really need to be looking at day/week plans and week/month plans. At senior levels, month/quarter and month/year plans are more appropriate.

An example of the whole cycle might look like the following (Figure 33):

- **Forecast** – Wednesday, week one: Create day/week forecast (i.e., create a daily forecast for each day starting on Monday of week two).
- **Plan** – Thursday, week one: Agree on the resource plan, who will be available, who will be away, which team members will be on training, when the team meeting will be held, and which team members can be seconded out.
- **Control** – Monday to Friday, week two: Check in every morning with the team to confirm whether the planning assumptions hold true. If not, decide what to do. Do you still expect the same amount of work? Are there any unplanned absences? If so, what actions will you take to adjust?
- **Review** – Tuesday, week two: Review the outcome from the week one plan, the control actions you had to take on a daily basis to address any issues, what went well and what can be done better next time.
- **Forecast** – Wednesday, week two: Create day/week forecast (i.e., create a daily forecast for each day of week three by incorporating lessons learned from week one).
- **Plan** – Thursday, week two: Agree on the resource plan, who will be available, who will be away, which team members will be on training, when the team meeting will be held, which team members can be seconded out and incorporate lessons learned from week one.

The same four steps are applied for long-term planning—for example, a month/year plan might look like the following:

- **Forecast** – Month 9 or 10, year one: Create the monthly forecast for year two.

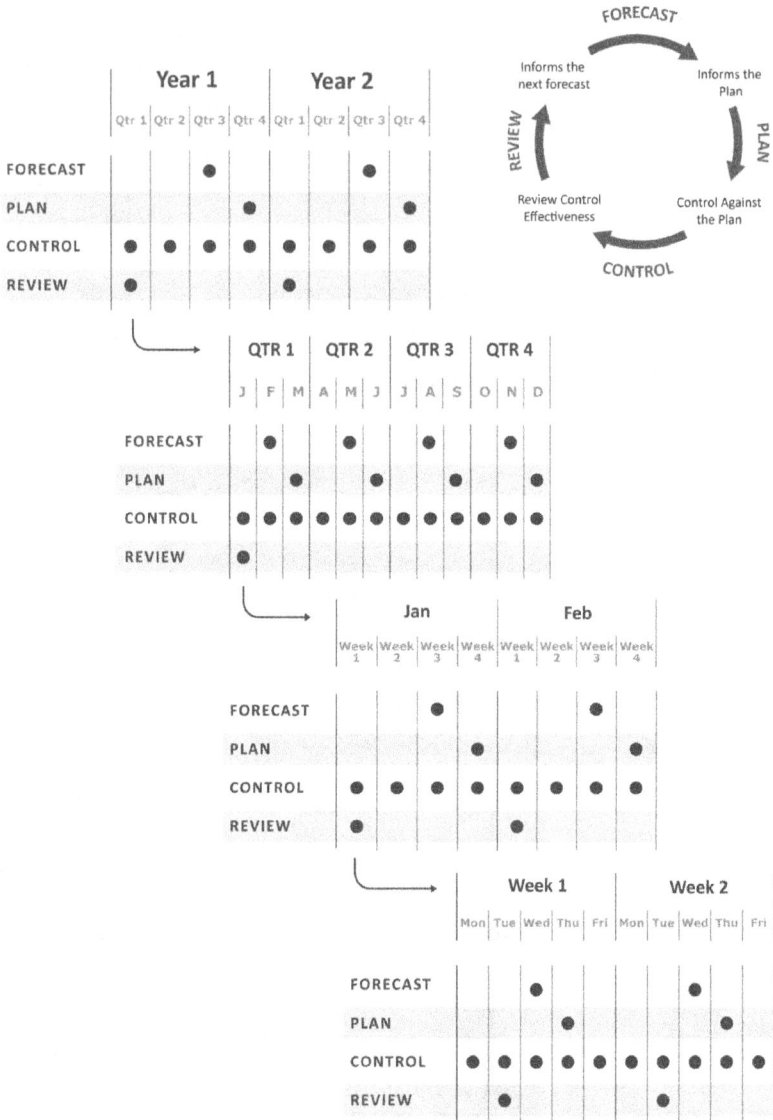

Figure 33 – Day/week and month/year planning cycle.

- **Plan** – Month 10 or 11, year one: Create the resource plan by month for year two.
- **Control** – Every month, year two: Run monthly control reports to check performance against plan and take corrective action as necessary.

- **Review** – Month 1 or 2, year two: Review year one performance— what went well and what can be done better in year two.

While some organisations run this through a centralised team, for the shorter-term cycles (e.g., day/week and week/month), my preference is for it to be run by the teams closest to the customer and the work. They are far better placed to understand what's going on. The techniques are simple enough to be learned by them, and this will increase their level of accountability.

However, it is important that the plans align. The longer-term plans, set by the executive team, should cascade down through the hierarchy and set the guidelines for the short time horizon plans. This is a way of cascading objectives and ensuring the outcomes required for the end of the financial year are met.

Building a good plan

Building a plan for the first time can be daunting. As mentioned earlier, the task is to find a way to ensure that there are just enough resources to complete the expected work. It's rarely that simple and, in nearly all cases, there will be some juggling required.

The steps are shown in Figure 34 and described in more detail in Appendix 10.

An important aspect of creating the plan is that it should be a collaborative effort. A critical question is, "Who will create the forecast?" For the medium to longer term, this may be the sales teams or the product teams, but all teams dependent on it need to be involved in the process. For the short term, it may be the team creating the plan, but they should still check in with the sales and product functions to make sure there's nothing unusual happening that they aren't aware of. I've lost count of the number of times I've come across a disgruntled operations manager who first heard about the latest sales campaign when he/she read it in the paper and his/her team are now drowning!

Similarly, resource planning should be a collaborative approach across teams, as lending and borrowing is a creative way to balance a plan as well as help team members build their skills and experience.

The third step (Adjust for current productivity level) is also critical,

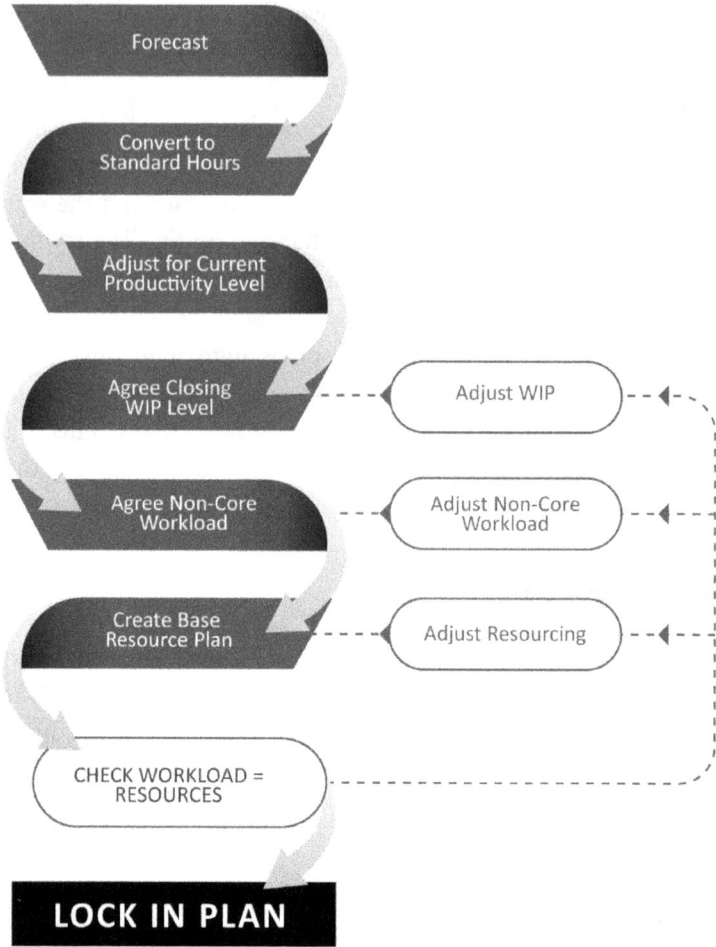

Figure 34 – Creating a good plan.

and this is where one of the easiest quick wins lies. As previously discussed, the team's productivity will "wobble" around. The most likely driver is demand variability. On low productivity days, this implies that there are more resources than actually required. To prevent this from happening, rather than plan at the average productivity level for the last few weeks, if you set it at the 85th percentile, you will create capacity. This is capacity that would be "idling" if you planned at the average rate. By planning at the higher level, you will get more done with less, and the resultant spare capacity can be put to more value-adding use (e.g., work on continuous improvement projects, upskill themselves through training, etc.). It's important to note that by choosing the 85th percentile, you are effectively discounting those exceptionally busy days when the teams would be working harder than normal. This is not "cracking the whip"! More to the point; why would you plan to be average?

As you can see from Figure 35, once you have identified that the plan doesn't balance, there are essentially three categories of actions you can take:

1. Adjust the core workload by allowing the closing WIP position to reduce or increase.
2. Adjust the non-core workload by rescheduling meetings, one-on-ones, training, etc.
3. Adjust the resource base by loaning or borrowing resources, changing leave, overtime, using flexitime and bringing in temporary resources or contractors.

Resources Required				Resources Available			
Item	Base Plan	Adj	Adj Plan	Item	Base Plan	Adj	Adj Plan
Opening WIP (hrs)	100	0	100	Staff complement (hrs)	600	0	600
Forecast work in (hrs)	550	0	550	Annual leave	-48	0	-48
Plan work out (hrs)	550	-50	500	Loan/borrow	-32	24	-8
Closing WIP (hrs)	100	50	150	Flexitime	0	0	0
Diverted work effort - training, team meetings, 1:1s, etc.	52	-26	26	Overtime	0	6	6
				Temps	0	0	0
				Downtime	-24	0	-24
Total resources required (hrs)	602	-76	526	Total resources available (hrs)	496	30	526
Balance					-106		0

Actions:
Allow WIP to increase by 50 hours, reducing work-out by 50 hours
Reduce team meetings by 30 mins, saving 26 hours in diverted time
Agree not to lend out 24 hours
Run 6 hours overtime if required

Figure 35 – Balancing a plan example.

There are three critical metrics that will help you track your performance:

- **Productivity** – I've already discussed how to calculate this and commented on the fact that if you analyse historical productivity, it will typically "wobble" around. The aim is to reduce the degree of "wobble" and trend upwards. This will reflect a team that is working at a steady pace rather than speeding up then slowing down. The upward trend should reflect the "more with less" challenge being met.
- **Utilisation** – This is the amount of time the team spend on non-core activities like training, team meetings, etc. Ideally, it should be in the 80–85% range. During busy periods it can go higher, but it is unsustainable to keep it in the high 90s for more than a couple of weeks. On the flip side, running utilisation below 70% for an extended period would raise questions about an overabundance of resources that may be better deployed elsewhere.
- **Planning accuracy** – Simply comparing your actual performance to your planned performance and understanding the reasons for the variances is a critical part of the review process. If you can forecast your workload and plan your resources to meet the forecast accurately, serving your customers and running your team becomes a whole lot easier.

Overcoming the roadblocks

I cannot overstate how critical it is to establish a robust, sustainable planning cycle. It requires discipline and rigour, but it will deliver. It is a change that may take some time to embed and there are a number of common roadblocks and issues the team may raise:

- "Our workload is so random it's impossible to forecast, so there's no point in planning." The more unpredictable the workload, the more important it is to plan.
- "We have a change coming up that will change how we do our work, so there's no point in planning." If you don't plan, how will you know the impact of the change?

- "We are too busy to plan." This is precisely why you should plan, to ensure your team is working at a steady rate.
- "It's only a couple of hours, there's no point in balancing to that level." A couple of hours a day is like turning down the offer of a full-time resource for thirteen weeks. No leader would do that.
- "There's no point in planning because it's never accurate." The more you understand about your processes, the better you will get at planning. There is no such thing as a perfect plan but learning from the cycle is a fundamental building block for any improvement.
- "I've added in a few more, just in case." Creating a buffer is just building in waste. Plan for what you realistically expect to happen and actively manage if it doesn't.

The key to effective capacity planning is discipline, rhythm and active management. Every minute counts. Every lost minute is a wasted opportunity when a team member could be cross-skilling, working on a continuous improvement project or helping out another team.

Besides a reasonable rhythm and active management, there are a couple of other things that are required to ensure you are set up for success.

Setting up for success

If it isn't already obvious by now, effective capacity management in a service environment is very much a question of how good you are at flexing capacity plus a smattering of workload management. Finding capacity quickly is almost always a good thing. With an understanding of the work profile, a strategy in place to address the mismatches between demand and capacity and a planning cycle to enforce the decision making, you are well set up to find the space and time the team need to get through their work and build their skills to equip themselves for the workforce of the future.

Choosing the right strategy and a good working knowledge of the available levers is key to managing capacity effectively. Unfortunately, the relative success of your actions will depend on whether other aspects of your operating environment are set up to enable success. The more items you can tick off below, the better the outcomes will be. The enabling factors are grouped into three categories (Figure 36):

- Capacity management toolkit such as an operating rhythm, capacity management system, visual management and the outlook matrix.
- People and structure including organisational alignment, consolidating like resources, effective skills matrixes, multiskilled teams and an active management approach.
- Process-oriented techniques such as creating a stable production environment, line balancing, removing bottlenecks, an effective continuous improvement and the wonderfully titled "runners, repeaters and strangers" technique.

These are all covered in more detail in Appendix 11.

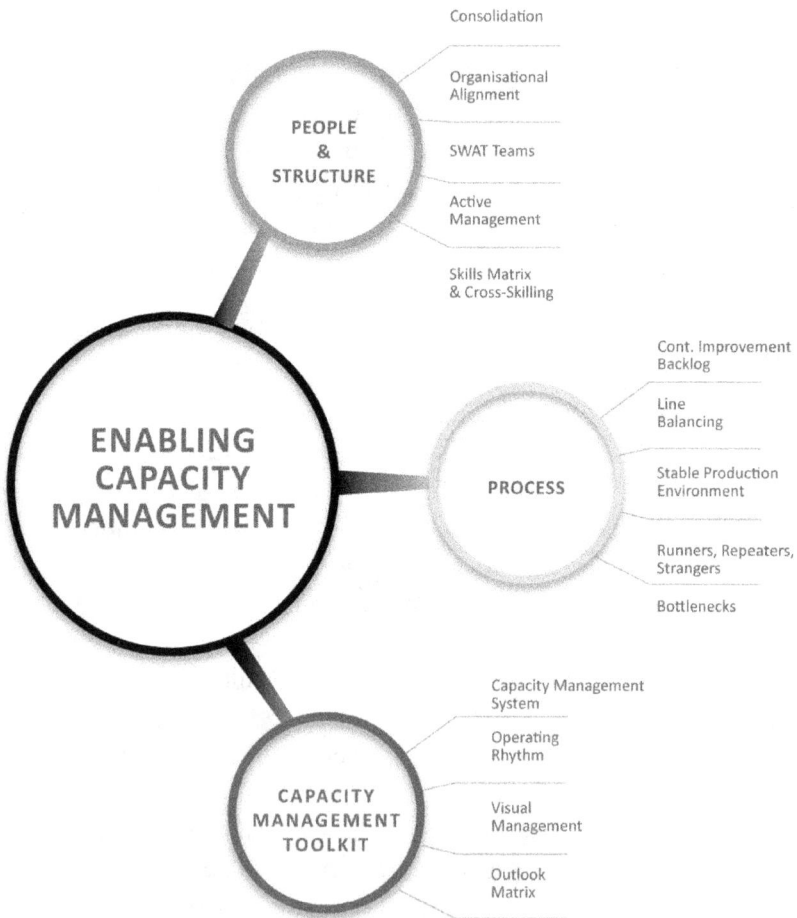

Figure 36 – Enabling effective capacity management.

Armed with this type of toolkit, finding 15–25% or more capacity is not uncommon. Apart from stabilising the production environment and implementing a capacity management system, this can be handled within the business-as-usual operating budget.

One final consideration for those teams that choose not to forecast but would rather focus on their responsiveness: a useful tool here is the "range-response curve" (Figure 37). This compares the time required to absorb a shift in capacity (positive or negative) with progressively larger shifts. For example, most teams can accommodate a 2–3% change in demand in the same day or at the very least by the following day. Ask the same team to take on double the amount of work, and the time required blows out—new premises will be required, additional staff will need to be hired, potentially a new platform may need to be built, etc. Precisely how long it takes to accommodate these shifts is an indication of flexibility.

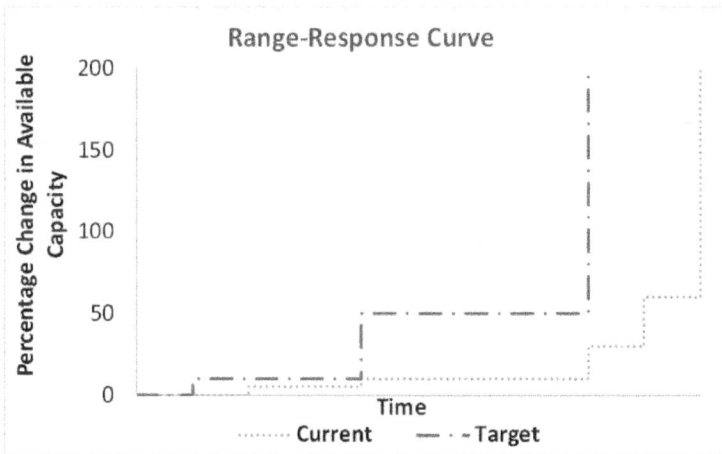

Figure 37 – Range-response curve (Slack, et al., 2015).

Drawing an as-is and a to-be curve is a great way to measure the increase in flexibility and responsiveness. It is particularly useful for both long-term planning and business continuity planning.

Finally, for teams providing service on a "best endeavours" basis, adopting the practices covered here will make "best endeavours" a thing of the past. You will be able to be far more specific in the service expectations you set for your customers and give your team far greater confidence that they can meet these expectations.

Managing individual productivity

Team members do not have a dial on their forehead that tells you how busy they are. Someone can look busy but be coasting. The effect of being very busy one day and bored the next is very damaging both for the individual and the team. A Match Fit team aims to operate at a steady pace. They achieve this in a couple of different ways:

1. By planning productivity at the 85th percentile, as mentioned previously, they can smooth out the peaks and troughs. This reduces the idle time and allows team members to focus on training and continuous improvement initiatives.
2. The leader understands and allows for individual differences to get the best possible out of each team member.
3. The morning "huddle" or "buzz" meeting is a critical event every day—the game is won or lost in the first 30 minutes of the day. By this time, the leader knows whether to expect a change in workload and which resources are and are not available.
4. By chunking the work down to 1- to 2-hour blocks and checking in at the end of each period, the leader has much greater line of sight if problems are on the horizon. Active management gives the leader ample opportunity to take corrective action.

In addition to these techniques, it's also important to know what the "theoretical" capacity of the team and each individual is. At a team member level, the option is to give the team member more work and then watch for the first tell-tale signs of stress (e.g., skipping lunch, leaving late and getting flustered). It is important that this is a two-way initiative between the team member and the leader. The team leader is allocating more challenging work, and the team member needs to know it's okay to say "Stop!" The team leader needs to carefully monitor the team member to ensure that they are not trying to "tough it out" with the associated detrimental stress and health implications.

At a team level, there are two opportunities:

1. Monitor performance during a business continuity event (e.g., a systems outage or when the pressure is on). The motto "don't

waste a crisis" is relevant here. After an outage, check back on the team's productivity and you will see it has peaked. This is close to the theoretical capacity of the team. Compare this to the average daily productivity and you'll be surprised at the difference. I've seen teams operate at twice their average rate! This is why it's okay to plan at the 85th percentile and not be too concerned that you are pushing the team too hard.

2. Every fortnight, increase the productivity target used in the planning process by 1%. A 1% increase is equivalent to less than five minutes per person, per day. No one will notice it for the first couple of months, but in aggregate it frees up more than enough capacity to introduce some continuous improvements that will make absorbing the 1% increases easier as time goes by.

Parkinson's law will always prevail without active management. Productivity is an outcome you can control, but you need to act, and act promptly.

Chapter summary

Having set the context, picked the team, set up the work environment, devised a performance management system to track progress and established a robust quality management program, this chapter has focussed on making sure you have enough resources to meet the workload.

The first step is to understand the work pattern for your team and how you are currently tracking. You must understand the profile for different time horizons from intraday to month/year. The more predictable and smoother the profile, the easier it is to manage resources.

Once you know your demand profile, you can assess which strategy is best suited to respond to it. Level scheduling is the default position, but it is rarely the most appropriate. Managing demand in a service environment tends to be difficult, which leaves a strategy of chasing demand to adapt to the peaks and troughs of demand.

The latter is the most common approach, and there is a range of techniques to help achieve this. The most significant factor is the level of individual productivity. It will ebb and flow with volume of work if not managed actively. This means that the team operates under stress some of the time and is underutilised the rest of the time. By calculating the productivity rate at the 85th percentile and using that level as an input to determine how many resources you need to meet demand, you will automatically free up capacity.

Finally, services are all about people. The output you get and the productivity level the team achieves is a function of each team member's aptitude, motivations and the opportunity—that is how much challenging, but achievable, work there is available. By working closely with each team member and managing their individual productivity, you will deliver:

- Greater consistency, which makes it easier to plan.
- A less stressful workplace with fewer peaks and troughs.
- Increased productivity, which frees up resources to be used on other things.

In most service organisations, actively managing capacity will yield 15–25% extra capacity.

Checklist:

Checklist Item	Status
Do your team understand the challenges in managing capacity and why it is so important?	❏
Do your team understand the demand profiles for the respective time periods, how well you currently manage capacity and the levers you can pull to adjust demand and capacity?	❏
Do your team understand and have a capacity management planning cycle in place, including how to forecast, adjust capacity, control the plan and review it?	❏
Do your team know how to build a plan, and do they do so routinely planning at the 85th percentile?	❏
Do your team have all the enablers in place to support effective capacity management?	❏
Does each team member understand their individual productivity performance, what's causing the variability and do they have a plan to improve?	❏

Part 3 – Mid-Season: Getting Fitter, Refining and Finessing

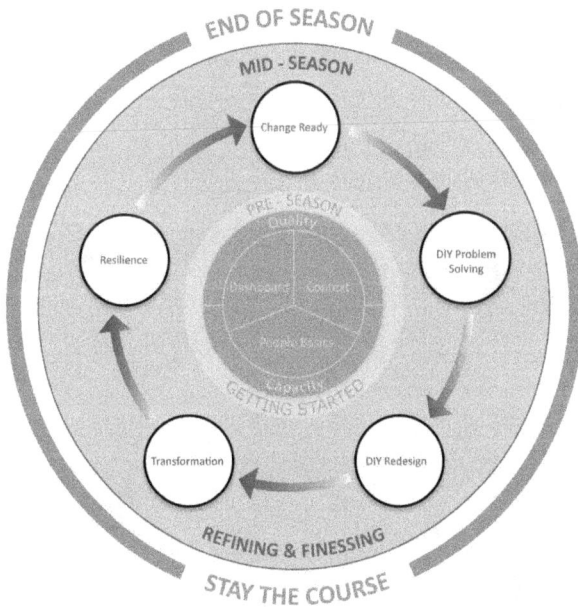

Chapter 8
The Need for Change

"My dear, here we must run as fast as we can, just to stay in place. And if you wish to go anywhere, you must run twice as fast as that." — *Lewis Carroll, Alice in Wonderland*

Once the pre-season ends and the season begins, life takes on a different rhythm. As the season progresses and the relentless pressure begins to take its toll, the success (or otherwise) of the pre-season preparation and conditioning is revealed. Hopefully, all the hard work at the start of the year begins to pay off as players are hardened: mentally, physically and technically.

Every game counts, every game is different and there's no such thing as an easy game. Between games, players continue to train hard. They are finessing skills, going over set moves and reviewing what worked well and what they can do better based on last week's performance. They are analysing playing conditions, the grounds and the weather outlook. Support staff will be researching next week's opposition— understanding their strengths and weaknesses and the impact that will have on team selection. They will also have to adapt where players are out due to injury or are not suited to certain conditions or the opponent's style of play.

At the same time, while the coaches may convince the media that they're only thinking about the team they play next week, they will be keeping a weather eye on the future— new rules, equipment or technology—and preparing for overseas competitions that involve different climates and time zones.

Successful teams take this in their stride. They perfect the art of improving their game by focussing on the small things, week in and week out, constantly tweaking performance to extract an extra 1% here or there. They are also constantly looking ahead at how they will innovate and adapt to take on the bigger changes.

It's no different running a service team. You need to be Match Fit to play, but once the season starts, you must get fitter.

Why innovate and improve?

Change is hard. Running an organisation with no change agenda would be far easier. So why do so many organisations put themselves under so much pressure to change? The answer is simple—the bar is constantly being raised. Customers' expectations are constantly changing, and the competition is responding accordingly. Even if you are world class now, just maintaining your current level of performance will see you drift backwards (Figure 38). The gap must be addressed through change initiatives. Any organisation worth its salt must innovate and improve to stay in business.

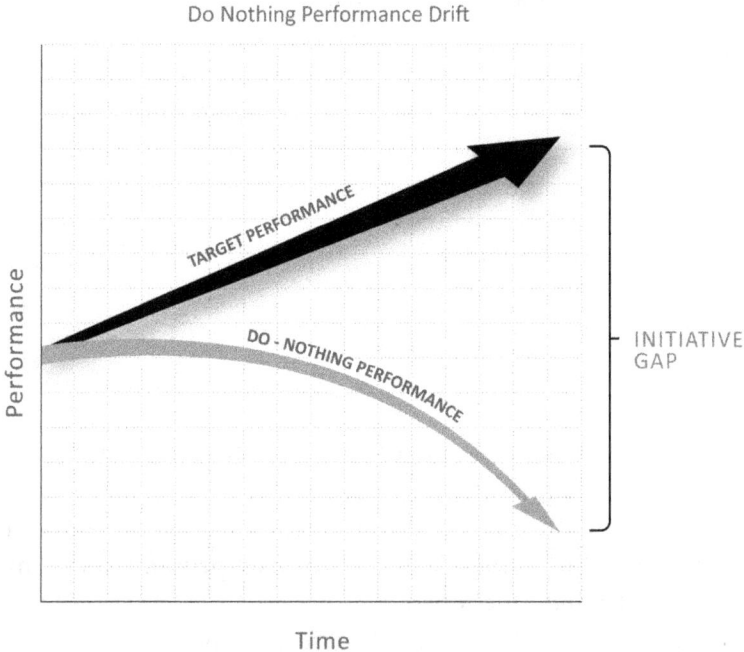

Figure 38 – Do-nothing performance drift.

In a digital context, it may not be your direct competition that is setting customer expectations. As more and more customers use services like Uber, Amazon, Airbnb, etc., their service level expectations of providers in financial services, education, healthcare and utilities are being reset. With such a shift, industry participants recognise that, if they don't respond to this change in their customers' expectations, their future may not be quite so rosy; hence, the need for change.

But it's one thing knowing you need to change; it's quite another knowing how to go about it and accessing the resources. For many large, mature, service organisations this presents numerous challenges:

- Their size and complexity stack the odds against them in terms of organisational agility. The speed of decision making in a hierarchical organisation, with complex matrix chains of command and process proliferation, will be slow.
- Many service organisations work in regulated industries where any change can potentially introduce significant risk. This compounds the bureaucratic inertia.
- Slow, bureaucratic decision-making processes make for slow projects. When projects take months and years to complete, there's a very good chance that a new project will overlap with, and have a dependency on, an in-flight project. This makes planning, sequencing and scheduling extraordinarily hard, which extends the time to get the projects finished. And slow projects run the risk of being out of date before they even land.
- Individual scorecards, at middle and senior leader levels, tend to reward transformation. However, the organisation cannot fund every transformation. This may lead to transformational change being initiated without the right support and resources. These projects are destined to fail but will chew up time and resources in the meantime, as well as adding to the volume of change and the complexity of managing the overall portfolio (Figure 39).

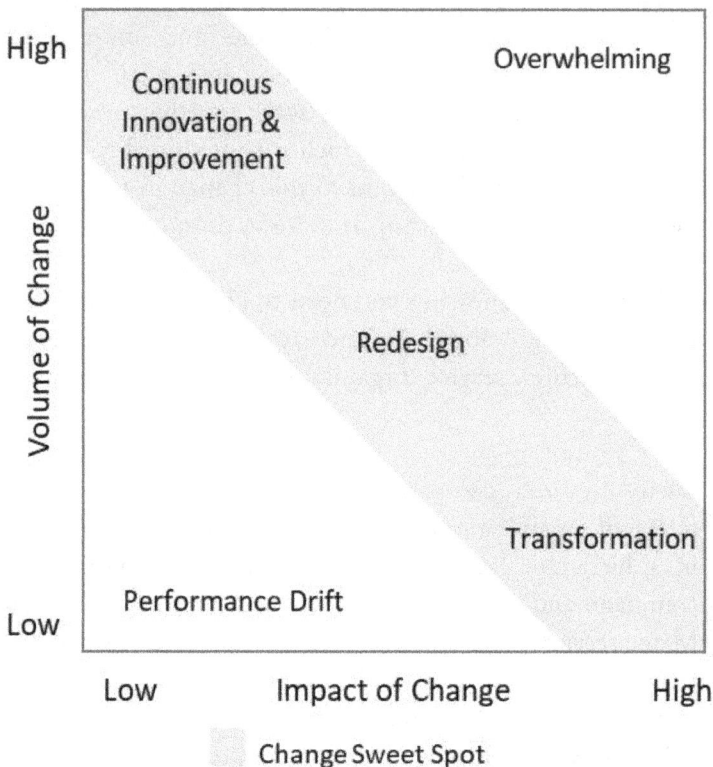

Figure 39 – Change volume v impact matrix.

In summary, organisations must innovate and improve, but in large, mature organisations, it's hard!

With this point in mind, it makes perfect sense to have dedicated teams of specialists working on large transformational change like digital, splitting the organisation into Run Teams and Change Teams as mentioned in Chapter 1. But it is rarely as clean-cut as that. It may seem contradictory, but Run Teams also need to innovate, improve and change. There are several reasons for this:

1. The Run Team are also subject to the perils of the performance drift. They need to innovate and improve to stay competitive.
2. Absorbing so much change from across the organisation consumes copious quantities of resources. The techniques discussed in Part 2 will free up a lot of capacity but not enough

to absorb all the change underway. More capacity is needed. The Run Team will need their own change agenda to find it.

3. From a completely different perspective, it makes sense that the teams closest to the customer and the work—the Run Team—should be the ones coming up with ideas to innovate and solve problems for customers. They see the problems firsthand. Why not let the Run Team address them?

4. Even using Agile methodologies, transformational change takes time, but the organisation can't stand still in the interim. The customer experience needs to be enhanced, productivity gains need to be made and risk needs to be managed more effectively. Innovation and improvement need to be continuous.

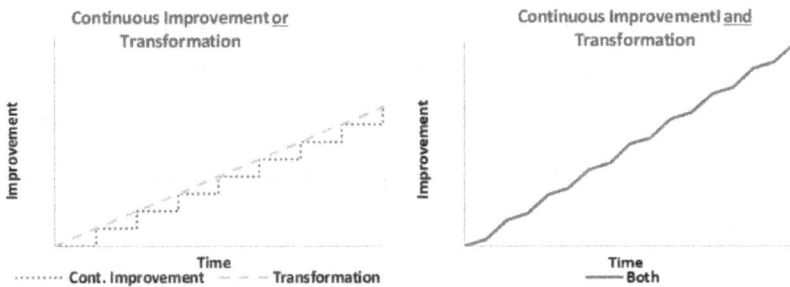

Figure 40 – Improvement strategy: continuous innovation, transformation or both.

As Figure 40 indicates, running continuous change and transformational change programs concurrently should increase the overall benefit profile for the organisation. It does, however, present additional challenges: turf wars!

Setting the boundaries

Some leaders who are running large transformation programs dismiss small, continuous change as a waste of resources. On the flip side, Run Team leaders may dismiss large change as a waste of money because it takes so long to deliver and is frequently underwhelming when it does. The reality, as we have seen above, is that both are necessary. The digital transformation will run for several years and consume significant chunks of the organisation's resources. In the meantime, the organisation needs to keep evolving, improving service to customers and driving productivity. This needs to be the culmination of lots of small change and innovation executed continuously across the Run Team.

Ideally, this difference in perspective wouldn't exist. In my experience, it takes work to ensure both sides can comfortably coexist. More specifically, each side must understand the aims and objectives of the other. Boundaries must be set to minimise the risk of overlap, duplication of resources, frustration and stress levels amongst the various team members.

One issue that complicates setting the boundaries is that many people think of transformation in terms of radical change but—for the most part—it is really a continuum of smaller steps. Take for example the Apollo 11 lunar landing, which was immortalised in Neil Armstrong's words: "One small step for man; one giant leap for mankind." However, Apollo 11 was just one of dozens of missions, starting with the X-15 rocket plane program, the Mercury and Gemini projects and subsequently the Apollo program. Each mission tested new aspects required to complete the mission of landing a person on the moon. Some aspects were simple tweaks and enhancements from prior missions and others were far more fundamental (e.g., testing a new launch vehicle). Apollo 11 was really the result of a series of small steps and experiments that, over the course of a decade or so, achieved something that in the 1950s seemed quite unimaginable.

To get around this issue, I prefer to look at change based on the resources and authority levels required to initiate the change by breaking it down into four distinct categories:

- **Just do it** – These are small changes that every individual can make to how they do their work; they don't need anybody's permission nor specific resources. Examples might include how someone arranges their computer desktop, the folder structure for their email, setting up rules for email, etc. These changes usually take a few minutes to a few hours to do.
- **Team-based problem solving** – These are changes that affect the team's work and can be introduced within the authority and the budget of the team and their leader. Examples might include introducing a common checklist, adding a control to a process, introducing visual management techniques and dashboard, and

setting the operating rhythm for their team meetings. These changes may take a couple of weeks to 2–3 months maximum, and they are particularly good for improving quality.

- **Redesigning** – This involves changes to processes and customer journeys that extend across multiple teams, either within and/or across functions. These changes typically, but by no means always, require technology enhancements. Coordinating the changes across boundaries and the resources required usually increases the cost of these projects; hence, more senior stakeholders authorise these types of projects. These changes can take anywhere from 1–2 months to 6–9 months to complete.

- **Transformation** – These are far more substantial in terms of impact and cost. Typical examples may be a system replacement, a fundamental transformation of a major customer journey or—even more fundamental—a digital transformation. These programs can run for multiple years. Chapter 11 will cover this in more detail.

As the above suggests, with each change in category there is a change in the authority level required to initiate a project or program of work (Figure 41). As you would probably expect, it's not quite as neat as this. There are elements in the redesign category that can and should be executed at a team level and other elements that have more than a hint of transformation about them if carried out at scale.

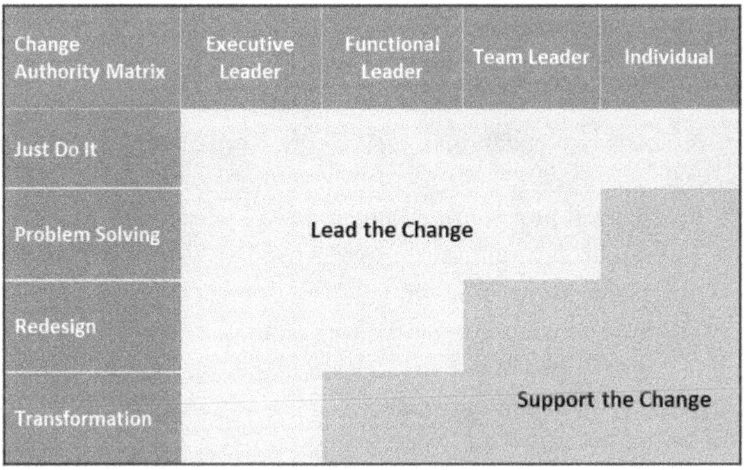

Change Authority Matrix	Executive Leader	Functional Leader	Team Leader	Individual
Just Do It				
Problem Solving		Lead the Change		
Redesign				
Transformation			Support the Change	

Figure 41 – Change authority matrix.

At each level there are suitable tools, techniques and methodologies to support the project that are appropriate for that type of change. "Just do it" speaks for itself, and I don't intend to cover this any further. I will cover the techniques associated with problem solving in Chapter 9 and redesigning in Chapter 10, as these are directly applicable to Run Team leaders. Chapter 11 is less about the techniques, given that the Run Team do not typically initiate transformation; it is more focussed on how the Run Team and Change Team can work more effectively together.

What's particularly interesting in NASA's lunar landing program is that all four programs overlapped chronologically. That is the same with the change categories. In all the organisations where I have worked, there were projects underway in each category that impacted my teams. These were projects of all shapes and sizes that originated from across the organisation. The volume of change can be overwhelming.

Coping with the volume of change

It is not just the transformation team or your own team that initiate change. Product teams may need to add new features and compliance teams may need to add or enhance controls. Technology may need to upgrade applications. All of these will have an impact and will have to be absorbed. At times it can feel like flying through an asteroid belt.

The way to avoid being overwhelmed by change is to ensure you have:

- A change calendar that lists all the initiatives impacting your team.
- An approval process for adding a new project to the calendar.
- The resources required from your team to define, test and ready the change for production.
- The time your team will need for training.
- A capacity marker that indicates the maximum amount of change the team can absorb at any time and the current predicted level.

Plotting this on a chart like Figure 42 quickly highlights areas of concern. There will be many dependencies and conflicts. You need to make the problem visible to all stakeholders to ensure they can see why you may need to say "No!"

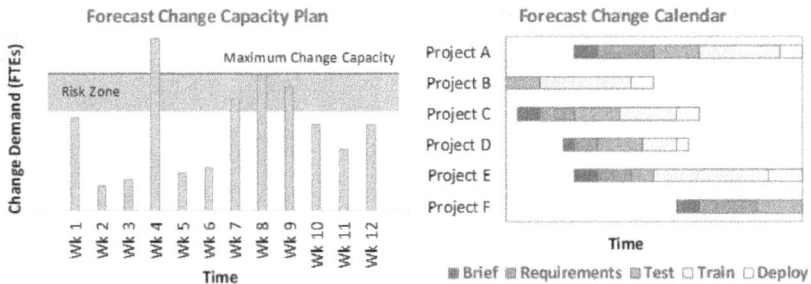

Figure 42 – Forecast change capacity plan and change calendar.

In many ways, this is like the capacity management issues discussed in the previous chapter. Instead of having to forecast customer requests, you now need to forecast the amount of work each change will introduce. The difference is that, for the most part, you can adjust the workload by how you schedule and sequence the different change initiatives. The workload created by each initiative will vary. Some changes will require little or no input for the team (e.g., a technology security update) or some people may require extensive training. What is essential is that the change workload is incorporated in the overall capacity plan as non-core work to ensure that there is one picture that shows what the team needs to do and the resources they have available to do it.

Many Run Teams find it hard to say "No!" Their natural bent is to try and do everything. When there is a significant change agenda, it's rarely possible to handle all the change and serve the customer at the same time. Every area initiating a change will view their change as the highest priority. As the leader of the team responsible for getting the change into production, it is easy to feel trapped by the conflicting priorities. Your team are telling you that they can't handle any more, and the change initiator is stating how critical the change is. Make the overall schedule transparent and share it with all stakeholders, with an expectation that individual change initiators need to negotiate amongst themselves if the change calendar is full. This is a great way to pre-empt any conflict and remove the responsibility from the leader absorbing the change.

This does not always mean that common sense will prevail. In these situations, where there is conflict over whose change goes first, the best approach, I find, is to ask three questions:

- What's best for the customer?
- What's best for the organisation overall?
- What's best for the staff?

Asking these three questions, in this order, usually gets the conflicted parties to a consensus decision.[4]

Leading the change

For the last section of this chapter, the focus is on change leadership. Leading a team is a big responsibility, and—for me—one of the key differentiators of leaders is how they lead their team through change. A former coach of mine once said, "Leadership is simple: all you need to do is to paint a picture of where you are going and inspire the team to follow you." This is all very well if you're in control of where you're going, but in a large organisation, there are invariably others who are contributing to setting that direction.

Many of the more authoritative voices on leading change would suggest that the key to successful change management is communication. It's hard to overstate just how critical communication is, particularly when your team are under so much pressure. It is not:

- A one-off town hall announcement.
- Placing a newsletter and a cup with the transformation's tagline on everyone's desk.
- A quick email.

It is:

- Being present with your team during the change.
- Continuous and consistent.

---

4. There are also methods that form part of the Agile methodology to help with prioritisation.

- Delivered with authentic empathy.
- Clear and concise.
- Connected to the bigger picture—the purpose, objectives, etc.
- Anchored on what you know, not speculation.
- Clear about "what's in it for me."
- Focussed on setting expectations for the next stage.
- Transparent and actively seeking participation in the change process.
- Appreciative of those who are actively embracing the change.

Finally, it is a timely reminder that leadership casts a long shadow. Everything you do or say in the line of sight of the team is open to interpretation and possibly misinterpretation. If you hear some bad news about a friend, and your head hangs low in full view of the team, they may interpret that to imply bad news for the team.

In some cases, you may not agree with the direction, but the decision is not yours to make. If you have given feedback and been unsuccessful in changing the direction, you must get behind the decision and speak positively for it. This can be very hard, and if you vehemently disagree, then you need to get another job. Although you may think you can mask your innermost feelings and bite your tongue, your team will pick up on the sentiment, and you will be unwittingly undermining the project in the process.

In this regard, your body language, facial expressions, the way you speak and the words you use all matter. And not just on the day you announce the change, but every day. Role-modelling behaviour takes energy, passion, care and discipline, but it is fundamental to creating the right environment for change to succeed.

Chapter summary

This chapter has focussed on describing the different types of change from the very small to a major transformation. Without innovation and change, businesses will cease to exist as their customers' needs develop and their competitors respond. But change is hard, particularly in large, mature organisations.

Given how hard it is to introduce change successfully, it is unsurprising that dedicated teams of transformation specialists exist in most large organisations. But change is not limited to the transformation teams alone. Change originates from across the organisation, and the Run Teams themselves should have their own change agenda. This may sound like a recipe for disaster, full of duplication and conflict. In fact, if handled well, it enhances the benefit profile.

One of the complicating factors is that even the largest transformation tends to comprise a linked series of smaller changes. This can lead to confusion, so it is useful to think about change in terms of four categories based on the scale of change and the authority level required to initiate it.

With so much change, the Run Team are often in conflict. They would like to say yes to everyone, but they just do not have the bandwidth to cope. It is essential to see all changes impacting the team and ensuring a rigorous change process is in place. This puts the onus on the change initiators to resolve capacity constraints and prioritise appropriately.

Finally, leading a team through any change is a challenge. Leading a team through a large portfolio of change, most of which has originated outside of the team, is even more challenging. Ongoing communication is critical, while remembering that, as a leader, you cast a long shadow. Everything you say and do will be analysed. You need to get the message right.

Checklist:

Checklist Item	Status
Do your team understand why you need to innovate and improve?	❑
Do your team have a catalogue of all change initiatives underway that impact them categorised into problem solving, redesign and transformation?	❑
Do your team have a change calendar in place that outlines the impact of all changes, when the changes must be adopted and has this been factored into your capacity plan?	❑
Is there a clear communication plan that your team understand to the extent that they know when, where and how change will be introduced and what is expected of them?	❑

Chapter 9

The 1 Percenters – DIY Problem Solving

"If the doors of perception were cleansed, everything would appear to man as it is—infinite." — *William Blake*

As the team progresses through the season, issues and opportunities will arise. Basic errors may creep in, key players may get injured and must be replaced, well-rehearsed tactics have now been learned by the opposition and are no longer effective, opponents change their strategy and reveal their new secret weapons, experimenting occurs with different combinations of players, additional set piece options, etc.

Some of these are opportunities that need to be capitalised on and others are threats that need to be countered. There is always more to do than the match schedule allows for. With limited resources and so many choices, prioritising the right things to finesse and the new techniques to work on is critical. Do you focus on the quick wins to build momentum or the harder changes that will take longer to implement but may yield better results?

These are decisions the team and coach can make as they are in control and set their own agenda. The changes must be owned by the team.

Running your own change agenda feels good. You get to choose what you work on and when. You are absolutely in control. Getting really good at executing problem solving and redesigning change, plus learning how to get the most out of transformational change, will significantly boost your career. In this chapter and Chapter 10 I will focus on the former, and in Chapter 11 I will focus on transformational change.

Problem solving

The trick to getting value out of continuous innovation and improvement is to execute it at scale. This involves leaders across the organisation identifying and prioritising the opportunities and then executing them every day. There are many toolkits and methodologies available on how to do team-based problem solving, but I've found a simple four-step approach is the easiest for leaders to learn and the fastest to implement.

1. **Identify** innovation and improvement opportunities.
2. **Prioritise** the opportunities.
3. **Solve** the problem.
4. **Sustain** within your operating rhythm.

The people closest to the work see issues and opportunities every day. They are the ones best placed to address these issues. Being armed with a simple toolkit and operating in an environment where it's okay to make mistakes and the team are encouraged to escalate and raise the lid on any issues to make them as transparent and visible as possible lies at the heart of a successful problem-solving mind-set.

Identify innovation and improvement opportunities

Gather a small group of people (8–10) around a table. Hand each person a pack of post-it notes and a pen. Give them five minutes to write down as many ideas as they can for improving the performance of the team (one idea per post-it note). Each idea must benefit either customers, staff or shareholders and be capable of being implemented by the team within three months (this will rule out big technology changes).

Every time I've done this, I've collected 80–100 post-it notes—sometimes many more—and even allowing for a lot of duplication, it's rare that I've come away with fewer than 20–30 ideas that can be implemented immediately.

The opportunities for innovation are everywhere, and those closest to the work are best placed to come up with the ideas, for a few reasons:

1. The people closest to the work know what really needs to be fixed.
2. Ideas from outside frequently fall victim to the "not invented here" syndrome.
3. The people who come up with the ideas must prioritise and implement them, so they need to buy in and assess them properly from the start.

Once you're clear that it's the frontline teams that will be running this, they have several options to generate ideas:

1. Ask "What went well?" and "What can we do better next time?" as part of the review process from the planning cycle.
2. Look for dashboard exceptions—items where performance is not as expected. The quality metrics (e.g., complaints, errors or defects) are always a good place to start.
3. Running a brainstorming session, as outlined in the introduction to this section, will always generate ideas.
4. Creating a "suggestions" space that's easily accessible and visible should capture ideas that the team think of in the moment.
5. Feedback from customers, suppliers and business partners is always a rich seam of ideas worth mining.
6. If your team are particularly negative or sceptical about the process, try to reframe the problem along the lines of "How might we…?"
7. Use the listening posts discussed earlier to generate ideas and opportunities.

It is important at this stage to introduce a filter to ensure the team's idea generation is focussed in the right direction. Team-based problem solving is about creating momentum within the team. The team must feel in control of its own destiny. Therefore, it is important to filter out any ideas that will require resources the team don't have or can't easily access in terms of money, skills, tools, etc. As noted above, no option may involve a major technology change or require more than three months to be implemented. Make note of these bigger opportunities and remind the team that you will raise them with your line manager, but they're out of scope for this session.

Collectively, these seven points should generate more than enough ideas on what you can do to improve and free up capacity. It's important to make the ideas visible to everyone, with credit given to the person coming up with the idea. Exactly how to do this should be left up to the team. Some creative ways that I've seen include a 2 m × 2 m picture on a wall of a lily pond, with each lily pad representing ideas at different stages in the pipeline, and each idea represented as a frog or a flower; and an apple tree on a wall, where each apple represented an idea and as an idea was implemented, it was placed in a basket next to the tree. There are also amazing web-based portals. The advantage of these is that they are easier to see in aggregate across multiple teams, but they must be visible to everyone, always.

This approach, however, does not guarantee success. There are many examples of "suggestion" schemes that fail. One common scenario is where a new leader arrives and asks for suggestions. The leader is then inundated with ideas but hasn't got the resources to implement them. In the eyes of the team, the new leader has already failed at the first hurdle.

Another scenario is where the leader asks for ideas and then dismisses them, usually in a disparaging way. One team leader told me that, occasionally, team members would come to him with suggestions, which he would think about for a few days before returning and telling the team member why it wouldn't work. I asked him if he received many suggestions, and you won't be surprised to hear his answer: "No, not many."

For the small steps to make a big difference, you need a lot of them. To generate not only a lot of ideas but also ideas that turn into action, you must empower and trust the team. Make sure they know from the outset that they will be responsible for generating the ideas and prioritising and executing them. They must feel safe and understand that it's okay to fail. You will need to put safeguards in place to reduce the risk of failure— without crushing momentum.

As you will remember from Chapter 5, nothing bad happens when you focus on quality. There is an endless supply of potential opportunities that can help improve the performance of a team, but there are very few that create a virtuous cycle the way that focussing on quality does. It's great for the customer—better accuracy, more timely responses and a better experience. It's great for productivity and freeing up capacity— less rework, fewer complaints, less time spent checking. It's great for staff—people take pride in excellence, and there is nothing more frustrating than having to correct errors. It's great for risk—fewer errors means fewer claims/penalties/refunds, etc., greater control and more predictable outcomes.

Using quality metrics, such as error rates, complaints/feedback from customers/suppliers/partners or monitoring competitors, generates a great deal of data that can trigger opportunities to improve.

One special case is the quality of the people on your team and their experience. For anyone that has led a team with high staff turnover, you will know the impact this has on quality. There is a misguided perception that everyone on a team is looking for the next promotion. I have found that there are many people who aspire to come to work in an environment they know and do the best job they can but see no need to seek promotion. These people are invaluable. It is their knowledge and experience that will anchor the team's performance. Yes, you need to ensure you bring new people and new ideas into the team but manage the ratio carefully and ensure you recognise and reward the stalwarts who underpin your capability.

Prioritise the opportunities

For most teams, the problem isn't generating ideas, it's prioritising which ones to work on. There are only so many hours in the day. Resources allocated to work on opportunities are, by default, not working on day-to-day customer activities. Occasionally, the prioritisation will be taken out of the team's hands when a senior leader makes a captain's pick and directs them to pursue a specific opportunity. Hopefully, this is the exception rather than the rule, as the success of these types of initiatives is dependent on the team feeling in control and making their own decisions.

While there are some complex prioritisation methods, at a team level, it doesn't need to be complex. There are two techniques that I think are particularly useful: importance-performance matrix (Slack, et al., 2015) and filtering and voting.

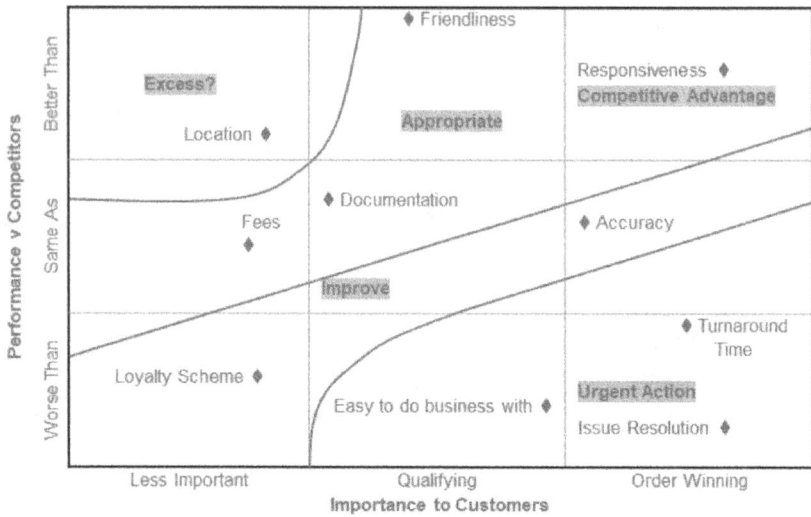

Figure 43 – Importance v performance matrix (Slack, et al., 2013).

The importance-performance matrix requires you to assess all the features of a product or service and assess how important each feature is to the customer and how well you perform relative to your competitors (Figure 43). Each feature is typically assessed on a nine-point scale and depending on where it fits in the resultant matrix there are recommended actions. Assessing the features is ideally done by the customers; however, if that's not appropriate, asking the sales, relationship and service teams to at least provide a proxy is a good start.

The various zones then help determine prioritisation. Any item falling in the "Urgent Action" zone needs to be addressed as a priority. Items in the "Competitive Advantage" zone must also be prioritised highly to defend the product/service positioning. If you have projects underway on items in the "Excess Resources" zone, you should consider stopping these activities.

This is an excellent tool to really help the team focus and filter out the noise, but it's likely that some further work will be required to nail the one or two opportunities you are going to work on. This is where the filtering and voting technique comes in.

In practice, the approach is straightforward:

1. **Screen** out ideas that are beyond the resources of the team to execute.

2. Cluster similar ideas and write a suitable problem statement.

3. Assess likely benefits and feasibility.

4. Vote on the filtered list of ideas.

Screen

The first prioritisation step happens at the idea generation stage, and that is to set up the boundaries. The following are good constraints to cull the more outlandish suggestions:

- The team needs to be able to implement any opportunity raised with the resources to hand (i.e., the people they have).
- They should be opportunities the team can implement within 90 days.
- The reliance on technology should be limited to simple automation tools or quick-fix configuration changes.

It's important to explain why you are applying this filtering approach to avoid leaving the team feeling discouraged. Bigger ideas can be captured and discussed in the appropriate forums. This session is about focussing on the things the team can control. If you missed this step at the idea generation stage, it is important to apply this filter now. The team can waste an enormous amount of time and effort trying to build support to fund a technology change that may well sit towards the bottom of a long, long list of priorities.

Having said that, be careful how you filter at this stage, and don't dismiss out-of-hand suggestions that breach these criteria. There may be some excellent ideas that a leader in another department can help you progress. For the purposes of this exercise, however, you want the team to focus on the things that they can control.

Cluster

The next step is to cluster ideas. It's highly likely that different team members will come up with the same or similar ideas. Capturing all of these on post-it notes, clustering similar post-it notes together and then asking the team to define each cluster as a single problem statement will also rationalise the number of ideas to prioritise. In practice, what the team writes on the post-it note will vary—some will couch their suggestion as an opportunity (e.g., "fix process A") and others will offer a solution (e.g., "get team A to do both steps and avoid the handoff that's causing the problems"). It's important you don't lose this context when you cluster. It's also important to let the debate run and tease out the nuances. At face value, what may appear to be the same issue can be something completely different in the mind of the team member who came up with the idea initially.

Assess

Plot each of the clustered opportunities on a simple 2 × 2 matrix (Figure 44). Potential benefits should be on the vertical axis and "doability" on the horizontal axis. Plotting is done with the knowledge and experience of the team. It's a best guess, and there is a risk that the guess is wrong—particularly the "doability" part, where team members frequently underestimate just how complex it is to change something. Over time, the team will learn, and the quality of their assessments will improve. It's important not to blame anyone if an assessment turns out to be wrong. Use it as an opportunity to learn and do better next time.

Figure 44 – Problem-solving assessment matrix.

Once you've plotted the opportunities, the labels in the matrix suggest the next steps. The ones in the "Gold" category—opportunities that are relatively straightforward to implement with high benefits—should move to the next stage of prioritisation. Avoid those with low benefits that are hard to do. Opportunities in the strategic category should be escalated for consideration at more senior levels. Quick wins are good "filler" opportunities. If someone has a couple of hours of spare capacity, this is a great way to use the time profitably.

Vote

All the opportunities that have made it through to this stage should be implemented. The question is, which one should go first? There is a straightforward technique called multi-voting that can help:

1. Put each idea on a post-it note and stick the notes on a wall.
2. Allocate each team member three sticky dots (three votes each), and ask each team member to pick their top three ideas by sticking one dot next to the relevant post-it note.
3. The idea with the most dots is the first opportunity to work on.

Having decided what opportunity to prioritise, the next step is to solve the problem.

Solve the problem

Some people prefer to use positive language (i.e., refer to an opportunity rather than a problem). Language aside, they are two sides of the same coin, and it really doesn't matter which term you use if it appeals to the team and motivates them to innovate and improve. Intuitively, I prefer to use the term "problem", as it simplifies the framing of what you need to do. In simple terms, the problem is that there is a gap between what you want to happen and what is currently happening, between your target state and your current state. The problem statement explains the gap.

It may be that there is a feature your customers would like but you don't currently offer, or your competitors can answer enquiries within one hour and you currently take two hours, or the number of complaints has risen unexpectedly, or your current productivity level is 90% and you must hit 95% to make your budget, or your team are complaining that they are doing too much overtime. Whatever the case, you must specify what the ideal state at the end of this project will be and what the current position is at the start of the project. This must be expressed in metrics and numbers with explanatory context of why the current state is not acceptable. The problem is then simple: "How do you close the gap?"

I try to minimise the use of jargon, but one of the most helpful problem-solving tools that I've found is called an "A3" (Figure 45 – A3 template). It is part of the Lean toolkit, and—as its name suggests—it is a template based on an A3-size sheet of paper. The aim is to get all the information relevant to the problem onto a single piece of paper (without resorting to 2-point font). It also acts as a communication tool, so using charts, photographs, tables and diagrams helps to bring the A3 to life. It should be visible to everyone on the team and stay visible for the duration of the project.

An A3 is broken into discrete sections:

- **Headings** – This section states the project name, sponsor, project lead and status.
- **Problem statement** – This section sets the context, current state, problem definition and target state.
- **Root cause analysis** – This is a "five whys" analysis and/or a fishbone analysis to identify the root cause.
- **Plan/Do** – This is where you state how you will address the root cause and prevent it from happening again (countermeasures) as well as the actions you will take to implement the plan.
- **Check** – This is where you test your hypotheses in a limited pilot.
- **Act** – Assuming the intervention is having the desired effect, this section is where you state how you will roll out the actions more broadly and reflect on what you've learned and who else might benefit from this solution.

Project Name:	Reduce Payment Failures		Status:	Green
Sponsor:	Sharon		Project Owner:	Ben

Background
- We have an objective to be the best-in-class delivery team
- The payments complete both manual and STP payments

Current State
Payment Process
- Daily – 3,250
- Peak – 5,650
Team not currently balanced

Quality
Current manual accuracy 99.3%

Problem Definition
420 payments must be reworked per month, which impacts customers by delaying receipt of funds. Subsequent customer and bank calls add to the workload.

Target State
Accuracy must be improved with a target of 99.99% for manual payments.

Root Cause

Top 3 Errors
1. Missed SLA
2. Wrong fees
3. Duplicates

5 Whys
Why 1
Why 2

Why 5

Root Cause
1. Forecasting
2. No validation
3. Training

Plan
We will implement the following countermeasures:
1. Improve volume forecasting
2. Cross-skill checkers
3. Apply validation rules

Do

Counter	Action	Who	When
Forecast	Improve	Ben	24/4
X-Skill	Manual	Ming	15/5
	Checkers	Ming	15/5
Validate	Design	Padma	20/4
	Develop	Padma	5/5
	Test	Padma	18/5
	Deploy	Padma	31/5

Check

- Benefits tracking to plan
- Missed SLA plateaued

Act

- Issue with time stamping
- All measures now tracking to plan
- Next steps to ensure improvements embedded

Action

Action	Who	When
Embed change into op rhythm	Sharon	15/6

Reflect
- Project went very well, even though not all errors resolved on 1st time
- Great team work

Figure 45 – A3 template.

For such a simple tool, it applies a significant amount of rigour and prevents people from jumping to conclusions and moving straight to solution mode. It pushes you to truly understand the root cause of the problem, using facts and data, and then determine ways to overcome the root cause. It's not a perfect science, and there's a chance that your hypotheses are flawed; hence, the recommended approach is to test the hypotheses in a limited pilot. Gather the results, and if performance improves and there is a clear trend towards the target state, then it is time to roll out the change more broadly. If the performance metrics don't change, it's time to revisit the root cause analysis, check your assumptions and come up with additional hypotheses. Finally, once you have rolled out the change, there is a placeholder for reflection. For example: "What went well and what can you do better next time? Are there other teams that might benefit from the same solution?"

There are a few dos and don'ts when completing an A3:

- It's primarily a communication tool, so do make it interesting and easy to read— colour, charts, pictures, highlights, tables, numbers, etc. All speak louder than words.
- It's a "living" document, so do make sure it is updated at each milestone (completing a section) or update to the status and action plan.
- Do make sure you assign an owner to each task on the action plan and a due date.
- Do remember that the Target State and the Ideal State are not necessarily the same thing. Don't be too hard on yourself when defining the Target State. It should be an achievable step towards the Ideal State. You may aspire to zero defects but solving all defect-creating problems within one project is probably unrealistic.
- Don't jump to conclusions too soon. Give yourself time to ensure the trend on your "Check" graph really is a trend.
- Don't be too upset if your original hypothesis turned out to be incorrect. Go back to the root cause analysis and work through the data and assumptions to see what you missed.
- Don't forget to celebrate your successes and reward/recognise those involved.

- Do remember that continuous innovation and improvement is very much about momentum. Showcasing completed templates is a great way to remind the team just how much they have achieved.
- Don't forget to complete the "Reflect" section. This is incredibly important, as it will influence how you can improve the A3 process as well as sharing best practices.

Sustain within your operating rhythm

As I've mentioned several times, a couple of small steps won't make a big difference, but lots of small steps will. To make this happen you must ensure that innovating and solving problems are very much part of your team's day-to-day operating rhythm. You must schedule time for it in your team meetings and at the end of every day when you ask: "What went well?" and "What can we do better next time?" Record the responses so you don't lose the insights.

Not only do you need to make it part of your operating rhythm, you need to make it part of the culture and a habit that is truly embedded. Organisations have different ways of doing this—some use the performance management system and set targets at an individual level, while others build momentum by using it as a team-building activity. For me, success is when it's just what we do. No one needs to be incentivised or rewarded specifically with coming up with better ways to do things. It's just part of the job.

There is an inherent conflict. On the one hand, in order to innovate and solve problems, people need to be creative; on the other hand, it takes discipline to turn it into a habit, and routine runs the risk of it going stale. There are ways around this. Setting a theme for the month such as customer, quality, risk or productivity is one way of keeping the ideas fresh. Another way is to turn continuous innovation into a game or a competition, which works well in some cultures. You can change the venue where the meeting is held, or run icebreakers that shake individuals out of their routine and release their creative juices. I've seen leaders run brainstorming sessions where the team had to stand on one leg and generate as many ideas as possible before someone put their other foot down (making sure you factor in safety/ability considerations). It is up to you as the leader to make this fun and engaging. Remember that in this context, "leader" doesn't necessarily mean the boss but the person leading the initiative or the champion.

One final point is to make sure the team are benefitting from the innovation and improvement ideas. It's great to improve the customer experience, reduce risk or drive productivity, but what's in it for the team? I typically like to encourage teams to split their efforts: one-third for the customer, one-third for productivity/risk and one-third for the team. And remember that your idea of what the team want and their idea of what they want is not necessarily the same thing. Many years ago, I had a boss who was concerned that the building our team worked in was looking tired and a little drab. He thought it would be good for morale if we painted the building. I suggested that we should ask the team what they would like us to do. The answer: replenish the cutlery in the kitchen regularly, as there were never enough knives and forks! A far simpler problem to solve, with a follow-up problem: "What's happening to the knives and forks?"

Chapter summary

This chapter has focussed on innovation and improvement within the Run Team at both the team and function level. With an ever-present requirement to free up capacity, deliver better quality and service to customers, reduce risk and empower and engage staff, embedding a continuous innovation mind-set and capability is critical to running a team during a digital transformation.

This chapter focussed on problem solving, which is relevant at all levels within an organisation, but it is particularly relevant at a team level. The people closest to the work are the ones best placed to identify, prioritise, and solve problems sustainably. Quality is a special case. The more you focus on quality, the more likely it is that you will see improvement in metrics across the board: customer, staff, risk and financial performance.

Finally, the benefits associated with these types of change are material. Embedding a problem-solving culture will deliver 5–15% p.a. in benefits. In a virtuous cycle, this approach will significantly enhance the customer experience, reduce risk and help build a far more engaged workforce. It is also far less risky than a transformational approach, as the risk is spread across many teams.

Checklist:

Checklist Item	Status
Do your team operate in a safe environment to freely raise issues without blame?	❑
Do your team follow a simple, standard approach to solve problems?	❑
Do your team know how to generate improvement opportunities, and is there a current list of problems to solve?	❑
Do your team practice a simple and effective way of filtering out and prioritising which problems they will work on?	❑
Do your team have a toolkit to solve problems?	❑
Do your team schedule time for solving problems regularly and deploy techniques to maintain momentum?	❑

Chapter 10

Timing the Peak – DIY Redesigning

"The Road goes ever on and on
Down from the door where it began.
Now far ahead the Road has gone,
And I must follow, if I can."
— *J.R.R. Tolkien, The Fellowship of the Ring*

Throughout the season, the team are making small tweaks each week; however, they are also focussed on bigger changes they need to implement as the season draws to a close. These may be changes that improve the team's recovery rate as the pace picks up towards the end of the season, set plays or team configurations, or it may just be simulating the pressure teams face at the "pointy end" of the season. The All Blacks are renowned for training in near-match-like conditions. That is, they don't stop if they make a mistake, they play on and they review the mistakes at the end of the session. This brings an intensity to the training that closely follows what they expect to experience on match day and makes sure their ability to adapt and respond when mistakes happen is also tested. World-class teams are constantly reviewing and redesigning aspects of their game. There is no complacency.

The redesigning category of change is usually a step up from problem solving in terms of resource requirements and sign-off authority. In this context, it is not about designing a new product or service; it is more about the design of the processes to deliver existing products or services. The tools and techniques can be applied to a single process through to an end-to-end customer journey covering many individual processes and departments. There are a range of methodologies in use such as Business Process Re-engineering, Lean/

Six Sigma and human-centred design, to name the most common ones. Going into detail on each of these is beyond the scope of this book, and there are many books dedicated to discussing each one.

I thought it would be more appropriate to highlight a typical redesign improvement pathway and some of the redesign considerations.

Where to start

Whether you're taking on a function/team for the first time or an established leader looking for the next challenge, implementing change is an exciting proposition. Most leaders aspire to leave the team in a better place than when they started. Coming up with the 100-day plan or the next phase of the strategy is one of those tasks that is both critical from a "doability" perspective as well as gaining a buy-in from the team. A plan with no buy-in is highly likely to fail. In some cases, there may be a strategy and a road map in place, and the task is simply to continue executing. In other cases, there may be a significant issue or pain point that your line manager has asked you to prioritise. For the rest, it's up to the leader to figure out what to do and where to start. We'll cover what to do in the next section. In this section we'll focus on where to start.

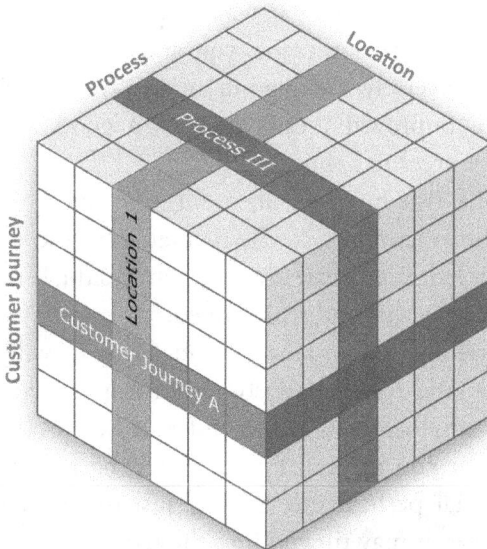

Figure 46 – Where to start options.

169

At a functional leader level, you have several options. You could take a team-by-team approach, customer journey-by-customer journey approach, process-by-process approach, location-by-location approach, etc. As you will realise by now, as a system, many of the options overlap (Figure 46). How do you choose? The most important thing is to get momentum and learn from your first venture. You need to pick an area where the odds of succeeding are stacked in your favour. Here are some of the criteria to consider:

- It must be large enough to be material but not so large that it puts the whole function at risk (e.g., don't bet the farm).
- The people working in the area need to be change hungry. A team that has had little change flow through or is actively change resistant will present enormous challenges.
- The opportunity needs to be clear (i.e., the dashboard, scorecard and other listening post data must point to this as an area where there is a clear performance uplift opportunity).
- Without pre-empting the "as-is" analysis, the underlying problems need to be visible (i.e., there must be some reasonable operational data).
- The stakeholders need to be aligned. Playing with a critical process when you haven't got any runs on the board will make stakeholders nervous and put you and the team under a lot of pressure. Conversely, seeking out an area that stakeholders would like to see improved means there is a good chance they will provide resources to help.
- What is the risk involved, including the underlying risk of the process, the execution risk, the reputational risk, etc? You should stay away from processes with high residual risk until your methodology is well and truly honed.
- Think carefully about timing and how it will impact your results. Kicking off a relatively resource-intensive piece of work a few months before the year-end and before any benefits will flow may set you up well for the following financial year, but if your financial performance is only just on track in the current financial year, it may tip you into the red.
- Where processes are distributed across multiple locations, it's a

reasonable assumption that they will be fragmented and there will be lots of opportunity. However, they are hard. Travel costs will be high and cultural differences can get in the way.
- Are you clear about the underlying problem you are trying to address? If you have a cost problem, and 80% of your costs are in one location, then where to start is obvious.

Notwithstanding the above, unless you have a very specific problem to address (e.g., leadership in a particular team or cost in a particular location), I would always choose to take a customer journey-by-customer journey approach. With the list of customer journeys you completed as part of Chapter 5 and Chapter 6 on customer and quality, it's a simple question of prioritising these. I would use the following criteria and score each customer journey out of five (Figure 47):

- Number of customers impacted.
- Benefit for customers.
- Size of team supporting the journey.
- Cost of supporting the journey.
- Number of locations supporting the journey.
- Change readiness of the people supporting the journey.
- Stakeholder support for improving the journey.
- Implementation risk.
- Known execution obstacles.

Criteria	CJ 1	CJ 2	CJ 3	CJ 4	CJ 5
Customers Impacted	1	4	2	2	4
Material Impact	5	2	3	1	2
# FTEs	2	5	4	2	1
Cost	4	4	1	5	5
# Locations*	1	5	4	1	1
Change Readiness	1	3	5	5	1
Stakeholder Support	4	3	2	1	2
Risk*	2	2	5	1	2
Known Obstacles*	1	4	4	3	2
Total Score	21	32	30	21	20

Inverse scoring applied
CJ = Customer Journey

Figure 47 – Redesign prioritisation matrix.

Now that you know which area to start work on, the next step is to figure out what to do.

An operational excellence journey

As the Change Authority Matrix (Figure 41) highlights, transformation is typically driven at a divisional or enterprise level. Problem solving is more commonly driven by individual functions and teams. Redesign can be at a divisional or enterprise level but also at a functional level.

Figure 48 – Operational excellence journey.

Knowing what to do can be overwhelming as there are always so many things that could be worked on. However, in these circumstances, once you've got the basics in place—which were discussed in Part 2—there is a logical, standard path (Figure 48):

- Control (i.e., Part 2).
- Stop.
- Consolidate.
- Standardise.
- Simplify.

- Re-engineer.
- Automate.
- Outsource/offshore.

Strangely, some service organisations tend to tackle this in the reverse order, which has led to the process proliferation and fragmentation that makes digital transformation so hard today. Trying to automate broken, fragmented processes with robotics (see Chapter 11 for a detailed description of what this entails), not only delivers limited benefit, it also makes the underlying operating environment far more complex. Following this sequence is a building-block approach, with each block setting the foundation for the next block to come.

Stop – The easiest way to create capacity is to create a "stop doing" list and stop doing whatever is on the list! Over time, the scope of activities that a team undertakes changes. What were once special requests or one-offs will become routine, reports will be produced that no one reads, multiple teams will each review a common process, etc. Simply listing all the team activities and asking, "Who is paying for this—either directly and indirectly—and are they happy to do so?" very quickly identifies those activities that are no longer required.

There is also a special case that falls into this category, which is commonly referred to as "failure demand". This is work that is done because something in the system has failed. Password resets, statement reprint requests, handling returned mail and help desks dealing with log-on issues are typical examples. In most service organisations, there are large, dedicated teams doing this type of work. A service centre walk-through, asking why the customer has called, will reveal just how endemic this is. The strategy is simple: find the root cause of why the underlying service/process is failing and fix it—this will stop the failure demand. The opportunity is enormous.

Consolidate – Consolidation is about trying to create scale and reverse the effects of the issues caused by fragmentation. Over time, jobs have become more and more specialised and dispersed across locations and functions. This creates unnecessary risk if an employee falls sick or decides to leave. It limits flexibility in terms of being able to adapt to changes in demand. The way to address this issue is to "sweep things up into piles". Activities, processes, people and functions that have similar characteristics are brought together. Co-locating where possible or putting these activities under the same leadership structure will help the team find synergies and reduce duplication, at the very least.

Team members don't always recognise the degree of fragmentation. One example I remember is where servicing teams for a specific function were country based. When both countries moved the work to an offshore location, this should have presented an ideal opportunity for consolidation. However, over time, the long-form names for each team had been substituted by three-letter acronyms: one team was ABC and the other was ACB. They did the same work but supported clients in different countries; however, because they had different names and different leaders, the teams couldn't see this as a simple consolidation opportunity. Another example is where people talk about their individual experience of a process as if it were the same as everyone else's experience. Ask the team to give you the process map for the claims process and you will get dozens of them—each process map incorporating a specific variant (e.g., regional variation)—one map for each region, client variation (e.g., unique maps for major clients), claim-size variation, etc. When you look at the maps, 80–90% of the steps will be the same. Unfortunately, most people don't have time to analyse them in detail. As such, what should be one process with some options ends up being dozens of processes that need to be documented, governed, maintained, audited, etc. Getting rid of this process proliferation is where the magic starts to happen. It is extraordinarily difficult to optimise processes without consolidating first.

It's worth noting that radical product rationalisation and consolidation will play a significant role in simplifying the business.

Standardise – If you have two people doing the same task in different locations, they will, in all likelihood, do it differently. In most services businesses that I've been involved with, even if you have two people sitting next to each other doing the same task, they will do it differently. This is highly inefficient and very risky. If an individual is absent and someone else needs to pick up their work, the chances of making mistakes are far higher. Moreover, if everyone follows the same process and one person comes up with an improvement, everyone benefits. If everyone does it differently, only the person coming up with the improvement will benefit. Standardise does not mean "any colour you like as long as it's black". Sensible uniformity is a far better expression (i.e., standardise where it makes commercial sense to do so).

When you decide to standardise, it's important that the people who do the work are the people who decide what the standard way of doing the work should be. There are two basic methods: a) identify the best version of the process and migrate to that one; b) merge the various versions—in which case, you should simplify the process at the same time.

You need the commitment of the team. Trying to impose standards without the team's buy-in is almost certain to fail. Bringing the discussion back to the need to deliver a consistent service and using the cake analogy (see Chapter 5) will help gain commitment.

Simplify – With a standard way of doing the work decided upon, the next step is to simplify the way the work is done. In Chapter 5, I discussed process complexity and how to simplify by removing steps, decision points, handoffs and the number of systems required to run a process. When deciding which steps to remove, the Lean waste toolkit is a good place to start. The toolkit describes the type of waste common in a process. After you identify it, try and eliminate it. There are eight types of waste:

- **Transport** – This is anything that needs to be moved or carried. In an office environment, a good example is filing hard copy documents or storing original documents.
- **Inventory** – This is where there is a store of something (work in progress or resources) that is not being worked on. This could be anything from office stationery, people "on the bench", files piled up on an individual's desk, an inbox overflowing with emails, or a to-do list. Multitasking creates inventory. You can only work on one thing at a time, so whatever is on your to-do list that you're not currently working on is inventory.
- **Motion** – This is any unnecessary movement. Examples include walking to a printer, searching for files on a computer and walking to meetings.
- **Waiting** – This is any time delay where the customer must wait, including being on hold, waiting for people to join a teleconference or a sign-off from an authoriser. There are

many euphemisms in use—such as backlogs, work baskets and queues—which are all areas on which to focus. Remember, if there's more than one item in a queue, there's an opportunity for improvement.

- **Overproduction** – This is waste where you produce more than the customer wants. Examples of this include bringing too many hard copies of a report to a meeting, creating reports that no one reads, keying the same data multiple times and "reply all" emails.

- **Overprocessing** – This is where you have done more work than the customer requires. Typical examples include unnecessary formatting on reports, too many signatures on a report, multiple iterations of a report and collecting unnecessary information.

- **Defects** – This is any work that needs to be reworked and checked. Examples include manual entry errors, lost files, incomplete information and incorrect calculations.

- **Skills** – This is where people's skills, knowledge, abilities and potential are not fully utilised. This is by far and away the most obvious waste I've seen in large, mature service organisations where those closest to the customer are not empowered to bring all that they have to offer to the job. Examples include inadequate tools and resources and setting people to work without providing basic skills training, such as how to use the phone system.

The acronym TIM WOODS is a useful way to remember the different types of waste.

Re-engineer – A simple, standard process is one that is ready for re-engineering and a focus on workflow. It is not simply enhancing the existing process; it requires a significant rethink of how the value the customer requires is delivered. The redesign toolkits mentioned above each have their own methodology and area of focus (e.g., Six sigma focusses on removing defects, whereas Lean focusses on reducing elapsed time between receiving a service request and completing the service request). Leveraging whatever is being used elsewhere in your organisation makes more sense than trying to introduce your own technique.

One other area worth mentioning in this section is workflow.

Controlling how work flows is particularly challenging in a modern service environment as, for the most part, you can't see the work. In a chocolate bar factory, you know there is a problem if there's a pool of chocolate oozing across the factory floor. In a service environment, most of the work in progress is hidden away in computers and stored in queues. It's not always easy to see how many items there are in a queue, how many queues there are across the whole service, which items should be prioritised, which ones are beyond deadline and which items have been misallocated. In short, queues are not only a form of waste but a major contributor to poor service delivery.

While many of these issues can be addressed with workflow or case management software, it's also an opportunity to consider switching from a "push" to a "pull" method of managing work. It is not particularly easy to implement, as in some ways it is counterintuitive, but the benefits are significant. When someone receives work to do, their natural inclination is to do it as quickly as possible and then pass it on to the next person in the chain. If the next person in the chain is busy, this new piece of work will just sit in a queue. The alternative is to "hold" the work at the start of the process and only release it when it can flow through the process without stopping (i.e., each operator would receive a new request just as they have completed the previous request). This is called "one-piece flow" or Kanban. There are a number of benefits:

- Holding all the work in progress from the start is not only cheaper, it's also easier to see and count.
- Every step in a process adds cost, so downstream queues are expensive.
- Removing the work in progress from the system means any production problems are immediately visible. If everyone has piles of work on their desk, and one team member is struggling, no one will know. If everyone only has the piece of work they are currently working on, and one team member has a problem, everyone knows because the whole flow stops. It exposes weaknesses, defects and problems in the system, which can then be fixed.

- Like a river, a process should only flow in one direction, which means defects are not passed on through the system.

Automate – There are two types of automation that you can consider: tactical and strategic. Tactical automation includes using techniques like macros, robotics or simple configuration changes. These changes are relatively limited in scope and cost. Typically, they can be implemented within a matter of days or a few weeks at most. Configuration and rule changes impact how a core system performs its tasks. Macros and robotics do not change the underlying systems but typically emulate the manual work a team member does (e.g., cutting and pasting from one system to another). Tools such as Blue Prism, Automation Anywhere and UiPath are seeing wide application. Bear in mind that tactical automation adds complexity to the overall technology landscape and there is a cost in terms of managing, maintaining and governing it. Be clear about the implications before you embark on this path.

Strategic automation, on the other hand, can cover everything from introducing artificial intelligence tools to re-platforming a process. The time to complete and cost can be significant. It is extremely important that you go through these steps in sequence before automation. Many automation projects fail to meet expectations because the processes they are trying to automate are too complex, fragmented and non-standard.

One area that consistently seems to be troublesome is where organisations try to automate a process without first consolidating, standardising and simplifying those processes. Trying to automate the most complex exceptions can be extremely expensive and, in many cases, futile. This will use up project funds, and as the project starts to run out of money, the project team will default to manual workarounds. It's far better to automate the whole process for the majority of cases and then handle the exceptions through a separate manual process.

There is one specific category of automation that merits further discussion and that is self-service. Enabling customers to lodge and fulfil a request, at a time that suits them, is both popular with customers and organisations. In essence, the customer is doing the work; therefore, it must be straightforward with a clear support path if the customer gets stuck. Getting this wrong can lead to significant customer frustration and complaints. Having said that, for me this is an eminently sensible approach that puts the customer in control, and assuming there is appropriate validation in place, quality should be significantly enhanced—not too many customers spell their own name incorrectly.

Outsource/offshore – The final step in the functional improvement strategy is to consider outsourcing and offshoring. The key point here is to understand why you are doing it and what you are giving away. Once you have outsourced a process, it is very difficult to bring it back. You need to be very clear on how the process contributes to your overall competitive advantage and why someone else can do it at a lower cost/better quality than you, especially after allowing for the third party to make a profit margin. As with automation, think very carefully about going down this path before you have completed the consolidate, standardise and simplify steps. There are success stories of third parties doing "lift-and-shift" and making it work well, but there are also horror stories.

The commercial arrangements obviously play a critical role in the success. I have seen organisations expect a third party, with no prior knowledge of the process, to run a process with a new team that involves the following issues:

- There are 10% fewer team members.
- All team members are one grade lower than the onshore team.
- There are wider spans of control and thus fewer managers.
- Overtime is not factored into the resource requirements.
- There is no allowance for a productivity ramp-up as experience increases.

This is very much a false economy. Trying to squeeze the provider in this way will almost certainly impact your customers. Once you have outsourced a process, if it then performs poorly, you will need to work through a third party to address the issue. This can be tricky. As a minimum, make sure the processes are well documented at work instruction level, you complete an FMEA before you transition the work and you hire the right number of people allowing for a longer time to competency.

It's also worth considering asking the Business Process Outsource provider (BPO) to redesign and/or transform the process over and above operating the base process. If you are charged on a "per seat" basis, there is no real incentive to do this. Whereas if you negotiate a "Lift, Shift and Transform" contract, you should end up with better processes.

You can execute the first four steps of the operational excellence journey within a team or function, with few if any additional resources. Tactical automation can also be included in this category. Workflow that introduces new technology, strategic automation and outsourcing/offshoring typically requires investment funding.

With this approach, you can go step by step or bundle steps together into a program of work (e.g., consolidate, standardise and simplify). The important point is that it's far easier to do these in sequence than to do at random.

Redesign considerations

Irrespective of the methodology you choose, it's important to consider the following when thinking about redesigning processes:

- **Customer** – Hopefully this goes without saying, but the most important point is to understand what the customer values about the service. If you listed all the activities required to deliver the service, which ones would the customers be prepared to pay for? This may be easier said than done in a service environment, as customers are not always able to articulate what they value, and even if they can, it may be subject to change—as covered in the section on defining quality. A critical customer-related discussion is where the same service is provided to different customer segments. If the segments value different things, the service may need to be designed differently for each segment.
- **Volume, variety, variation and visibility** – These are the 4 Vs of design (Slack, et al., 2015). Profiling the process in terms of how much volume it will need to handle, how seasonal that demand is (variation), the range of variants that customers will expect and how visible the process is to customers will determine the type of technology you will need, the skills required to run the process, the location of the process, the type of layout and how flexible the process needs to be to cope with demand changes.

They also determine how complex the design decisions will be. A high-volume process that must cope with a lot of variety will typically be complex and expensive to design. The higher the volume, the more likely it is to use highly automated solutions, but the more variety there is, the more expensive the solutions are to build. This is why a digital transformation that essentially tries to digitise legacy processes in a mature service organisation is doomed to fail!

- **Overall objective** – The overall objective for any service delivery team should be to deliver the service as specified at the lowest possible cost. That does not imply it has to be a low-cost solution—quite the opposite. For example, if a service specification includes client-embedded resources fluent in a minimum of five languages and detailed "fail-fix" knowledge of your core applications, this would be a very expensive service to provide. But cost does matter. It is not about cutting costs; it is about finding the most cost-effective way of meeting your customer obligations.

- **Long–thin v short–fat** – This is a design decision about how specialised you want your resources to be. Breaking a process into many steps with specialist resources at each step (long–thin) ensures you pay for precisely the skill that is required at each step, but there is a cost of transferring the work from one person to the next and the risk of on-the-job boredom. Alternatively, if you consolidate the steps and recruit resources capable of performing the whole process (short--fat), the skill level required will be set by the most complex task, hence you may be overpaying for other simpler tasks in the process. Take laser eye surgery as an example. The ophthalmic surgeon could do (almost) everything: admit the patient, brief the patient, prep the patient, perform the surgery, administer recovery and discharge the patient. However, many of these tasks do not require the skills of a qualified ophthalmic surgeon. At the same time, some of those tasks—such as admitting the patient—require skills that are more readily available and cost less, such as clerical skills, and they may be skills that the surgeon is not particularly adept at.

- **Technology choice** – Many would have heard the story of

NASA investing millions of dollars to develop a ballpoint pen that would work in zero gravity, whereas the Russians chose to use a pencil for their early space flights. When designing a process, it is often tempting to jump to the latest, bleeding-edge software, but one of the underlying principles of the Toyota Production System called out in *The Toyota Way* (Liker, 2004) is the need for stable technology. It's also important to recognise that technology doesn't just mean computer hardware and software—if your job is to remove staples, a staple remover is a possible technology choice. In many services, the decision often comes down to the degree of automation. The 4 Vs discussed above suggest an approach: high volume and low variety lends itself to automation, whereas low volume and high variety is more about facilitating and enabling than fulfilling the process. One final point to consider is the relevant labour rate. In high-cost countries, there may be a valid business case to automate processes with a handful of resources, whereas in low-cost countries, to generate the same return on investment (ROI) may require processes with hundreds of people working on them.

- **Centralise v decentralise** – There is no doubt that it is far easier running a team that is located in the same space. But this isn't always practical. Some team members may need to be close to the customer. Teams may need to be split to provide resilience in case one site goes offline. Many teams operate onshore and offshore. This is usually a simple cost-benefit exercise. Centralised teams, in my experience, tend to be at least 10–15% more efficient. The question is whether the reasons for decentralising merit giving up this efficiency.

- **Capacity lead v lag** – With growth comes the need for new capacity. There are two choices: bring on the capacity early, ahead of the growth, knowing that the growth projection is a forecast and may be wrong; or bring on the capacity as the growth hits. The former delivers better service but can be a costly overinvestment, and the latter can have a negative impact on service if you are too slow to respond. The right approach will usually depend on how big the chunks of incremental capacity are. If it's just a question of adding a few people, then you can wait; however, if you need to build or source new facilities, then it's a trickier problem.

- **Location** – Deciding where you locate your capacity is one of the most significant and politically sensitive design decisions an organisation can make. Choosing how many sites to run and where to locate them are difficult decisions to make. There are many factors to consider:
  - ○ The need to be close to customers.
  - ○ The availability and depth of labour pools with the required skills.
  - ○ Language and cultural considerations (e.g., Manila has built a reputation as an offshore contact centre hub because of its strong English language skills, low-cost labour and positive customer service attitude).
  - ○ Operating global businesses across many time zones has seen businesses develop "follow-the-sun" models.
  - ○ Geopolitical considerations (e.g., establishing a site may be the price of entering a market).
  - ○ Labour cost and tax considerations are also strong drivers (e.g., labour arbitrage was one of the main reasons for the rapid growth of the business process outsourcing industry in India, and many governments offer regional tax incentives to locate sites in deindustrialised, redevelopment zones).
- **Suppliers and partners** – Choosing the right suppliers and partners is also a complex decision:
  - ○ Will the relationship be transactional or more of a partnership?
  - ○ Are the potential partners culturally aligned?
  - ○ How is performance measured and rewarded/compensated for?
  - ○ Can the partner provide support in all markets?
  - ○ What are the risks in terms of key resources, financial stability and access to technology?

With an increasing focus on ecosystems and platforms, this area of consideration is gaining increased focus.

- **Risk and resilience** – All teams must be prepared to operate in two modes: business as usual or business continuity planning mode. The latter is invoked when something fails in BAU. When designing a process, you must design for both BAU and BCP mode. This involves:

- ○ Understanding the criticality of the process—some processes must be "always on", while for others it's okay if they are offline for a few days (e.g., an internal reporting process).
- ○ Completing an FMEA (see Chapter 6) to understand what can go wrong, how to design out the possible failure modes and mitigate the impact of those that can't be designed out.
- ○ Developing recovery plans for each scenario.

- **Redesign approach** – There are several tools available to assist the redesign approach. The human-centred design/design thinking approach is one, many business process management (BPM) tools have their own and for end-to-end processes that span multiple departments, there's no substitute for getting everyone in the room with a bunch of post-it notes and working it out on a wall. It is somewhat old fashioned, but it is also very effective as a visual tool and great for collaboration.

- **Process design principles** – At a more detailed level highlighted in Figure 49, the core elements to bear in mind are to keep a customer focus, design in quality and control, keep it simple, balance the work across the process, minimise complexity and remove waste.

CUSTOMER FOCUS	• Design processes for the customer first - what do they truly value • Design work flow around value adding activities, not functions or departments • Provide a single point of contact for customers and suppliers whenever possible
QUALITY & CONTROL	• Ensure defects are not able to pass from one stage to the next • Control input quality ferociously • Design processes so they cannot fail
KEEP IT SIMPLE	• Capture information once • Eliminate "just in case" activities • Minimise the opportunity for variation • Ensure process data is available and visible
BALANCE WORK	• Distribute work evenly across subprocesses • Break work into "small" packages and process continuously • Minimise wating and delays • Work is performed where it makes the most sense • Design processes for flow
MINIMISE COMPLEXITY	• Minimise the number of steps • Minimise the number of handoffs – they drive errors • Minimise the number of decisions — but empower the front line to make these decisions • Minimise the number of applications / technologies used
REMOVE WASTE	• Re-engineer first then automate • Clearly identify all waste and eradicate ruthlessly

Figure 49 – Process design principles.

Picking the team to do the work

The teams that lead this type of redesign work tend to be small – 3–5 FTEs typically. In my opinion, they should be drawn from the line with support from one or two specialists (e.g., a lean coach or tactical automation specialist). The project should be owned and run by a manager from the area impacted—whether they do this as a full-time or part-time secondment opportunity, fitting under their overall scope will depend on the nature and scale of the project. If the project spans across other departments, then representatives from those teams need to be involved. In addition, if there is significant cross-functional impact, then joint sponsorship should also be considered.

Teams that work on these types of activities must be set up for success. It should be a cherished opportunity that is critical to any aspiring leader's development path. Team members working on these types of projects must have their efforts recognised in their overall performance appraisal. They should be given every opportunity to share their learning both about the project and the process of managing the project so that other team members moving on to these projects get up to speed quickly and the early pioneers are given kudos for the risk they've taken.

In terms of the methodology the team should use, that will depend on whether the organisation already has a methodology in place (e.g., Agile). Failing that, the A3 approach is more than capable of supporting this type of project. As with all change work, getting the baseline right and establishing the success metrics is a fundamental part of the overall design.

There are a few conditions that will increase the chances of success:

- The team must be visible to the rest of the Run Team—not locked away in a different building.
- They must be accessible for the Run Team to ask them questions and vice versa.
- Project tracking and reporting must be weekly at a minimum or daily if using Agile.
- Progress must be visible to the Run Team.
- The sponsor must focus on momentum and ensure roadblocks are cleared in a timely manner.

- Ensure there is a "visual wall" tracking progress on each initiative for all to see.
- Initiatives must be included in the overall change calendar.
- Showcasing the work to senior management is both good for morale and a powerful incentive to complete it on time.
- As the first project nears completion, reflect on what's gone well and what can be done better next time.

With this in mind, the next task is to look at how you can scale the approach. This is both a function of change capacity, opportunity, capability and management bandwidth. My advice would be to not rush it. Complete the first project before you move on to the next and then run two concurrently, then three or four. It's hard to put a time frame on completing the whole cycle but completing the steps from stop through to tactical automation within 6–18 months should be achievable.

Business benefits

It is very hard to put a precise benefit figure on these techniques, as so much depends on the state of the processes to start with, the quality of the team and the underlying environment—particularly the degree of trust. It's also difficult to quantify the impact on the customer experience or risk reduction, but both will benefit directly from this approach. In terms of productivity, I would expect the following:

- **Control** – 15–25%
- **Stop** – It will depend on how much failure demand the team supports. When excluding failure demand, 5–10% is reasonable.
- **Consolidate** – 10–15%
- **Standardise** – Direct benefit, 5–10%; indirect benefit, 10–15% (many of the costs are hidden and dispersed across the organisation).
- **Simplify** – 5–15%
- **Re-engineer** – 10–20%
- **Automate** – 10–30% (tactical); 20–70% (strategic)
- **Outsource/offshore** – 10–40%

The ranges are indicative and not necessarily cumulative, but if you work your way through the entire program, productivity benefits of 50–75% are eminently achievable over a 3–5 year period (Figure 50). Double the quality and half the cost has a nice ring to it!

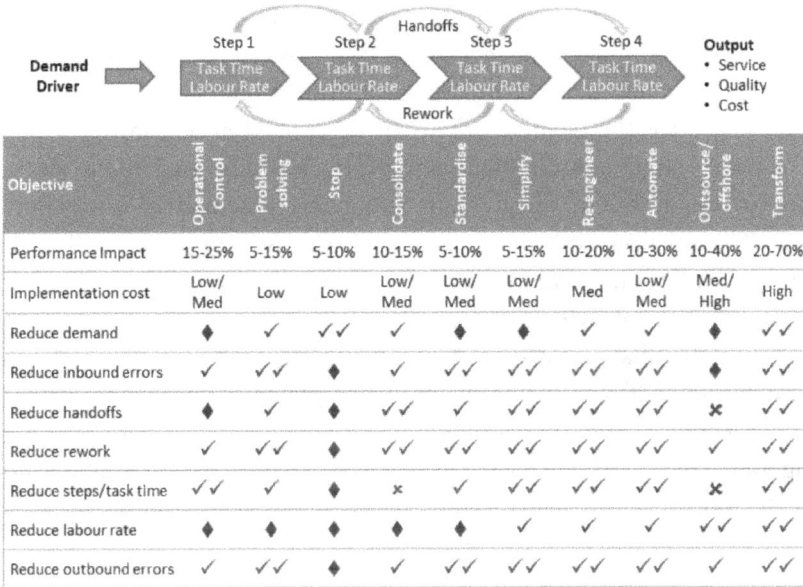

Objective	Operational Control	Problem solving	Stop	Consolidate	Standardise	Simplify	Re-engineer	Automate	Outsource/ offshore	Transform
Performance Impact	15-25%	5-15%	5-10%	10-15%	5-10%	5-15%	10-20%	10-30%	10-40%	20-70%
Implementation cost	Low/ Med	Low	Low	Low/ Med	Low/ Med	Low/ Med	Med	Low/ Med	Med/ High	High
Reduce demand	◆	✓	✓✓	✓	◆	◆	✓	✓	◆	✓✓
Reduce inbound errors	✓	✓✓	◆	✓	✓✓	✓✓	✓✓	✓✓	◆	✓✓
Reduce handoffs	◆	✓	◆	✓✓	✓	✓✓	✓✓	✓✓	✗	✓✓
Reduce rework	✓	✓✓	◆	✓✓	✓✓	✓✓	✓✓	✓✓	✓	✓✓
Reduce steps/task time	✓✓	✓	◆	✗	✓	✓✓	✓✓	✓✓	✗	✓✓
Reduce labour rate	◆	◆	◆	◆	◆	✓	✓	✓	✓✓	✓✓
Reduce outbound errors	✓	✓✓	◆	✓	✓✓	✓✓	✓✓	✓✓	✓	✓✓

Figure 50 – Benefit matrix.

Finally, there is the impact on the team. Empowering and unleashing a self-directed team is a thing of beauty. The energy, passion, creativity and commitment are extraordinary. The difference it makes knowing that you are in control and you set and execute the agenda is a very powerful stimulant. Creating an environment for this to happen is predicated on trust. Given the goals for the organisation may be to lower costs by reducing its workforce, being open and transparent is crucial.

Chapter summary

This chapter has again concentrated on innovation and improvement within the Run Team, but with a focus on redesigning.

For any leader, whether new to the team or looking for the next initiative, there is always so much to do that knowing where to start is a challenge in itself. Unless there is a specific problem requiring a team-based approach or a location-based approach, starting with customer journeys should be the default position. A simple prioritisation approach—scoring the customer journeys across a range of criteria—will help sequence and prioritise the relevant customer journeys.

With an area to focus on, the next step is to figure out what to do to improve. Following a standard eight-step pathway will ensure the problems are tackled in a logical way. Each step facilitates the next. There are the elements that can be applied at a team level, such as control, stop, consolidate, standardise, simplify and some tactical automation. But it is ideally suited to being executed at a functional level. Completing the eight steps will require support funding for strategic automation and outsourcing/offshoring.

Irrespective of which methodology you choose, there are design considerations that you need to factor into your decision making. Bearing these in mind will ensure that the improved processes are fit for purpose.

Collectively, these techniques will deliver substantial benefits on an ongoing basis. They are relatively low risk as they are distributed, and for the most part they will deliver a payback within 9–18 months.

Checklist:

Checklist Item	Status
Do your team understand the options available in terms of where to start your redesign journey, and have you agreed on the prioritisation criteria?	❑
Do your team understand the stages in the redesign journey, what each means and how they will impact the team?	❑
Do your team understand the factors that must be considered when deciding how to redesign?	❑
Have the team that will be running the redesign been selected and do they have the breadth of skills and support to run the redesign effort?	❑
Have your team committed to the redesign benefits plan? Do they know how the changes introduced will release the expected benefits?	❑

Chapter 11

Reinvent Your Game – Supporting Transformational Change

"You can't stay in your corner of the Forest waiting for others to come to you. You have to go to them sometimes."
— *A.A. Milne, Winnie-the-Pooh*

You'd be forgiven for stifling a groan when listening to a post-game interview if you heard the coach or captain utter the clichéd, "We're taking it one game at a time" or words to that effect. It may be overused, but that is absolutely the focus of the team. Focus on the next game. What skills do they need to hone, what drills do they need to practice again, what tactics will they need to employ and what's the right mix of players to take to the field? At the same time, backroom staff have a range of initiatives underway to ensure the club stays competitive in future seasons. This may include trying out new technology, new uniforms, new techniques, new equipment and new set pieces.

For all the tactical talk of focussing on the next game, a key characteristic of world-class teams is to look further ahead and to reinvent themselves when they are at the top of their game. When to drop star players, when to bring in new talent, when to turn the game plan on its head—making these decisions at the right time is the hallmark of a world-class team. It may mean going backwards for a short period, but they come out again on top. Manchester United, the world's most valuable soccer club in 2018, has been winning trophies—more than any other English club—since the early 1900s. Yet in that period it has suffered setbacks, been relegated and continues to reinvent itself and transform. Similarly, the All Blacks notably reinvented their whole approach to leadership in the early 2000s by pushing more responsibility from the coaches onto the players. By creating a leadership group and individual operating units, the club rebuilt the culture from the ground up, with players at all levels directly involved in the transformation.

Trying to transform and build for the future without involving those who lace up their boots and walk out onto the field every week is a recipe for disaster.

Supporting the cause

I overheard a comment on a train a year or so ago that really crystallised the challenge of executing a digital transformation. I didn't know the person who made the comment, nor the organisation they worked for, but they said, "They're getting paid more money than me, to do a job that they need my skills to execute, but I'm the one who'll be without a job when it's done." This seemed to articulate the challenge so well. It is a sentiment that is not uncommon, but as a leader, if this is the mindset of the team responsible for serving customers on a day-to-day basis, it doesn't augur well.

At face value, the individual may have a point, but it is the responsibility of both the individual and the leader to take charge and not allow themselves or their team to fall victim to the circumstances. What is clear, as I explained in Chapter 1, is that for a digital transformation to succeed, it takes both the Run Team and the Change Team to deliver on their individual and collective goals. That means they must work together.

Senior management may recognise this to be the case. The question is how to convince the Run Team member that it's in their best interest to work closely with the Change Team? I believe there are several good reasons for this collaboration:

- The Change Team need you to do the groundwork: consolidate, standardise and simplify.
- It's better to be inside the tent than outside. If you collaborate with the Change Team, you may be able to influence them. You

can influence prioritisation of the backlog, so that changes that have a greater or lesser impact are scheduled in line with your demand profile. You can influence them to add items to the backlog that directly benefit the team. You can influence their understanding of the problem based on your knowledge of the customer. If you ignore them, then you really are at their mercy when changes "go live".

- You can learn new skills. By working closely with the Change Team, you will acquire new skills, such as learning about the Agile operating rhythm, what a scrum master or product owner does and how to manage a backlog. All these skills will add to your resume when you look for your next job.
- You will be more credible if the changes do not go to plan. If you're seen to be part of the team, the team are more likely to listen to you when you say something isn't working.
- You will be seen as actively supporting the strategy and can improve team visibility by encouraging senior executives to see the change in action.
- You will be seen as embracing change and demonstrating that you have a "growth" mind-set, which positions you well for future career opportunities.

These are all reasons why it makes sense to embrace the transformation and get as close as possible.

Digital Zeitgeist

One of the many challenges that has arisen in parallel with the digital revolution is the explosion of jargon and acronyms that has accompanied it. This ranges from the labels used to describe new technologies (e.g., AI, machine learning (ML) and robotics (RPA) to the language associated with the methodologies (e.g., Agile and HCD) and the tools used to support them (e.g., Jira, Lean Canvas, etc.).

There are now many books written on these individual topics that go into great detail to explain what they are, and why and when they are used. For the purposes of this book, I have touched on a couple of these that are particularly relevant to the Run Team and some aspects to be aware of.

Agile – In simple terms, Agile is a project methodology that was developed in the software industry to speed up development; however, it contrasts with a structured "waterfall" approach in project management. With waterfall projects, requirements are gathered and the system is designed, developed, tested and implemented. This process can take several years for large projects, which means that it is too slow, you must wait too long for benefits, and by the time the project is delivered, the environment will have changed and it may not be fit for purpose. Agile is seen to be much more customer focussed, as the "product owner" is constantly prioritising what gets done and can respond and react quickly. The work is chunked down into "sprints" that are delivered by small cross-functional squads every two to four weeks, so the time to value is far shorter and much more responsive to changes in the environment. The debate about which methodology is more appropriate is well beyond the scope of this book.

For Run Team leaders, there are key points to be aware of:

- The pace of change will accelerate, and your team will need to absorb more change.
- There is a notion of "fail fast", so rather than take a long time to get it absolutely right, experiment and test a solution on a limited scale. If it doesn't work, back it out. This can save significant amounts of time and resources overall but can be frustrating for Run Teams picking up the pieces when a change fails.
- It is much more time intensive. In a waterfall approach, a few workshops may be held to gather requirements, and then it's hands off until testing time. With Agile, the Run Teams need to actively engage in the sprints.
- Some organisations will use a combination of project methodologies (e.g., Agile and Waterfall). This can be confusing, and you need to be clear about which change is being managed by which approach.
- In Agile, there is usually an "epic"—a high-level narrative of what the squad is trying to achieve—but it is not laid out in

milestones over the next few months and quarters. Hence, the road map may not be clear.

- Within the Run Team, it may be appropriate to think about using Agile to manage your own change but be circumspect if there is a suggestion to run day-to-day business on Agile principles.

Human-centred design (HCD) and design thinking – In many ways, these terms get used interchangeably. Design thinking is technically broader in scope, and there are some small differences in approach. Their principal focus is to use cross-functional teams to take a continuous and iterative approach to innovating and problem solving, with the end user actively in mind and engaged throughout the process. This approach builds a greater customer focus within an organisation and a simpler, better experience for customers. Acronyms such as CX for customer experience and UX for user experience, and terms such as "ideate" are common within the HCD approach.

Some key points to consider:

- It is a great development opportunity and a real benefit to the HCD teams to get Run Team people involved in these projects. The Run Teams have a wealth of knowledge and understand the challenges that customers face with existing products and services.
- In the examples I've seen, a lot of effort goes into the browser/ mobile interface design. Far less effort is extended to the exception handling queues. A customer starts their journey with a beautiful experience, and because of some exception, they end up in a Kafkaesque process nightmare.
- Run Teams need to be open-minded about these projects. Given their depth of knowledge, there is a tendency to want to incorporate far more detail and complexity than a customer can cope with.
- The approach is equally relevant to developing both end-customer solutions as well as solutions for staff. If you consider the time to competency for a new hire, as they struggle to learn

multiple, detailed mainframe "green" screens with arcane codes, the benefits can be significant.

The Lean Startup – This is a book by Eric Reis. It focusses on eliminating waste when starting up a business and experimenting. It is being used in more mature organisations to try and build a more entrepreneurial spirit. The book was the source of the MVP concept. Like Agile, it has principles, but the key point is that it is concerned with validating learning through experiments, doing small things and testing to see the customer value. There is also a strong theme of the build-measure-learn feedback loop—starting small and building the MVP, testing it with the market and then starting again, while continually improving and adapting the product or service. It also emphasises the importance of actionable v vanity metrics to improve decision making. The book also popularised the idea of "pivoting" when the original plan doesn't appear to be working out.

Some key points to consider:

- It has many similarities with the A3 methodology discussed in the problem-solving section.
- Test and learn is a very powerful concept and should be encouraged with your teams.
- Encouraging entrepreneurial behaviour requires the leader to create a safe environment and make the boundaries very clear.
- Pivoting when you have a very small customer base is one thing—it's a very different proposition when you have millions of customers.
- The idea of a mature organisation learning from start-ups may seem ironic given so many of them fail (the statistics I've seen vary dramatically, but anything from a half to over 90% seems possible). However, the lessons learned are more than pertinent. The real focus is on accelerating decision making, deploying lots of experiments and using facts and data to make decisions.
- There's no definition of what constitutes an MVP, and you must understand the consequences of failure before accepting someone else's definition of MVP.

Digital ecosystems and platforms – A digital ecosystem is a collection of organisations, people and things that share standardised digital assets (the platform) centred on a unifying area of interest (e.g., healthcare, retail, financial services and entertainment). Amazon, Google and Apple are frequently cited as leading examples. Interoperability is critical to an ecosystem, and it's not unusual for the ecosystem provider to allow direct competitors to operate on the platform with the intent of trying to create a one-stop shop.

Questions for the Run Team are:

- To what extent will they need to interact with other ecosystem participants?
- How resilient is the platform and what happens when it fails?
- How can the Run Team's knowledge of the customer be extended and leveraged across the ecosystem?
- How will they interact with other participants?
- Which processes will be standard and common across participants and which will be unique?

Cloud computing – Cloud computing covers a broad spectrum of services delivered via the internet. These services can include computing infrastructure such as storage, application development, platforms and software as a service (e.g., MS Office 365). The services can be public, private or a combination of both, and they deliver significant benefits. They are typically available by self-service and on demand so that they are faster to set up. They can scale very quickly and tend to be lower cost, as maintenance and security costs are spread over a wider base. In high-risk service areas, there are still some residual concerns over security.

In terms of the implications for the Run Team, it's highly likely your organisation is already using cloud computing. The role of the Run Team is to work with IT to help them understand the underlying customer data and other confidential data risks. There is also the opportunity to participate in testing and gain an understanding of technology resource constraints, for example latency and capacity issues that may impact ongoing delivery. This is more for the Run Team's understanding than anything else.

Application programming interface (API) – An API simplifies how applications talk to each other by providing a standard way to interact with a system. It is fundamental to rapid application development. Rather than write many lines of code, the programmer can insert a function provided by the information owner (writer of the API) and pass some parameters (share some specific details). The API provider then returns the requested information to the programmer. For example, if you're building a website for a new cafe and you want to show a map of where your cafe is located, you can use the Google Maps API (for a fee). This will save hours of programming.

Organisations use APIs internally to simplify repeat routine requests (e.g., returning a customer's address from the mainframe). This saves people who want to access this information (e.g., when designing a new channel) from having to write a specific interface to the mainframe.

The Run Team should think about:

- How can they help the Change Team prioritise which APIs to build first based on the degree of switching they do between applications?
- Where are the bear traps (e.g., outdated database fields, which in some cases still hold data that looks like it's still relevant)?
- Which fields should be included in APIs intended for customers to use?

Microservices – Building off an API foundation, microservices is an approach to simplify rapid application development in large, complex organisations. Think about how many different parts of an organisation need to know customer details, such as an address or date of birth. Creating a dedicated function to share this information (via an API) is a way of consolidating, standardising, simplifying and automating computer code. There are no longer multiple versions of software and code all trying to do the same thing but in different ways. Because each microservice has a very specific purpose, it is, by design, far simpler. As a single, standard service that is leveraged multiple times, it is easy to maintain and control.

The Run Team can:

- Provide feedback on the specific services where they have noted inconsistencies.
- Identify those services that are frequently updated but take a long time, as the changes must be replicated in many different applications.
- Inform the Change Team on which parameters are easy to access and which are more difficult.

Blockchain – Perhaps most famously or infamously, Blockchain is the technology that underpins Bitcoin and other cryptocurrencies like Ethereum. It is essentially a ledger that is distributed across a network (not held in one place) that records and timestamps transactions in a cryptographical, permanent way that all parties to the transaction can verify. A transaction is recorded once and accessed by many, as opposed to each entity maintaining its own record of the transaction. This overcomes version management risk.

The technology has moved beyond cryptocurrencies into areas such as smart contracts, payments, trade and supply chain management and financial markets.

There are some points you should consider:

- It can be slow—processing at a rate of 5–15 transactions per second as opposed to the many thousands of transactions per second in some transaction processing systems (e.g., payments).
- It can take time for a transaction to be validated.
- There's no standardisation yet, so it's possible you will need to work with different protocols for different applications.
- Regulation hasn't caught up with the technology in many ways, and this needs to be an active watchpoint.

Robotics (RPA) – There are few areas that have captured the corporate imagination as much as RPA and AI. RPA is a way to automate repetitive tasks without changing the underlying systems and applications. For those of you familiar with Excel macros and visual basic, in many ways the tools are an evolution of this concept, albeit with better audit trails and far more sophisticated features. By detailing what a user does, keystroke by keystroke, this can all be codified and then automated to run without an operator. This can both speed up the process and cut down on the number of manual processing errors. The other benefit is that staff can be retrained to work on more challenging tasks.

There are certain key points to watch out for:

- You must first consolidate, standardise and simplify. You can waste a lot of time trying to automate complex processes with many variants. These invariably fail, although some of the RPA tools will help you consolidate, standardise and simplify.
- This is a great development opportunity for team members. The projects require deep SME knowledge. By equipping the SMEs with some basic robotics and then training and buddying them with an experienced developer, team members can quickly learn a new skill.
- There is significant governance required, particularly for change management. If there is a change to the underlying application, the "robot" will not be aware of the change. Imagine what would happen if the "buy" and "sell" rate fields on a foreign currency exchange screen were swapped. The robot doesn't know what buy and sell fields are—it just knows to go to a specific position on a screen. Documenting each robotic process, peer reviews, testing, cataloguing and auditing are just as critical here as for any other process.
- There is a significant degree of maintenance. The robots need "logins", they need to be monitored for performance, they are subject to issues such as latency and they take up space on the desktop.
- RPA is potentially a great way to remove the more mundane, repetitive tasks that team members perform, which then frees them up to do more value-adding work.

Artificial intelligence (AI) and machine learning (ML) – Both AI and ML have received significant publicity in the last couple of years. The premise is that it's easier to teach computers how to learn than it is to program them to do all the things we want them to do. Add to this advances in neural network programming, which allow computers to "think" and classify information more like the human brain but faster and with greater accuracy, plus accessibility to vast data stores via the internet, and you have a very powerful toolset. Applications of AI are now relatively common in our everyday lives: chatbots on websites that can triage a customer problem and find the right solution; Google Home and Alexa; and Amazon's "you might also like …" algorithm. There are exotic new tools and programming languages used to develop these applications such as R, Python or Scala.

Things you need to know:

- AI takes time to "learn" and will need help in such things as "labelling". These are not quick initiatives and AI can take many months to learn the behaviour patterns that allow the applications to predict.
- In its early stages, it is not infallible (neither are we!), so be careful with where you trial it and understand the consequences of it going wrong.
- It can slow the team down. If an application can only handle 60% of the cases, and the rest are rejected for human intervention, the team may second guess why it's been rejected.
- It requires a lot of data, and getting access to that data is not always easy.
- AI is also great for removing the more mundane work from team members, which then frees them up to do other activities.

Big data and data analytics – Data analytics is a wide field covering everything from data capture tools and processes to storage and processing environments and the AI/ML tools described above. In recent times, it has attracted some notoriety with the exposé on Cambridge Analytica, Facebook and allegations of election meddling. Linking together multiple data sources using APIs and then running algorithms over these huge data sets has given companies the ability to pinpoint smaller segments of customers with more targeted messages and offers, and this has created new revenue streams and business models. Most people are familiar with the scenario where after a conversation about a topic, that very product or holiday destination appears in an advertisement on social media just moments later.

In a services environment, Run Teams play a critical role in enabling data analytics. The key points are as follows:

- Run Teams typically play a significant role in determining how customers submit requests (e.g., through electronic channels, over the phone, faxes, emails or handwritten letters delivered by post). The first step in any analytics program is to digitise the data; hence, a push towards digital channels is a rare opportunity for the Run Team to access investment. There will typically be an uplift in quality, when teams no longer have to decipher handwritten notes!

- Data quality is a significant problem for analytics teams. The Run Team plays a major role in ensuring the integrity and quality of the data. This is an opportunity to find a powerful ally to tackle the issue of input quality. One of the most common grievances from Run Teams is that the frontline sales and service teams send through incomplete and incorrect requests.

- There are solutions available that will claim to convert forms/faxes/documents into structured digital data and then classify, categorise and tag them appropriately. Digitising a faxed document that was scanned at an angle on poor quality thermal paper with coffee stains and faint handwriting can be a real challenge, so be clear about the quality levels for the documents you want to capture and test these before committing. The read rates may not be as high as expected.

The elephant in the room

There are aspects of change that can present enormous challenges for Run Teams:

- **Minimum viable product** – Just how many workarounds will the Run Team have to manage in production?
- **Fail fast** – The Change Team may fail fast and move on to the

next product feature, but how much mess will the Run Team need to clean up and how long will it take?

- **Minimal documentation** – It must be done to capture the knowledge and be used for training purposes and good governance, but who will do it—the Run Teams or the Change Teams?

- **Short time horizon sprints** – How can the Run Team plan their resources in the medium to long term if there is no long-term road map? In practice, Agile teams work on a level scheduling approach with fixed capacity; hence, the amount of change the team produces is relatively known. What's unknown is the impact this will have on the Run Team.

- **Volume of change** – The pace and volume of change has accelerated, but the Run Team have barely enough resources to manage day-to-day service without worrying about learning new processes. How much change can the team cope with?

- **Level of detail** – The Run Team will always know more about the current state than the Change Team. The transformation should be aspiring far higher than just moving the current state on to a new platform, and they shouldn't be expected to know everything. The Run Team, in this case, need to be tolerant. They also need to recognise that a lot of the detail that is required to run the system now will be irrelevant in a reimagined process.

All of these are very real issues and concerns for the Run Team. Handled the wrong way, "us v them" positions can become deeply entrenched. Adopting some of the following techniques can help both the Run Team and Change Team succeed.

What are my options?

There are many ways that the Run Team can get involved with the transformation. As the leader of a team, it is important that you seize as many opportunities as possible. The more intertwined you are, the better. Some of the options include:

- **Shared KPIs** – Ensure that at least one or two KPIs are owned by both the Run Team and the Change Team so that the Change Team feels a sense of joint responsibility.
- **Floor walks** – Invite the Change Team to visit your team and show them what you do and the challenges you face. By engaging them in a constructive way, you should see them focus some of their effort on addressing your pain points.
- **Embedded resources** – Set up a small SME unit within the Change Team that is staffed and funded by Run Team resources. Their role is to communicate and liaise between the Run Team and Change Team by pre-empting issues and preventing them from turning into problems.
- **Secondments** – Second Run Team resources into vacant Change Team roles. This creates both development opportunities for team members but also ensures there is a direct feedback line.
- **Showcases** – Ensure your team are present at any Change Team showcases (playbacks of what they've achieved). This is a great opportunity to rotate various team members through and expose them to how a Change Team works.
- **Steering committee** – Access to the steering committee may be restricted to more senior members, but it is vitally important that the Run Team have a seat on the steering committee and play an active role—not just make up the numbers. It's also important that the steering committee representatives share key messages and action items with the team.
- **Working groups, tribes and squads** – Below the steering committee there are usually working groups or squads if your organisation operates in an Agile environment. Representation at this level is critical to ensure the changes are introduced smoothly, the quality is fit for purpose and the likelihood of success is increased.
- **Guest speakers** – Invite Change Team members to your team meetings to provide updates and participate in Q&A sessions. This builds relationships, provides clear insight into the strategic direction and ensures the voice of the Run Team is heard.
- **Internal communications** – Whether it's email updates,

newsletters or any other form of communication about the transformation, make sure your team are on the distribution list.

- **Shared reporting** – Share your performance updates with the Change Team, and don't be afraid to share your pain points. Similarly, ask to see the project updates and performance packs and offer support where required.
- **Social media communities** – Many organisations have introduced internal social media and collaboration platforms such as Slack or Yammer. Encouraging your team to participate in these forums is another great way to make sure the Run Team voice is heard and to keep up to date with progress and what's planned.
- **Change calendars** – Work with the Change Team to develop a common change calendar where you highlight when changes will be introduced, when the communication will go out, when training will begin, how long it will take, how big the change is, etc.
- **Insight generator** – Use the Run Team's specialist knowledge to capture current insights that may impact how the Change Team prioritises and defines what it is working on. Any change in customer behaviour is relevant. How customers interact with your products and services and what they are saying about the competition are valuable insights that need to be shared with the Change Team.

The more of these options you can employ, the better. This is about making you and your team visible and part of the solution.

How to interact

Once you have created the bridges to the Change Team, you need to make sure that the support is well received. As well as the corporate values and expected behavioural norms, there is very much a "way" to interact. Everyone on your team must learn and understand how important this is. If not, the team will be perceived to be change resistant and not "on strategy". This is not a great place to be. However, the role at these forums is to challenge, raise concerns and question underlying assumptions. You just need to do it in the right way!

- **Customer focussed** – Always frame a potentially controversial comment in terms of the impact on the customer. This is not an "us v them" situation. Both teams are marching towards the same goal. Simply asking, "How will this impact the customer?" or "Customer A currently works in a different way—how will we manage the transition?" are ways to desensitise the situation. If you can't frame the concern relative to the customer, frame its impact relative to people and risk.

- **"Yes, and" not "yes, but"** – This is very difficult to do when you are presented with something that you disagree with, but it's a very powerful skill to learn given the negative connotations of the word "but", which immediately makes people feel defensive. You can do this by turning your concern into a question and giving the Change Team an opportunity to clarify their position in a constructive way, without feeling that they are under attack. For example, if you are concerned that a change will slow down the service for the customer, you could say, "Yes, and this will make it faster, won't it? I am right in assuming that?"

- **Use facts and data** – Don't make vague assumptions, and don't criticise individuals, but do phrase concerns in a way that suggests you are trying to check your own understanding (e.g., "I thought the monthly report showed the trend going in the opposite direction. I may be mistaken.")

- **Open-ended questions** – Use open-ended questions to seek clarity (e.g., "Can you explain that to me again? I just want to make sure I understand how the customer will benefit from this change.")

- **Body language** – Be very aware of your body language. Adopting an open posture, smiling, sitting upright, being actively engaged and not checking your phone the whole time makes a world of difference.

- **Tone and language** – It's important to consider how you phrase questions and how you make your points. Use positive language—avoid negatives and the passive voice. Speak calmly and clearly. You may feel exasperated or frustrated but resist the temptation to raise your voice and speak hurriedly, sarcastically or aggressively.

- **Do your homework** – If papers or documents are sent out for review or if briefing sessions are held, make sure you read them before you participate. You do not want the team to feel that they are always having to help you catch up.

- **Find allies** – If there are concerns being echoed by multiple voices, it is far more powerful than a sole voice—especially if the concerns are shared amongst members of the Change Team. This can be quite political, but to encourage someone else (particularly an SME) to air the concern can get the issue on the table without it always coming from the one voice (e.g., "Is this the issue we spoke about this morning, Tina [the SME]? Didn't you say it would be quite difficult to do this?" Or, "What are your thoughts on this matter, Tina?") Clearly you can't betray a confidence, and you need to know that the SME is comfortable sharing their thoughts.

- **Be positive** – Implementing change is hard, and there will always be problems; however, people gravitate towards those who take on a positive attitude. If you share a concern, always suggest a couple of different options to address it (e.g., "I think this will be really difficult to implement if we go down path A, but I think if we adapt it slightly, path B or path C are much more viable and will help us achieve the same goal.")

- **Can-do attitude** – A Run Team leader with a can-do attitude is a breath of fresh air as far as most Change Team leaders are concerned. This is not about just saying "yes"; it is about understanding the problem to be solved and then figuring out a way to make it happen.

- **Turn up** – Make sure you attend meetings and don't send delegates. The Change Team need to know it is important for you. Outside of events such as sickness or annual leave, when you should send a respected delegate, you need to prioritise this personally.

- **No surprises** – There are times when significant points of difference need to be worked through. For me, it is both common courtesy and good practice to let the meeting chair know that a particular agenda item may be contentious. This will help ensure there is enough time to debate the point and give you an opportunity to share your perspective with the chairperson ahead of time.

- **Sell the change** – Ensure you have the Change Team collateral on display in your Run Team's work areas (e.g., posters, banners, lanyards, etc.). Talk positively and frequently about the transformation to your team, making sure they feel part of it.

- **"We" not "you"** – Wherever possible, always refer to "we". "You" can be accusatory and seen as finger-pointing.
- **Walk in their shoes** – Imagine you were part of the Change Team. What are your goals? What is stopping you from achieving your goals? No one has an easy job. Every job has its own challenges and complexities, and the more you understand these and can see the difficulty through another lens, the more able you will be to address issues in a win-win way.

It is not a competition. It is not about scoring points or a zero-sum game. Lead by example, role model the leadership behaviours that are expected, encourage your team to take your lead and work openly, honestly, collaboratively, at a fast pace and with respect, and you will be amazed at how smooth the relationship can be.

Using these engagement options and techniques will ensure both the Run Team and the Change Team are aligned. This is about keeping communication channels open and building trust. It takes time and effort. You need to lock this into an operating rhythm. It can't be a series of one-off events. If you are doing secondments, make sure that they are timeboxed and rotated. With steering committees and working groups, make sure that they are held frequently enough and that you are present. Do not send a delegate to a meeting if you could go yourself. Take every opportunity possible to get senior leaders on the floor, meeting your teams and hearing from them about how they are actively supporting the transformation and addressing the issues. Keep asking questions, be visible, be humble and be present.

Chapter summary

This chapter covered the importance of the Run Team and the Change Team working together effectively. There are, however, challenges that will need to be overcome, which will naturally create tension between the teams, but it is critical that it is a constructive tension.

There are a whole raft of techniques and there is a whole new lexicon associated with digital transformation that have implications for the Run Team. Sharing a basic understanding ensures that any interaction with the Change Team is off to a good start.

Run Teams can lapse into feeling hard done by. They may feel that they are undervalued and expendable, but they need to see the transformation as an opportunity to learn and grow. They must take control of the situation and position themselves as equal partners responsible for driving the transformation.

Doing this requires extra effort from the Run Team, and there is a range of techniques they need to adopt to foster this relationship. But it's not just about embedding some new techniques. The way the team interacts is just as important, if not more so.

This is an opportunity for the Run Team to demonstrate maturity and leadership, to role model expected behaviours and to significantly increase the visibility of the role they play in successfully delivering the transformation.

Checklist:

Checklist Item	Status
Do your team know the role they play in supporting the transformation?	❑
Do your team understand the new terminology introduced to support the digital transformation and how each aspect will impact them?	❑
Do your team understand the challenges that the digital transformation will bring, and do they have a plan to address the challenges?	❑
Do your team know the options available to get closer to the digital transformation, and are they utilising the options effectively?	❑
Do your team understand how to interact effectively with the digital transformation team and role model these behaviours in practice?	❑

Chapter 12

A Game of Hard Knocks – Resilience and Workforce of the Future

"I get knocked down, but I get up again. You're never going to keep me down." — *Chumbawamba, "Tubthumping"*

Throughout the season, the team know that the coaching staff have one eye on the future. Who's retiring at the end of the season? What are they looking to do? Can we retain them in the coaching staff, and do we want to? Who is past their prime? What gaps are opening up? Are there any long-term injury concerns? Is there a missing piece of the puzzle that will unlock future potential? Who is showing promise in the development squads? Are there target individuals to go after in the transfer market? What is the pipeline of talent looking like in the junior and school programs? What skills are we lacking? What are the winning combinations that we need to strengthen? These are questions constantly asked. In short, how do I set up the club for future success?

Running out on to the field, knowing that this might be your last game, certainly adds to the pressure. As an individual, will your fitness hold up? Will you perform at your best? Is your best better than anyone else's on the squad in your position? Are your team a winning team? A losing team is more likely to see wholesale changes in coaching and playing staff, and you could just be collateral damage. The mental toughness and resilience to cope with this pressure is extraordinary. Since 2004, the All Blacks have been behind at halftime in 42 games, but they have come back to win 28 of those games. Conditioning, skills, attitude, mental toughness and mind-set are what it takes to survive and thrive in this type of environment.

It is exactly the same with a digital transformation. There is no doubt that many of the skills required to execute the transformation are new. There is no doubt that post-transformation, many of the roles required to run the organisation will be different. Some people will go into this with an open mind and willingness to change. Others will be change resistant. As a leader, the decisions you make about your workforce of the future are some of the most significant you will make. They will impact people's livelihoods and the future success of the organisation.

Why building resilience matters

It is tough operating in the type of environment I have portrayed. The relentless focus on freeing up capacity to meet targets, enhancing the customer experience, seconding and moving team members into new roles all happens under a cloud of uncertainty. Will my role exist when the transformation finishes? What will I be doing? Will the transformation mean changes to my workplace and to the nature of my role? How individuals cope with this type of environment will vary widely across the team. Some will relish the challenge, the adventure and the opportunity to learn something new and grow. Others will be frightened, concerned about being able to maintain their financial commitments, support their families or maintain their dignity.

Change is a clichéd constant, but the accelerating pace and breadth of change is, perhaps, what is unparalleled. A digital transformation epitomises the frenetic nature of change currently underway in so many organisations. The need to plan and control, forewarned is forearmed and other maxims—which are predicated on a known or at least predictable future—are being thrown out of the window, and organisations are using analogies comparing the nature of the environment to being in a free-form, experimental jazz band, ready to pivot at a moment's notice.

Surviving and thriving in this type of environment demands both organisational and individual resilience. If people are not change ready, the negative consequences in terms of stress levels for the individual and impacted performance for the organisation will be material. The impact and scale of workplace stress has been described by the World

Health Organisation as the global health epidemic of the twenty-first century. The good news, according to Rich Fernandez, is that "more than five decades of research point to the fact that resilience is built by attitudes, behaviours and social supports that can be adopted and cultivated by anyone." He goes on to outline five ways individuals can build their resilience:

- **Exercise mindfulness** – Mindfulness tools and techniques have gained in popularity over the last few years. Numerous studies have demonstrated a positive correlation between mindfulness, resilience, cognitive ability and overall job performance.
- **Compartmentalise your cognitive workload** – The key here is to avoid continuous task switching. Block out chunks of time to focus on specific tasks and try to avoid being disrupted.
- **Take detachment breaks** – Our ability to stay energised and focus for long periods of time is limited—the precise amount of time is very dependent on the intensity of the focus required. Standing up, having a stretch, going for a quick walk and doing some breathing exercises help improve energy levels, mental clarity, creativity and focus.
- **Develop mental agility** – This technique is the ability to take a mental step back from a situation and view it objectively.
- **Cultivate compassion** – Increasing compassion helps create positive emotions and build better workplace relationships, which in turn increases cooperation and collaboration.

These activities are clearly focussed on the individual. To build a resilient workforce, leaders need to understand what they can do to support their teams to become more resilient. From a leader's perspective, the action is to create an environment that enables resilience. This means:

- Creating space for the team.
- Finding appropriate material and programs for the team to participate in.
- Role modelling to demonstrate that this is important.
- Building detachment breaks into lengthy meetings.
- Sharing ideas on how to compartmentalise the workload.

- In tense meetings, asking the question "What would X do?" (X is an individual with a different perspective, who will view the situation objectively, but is external to the meeting.)

Build resilience, communicate the necessary change patiently and frequently, and lay the foundations. The next step is to think through the types of roles that you will require in the future.

What do the roles of the future look like?

Technology change has impacted the workforce for centuries, with the Luddites possibly being the most famous example. Most economists agree that, in the short term, technological change will impact jobs, while in the long term, different jobs will be created. There is no doubt that AI, robotics, etc. will impact the way people work, but the doom and gloom that over 40% of jobs will be lost to automation, as predicted by Oxford University economists Dr. Carl Frey and Dr. Michael Osborne, fortunately seems to be waning. Current research suggests that there will be different jobs, which is precisely what has happened since the start of the Industrial Revolution. Twenty years ago, there were no social media analysts or Instagram influencers. AI was restricted to the research institutions, and Agile coaches and scrum masters were unheard of. Accenture refers to three categories of roles that AI will require:

- **Trainers** – Will help develop the algorithms the machines use.
- **Explainers** – Will clarify why the machines have made the decisions they have; thus, explaining the "black box".
- **Sustainers** – Will ensure the machines operate as intended.

For many, their roles will be augmented, not replaced, by technology. Asking Alexa to search for and play a piece of music is a simple productivity tool. Asking a work-related Alexa to source case studies of organisations that have successfully entered a specific market is far easier than having someone trawling through the internet or cheaper than using consultants. The analyst can spend more time interpreting the case studies and less time finding them.

One other interesting aspect, particularly concerning many of the newer roles, is the importance of getting beyond the hype. Many roles with exotic, futuristic titles are not necessarily radically new but rather a variation on a theme or an enhancement to a role that has existed before. For example, anyone that has written macros in Excel is already well set up for roles in robotics. People who have worked as a Lean coach over the last few years will find the transition to Agile scrum master relatively straightforward, and people working in reporting teams using Excel and pivot tables should find the transition to analytics and data science within their grasp. Even the origins of AI and machine learning have been around for a very long time.

It's also not just about the technical skills. There is a focus on people developing better "soft" skills and emotional intelligence. More and more research has shown that the key to building effective teams is dependent on the ability of the people within the teams to build effective relationships. Skills such as goal-centric thinking, communication, collaboration, playfulness, learning and troubleshooting are seen as particularly important in building great digital organisations (Samuel, 2016).

To participate in the workforce of the future, people will need to develop new skills. They will need to become far more familiar with technology and data, and they will need to work better with others.

Build or buy?

The age-old question of "build or buy" applies as much to the workforce of the future as it does to any other procurement decision. It's highly likely that an organisation embarking on a digital transformation has already bought in a number of the new skills required, either as new hires or consultants. Being able to seed an initiative in this way seems to make sense, but it's what happens next that matters. With such a disruptive change, an organisation must rapidly scale-up these new skills.

The question is "How to scale?" Do you continue to buy in new people with the new skills but no understanding of the organisation, or do you retrain and reskill your existing workforce? At face value, buying in talent might appear to be the fastest and cheapest way, although these resources are in high demand and may charge a premium, but it also creates a medium- to longer-term problem.

What do you do with an existing workforce that hasn't been able to acquire the new skills but is steeped in corporate memory, organisational history, detailed knowledge of its customer base, the intricacies of the legacy systems and are current custodians of the culture? It is no mean feat to get a group of new hires, who have never worked together and are from different backgrounds, to respect and build on the successes of the past and converge on a shared view of the future.

The argument would run something like, "It will take a long time to train people in the new skills, and they probably don't have the aptitude or the right attitude. At the same time, we can't free them up to train them because they need to keep the old system running and continue serving customers." In my mind, this is incorrect and a disappointing line of argument. Yes, there will be people who don't want to learn how to become data scientists. Yes, someone does need to keep the old systems and processes running to serve customers today. It does not mean that you limit investment in the current workforce. You must give them the opportunity to join the workforce of the future, which means that leaders of Run Teams must get their teams Match Fit. They need to free up capacity to be able to place their people in the right development programs. This is both a moral obligation and commercial common sense. The risk to the fabric of an organisation of bringing in large numbers of new people, with no emotional commitment to the organisation, is great. The medium- to long-term impact of the "hot" talent, selling their services to the highest bidder, will ultimately impact the ability of an organisation to survive and thrive.

A recent survey for Harvard Business School's Managing the Future of Work project in collaboration with Boston Consulting Group's Henderson Institute highlighted the fact that employees are more willing to learn and adapt than their leaders give them credit for (Fuller, et al., 2019). It also found that a majority of workers feel that automation will have a positive impact on their future and that employers need to embrace this energy and provide the right support for their staff.

For me, there are two factors that are important if you choose to go down the "build" path:

- **Growth mind-set** – As anyone that has ever tried will know, trying to teach a topic to a disengaged audience is particularly challenging. If the team are not receptive to learning and personal growth, anything you do to encourage the team to acquire new skills will be a waste of time. The first step is to awaken the need to learn. Carol Dweck's work in this area has gained momentum in recent years. The key points to creating an environment that fosters a growth mind-set according to Dweck are:

- Presenting skills as learnable.
- Conveying that the organisation values learning and perseverance and not just ready-made genius or talent.
- Giving feedback in a way that promotes learning and future success.
- Presenting managers as resources for learning.

- **Learning as a day-to-day proposition** – Long gone are the days where training was a matter of being sent off for an induction week at an off-site development centre and then the occasional 3–5 day off-site for a technical program or leadership development program. Today, every day is training day. The role of the leader is to facilitate and encourage the experience, with many options to choose from:
  - **Secondments** – Short-term assignments in different areas of the organisation that already practices the new skills and techniques.
  - **Leverage the ecosystem** – Look beyond your own organisation to provide secondment opportunities. Finding opportunities with ecosystem partners is an obvious place to look.
  - **Buddy system** – Assign people to a "buddy" who has already acquired the new skills.
  - **Bite-size learning** – Sourcing short articles, podcasts, blogs and vlogs that introduce new topics.
  - **Feedback and reflection** – As part of the end-of-day review cycle, simply asking the team to reflect and answer the questions, "What went well? What can we do better tomorrow?" provides an opportunity to learn.
  - **Leader as coach** – Rather than tell, ask. It never ceases to amaze me that the most important lessons many leaders have learned, they have learned through getting something wrong— trying something new that didn't work out. The learning really

comes when they are asked to reflect on why it didn't work and if they had their time again, what they would do differently.

- ○ **Lunch and learn sessions** – Inviting guest speakers, either from other parts of the organisation or external to the organisation, to discuss topics of interest, new techniques, etc.
- ○ **Reading lists** – Which should be fairly self-explanatory.
- ○ **Hands-on learning** – Where the team is being introduced to a new idea or concept such as Kanban or AI, I have often found that using games and practical exercises is a great way to convey meaning (e.g., use Lego, puzzles, etc.).
- ○ **External programs** – There are an amazing number of online training programs now available that are either free or relatively modestly priced.
- ○ **Gamification** – Many organisations are turning to apps that use gamification techniques to build new skills. These have been particularly successful in areas such as compliance or technical skills.
- ○ **Look outside** – Which organisations in other industries can you learn from? The All Blacks worked with the US Marines, ballet dancers and cage fighters to learn how to lead, lift and grapple better (Hill, et al., 2018). I've taken teams to zoos, cafes, supermarkets, the post office and rarely had difficulty in convincing people to host.

As a leader, making this happen means you need to:

- Prioritise this.
- Free up capacity.
- Lock it into individual development plans.
- Schedule time in the capacity plan.
- Role model learning and growth behaviour.
- Where possible remove the uncertainty—be up front and engage with your team early.

There is no doubt that in the short term it is quicker to bring in new people, but in the long term, it is far more rewarding to watch your people grow and move into new roles with new skills.

Parting of the ways

In some cases, there will be transformations that lead to a reduction in the workforce. The team you have been dependent on to meet customer needs during the transition may face a very uncertain future. This is clearly a critical decision that will potentially impact the livelihood of many people. It is one thing to manage a team that will be acquiring new skills and moving into different roles. It is quite a different matter to lead a team that will no longer have roles in the organisation in the future.

Leading a team through a downsizing program is possibly one of the most challenging leadership tasks. It is emotionally draining for all concerned and is time intensive as you work with each individual to plan their next steps. It exposes the organisation to a range of new risks, such as people leaving en masse and jumping ship as soon as they become aware of a downsizing program, loss of corporate knowledge and in extreme cases, impacted staff members acting with malicious intent. All of this will have a negative effect on quality, customer service, reputation and ultimately the shareholder.

There are, however, examples of organisations that have managed this remarkably well. In 2014, Toyota decided to close their Altona plant in Australia. It was the first plant that the global automotive giant had ever closed. It set a goal of "last car = best global car" and despite a four-year transition period, the number of people prepared to go above and beyond and those responding positively to the staff survey went up. And they were already well above industry standards. To do this, Toyota established the DRIVE program to upskill and reskill 2,200 people who would no longer have a role when the Australian business exited manufacturing and focussed on sales and distribution. How did the company do this? (Samson, 2017)

- Its primary focus was on the people. When asked what the ROI of the program was, the response was reputation and respect for the people.
- The announcement was made by the President of Toyota Motor Corporation in person, and he was there at the start of the program and just before the plant closed.

- Individuals were given choices and helped to develop their own transition plan.
- Recognising that automotive manufacturing skills were unlikely to be required (the other two manufacturers—Holden and Ford—also closed their facilities about the same time), they focussed on building generic skills.
- Employees were given a generous severance package, funding of internal and external training programs chosen by the impacted employee and ongoing support.

This would seem to be a template for digital transformations that will lead to large-scale job cuts. It was a significant enterprise-wide undertaking. Not every organisation will adopt such an approach. If you are a leader in an organisation that does not have such a program, there are still many things you can do:

- Recognise that everyone will respond differently—some may be in denial, some may be devasted, some will be angry, and some may be delighted if they are getting a large payout. Treat everyone as an individual and with respect.
- Create the time and space for each individual to build their career plan.
- Source whatever you can to help your teams, whether it is access to training budgets, redeployment budgets, further education grants, etc.
- Provide introductions and help build their networking skills.
- Showcase the team's talent with recruitment agencies.
- Help develop their LinkedIn profiles, help update resumes, etc.
- Role-play interviewing techniques.
- Market your people to your network.
- Make sure that everyone has a buddy who will keep an eye out for a colleague.
- Take advantage of any secondments, job rotations and buddying programs.
- Above all, communicate regularly, check in constantly and always be there for your team when they need you.

Last and not least, particularly if you will also be impacted by the transformation, remember to look after your own well-being. I have seen leaders so focussed on their team that they have ignored their own stress indicators. This has had a detrimental effect on their health and consequently inhibited their ability to support their team.

Designing your workforce of the future

Designing the workforce of the future may seem like a daunting task. At a time when there is so much uncertainty and the pace of change is so rapid, how can you plan to make sure you are prepared when redesigning structures, creating new positions and reskilling people takes time? In some ways, this is similar to a capacity management problem. There is change we know about, or at least are fairly confident about anticipating, and then there is change we will just have to react to.

We have already covered the types of skills that are likely to be needed in the workforce of the future. This section will focus on how to bring those skills to life.

For me, the difference between capabilities and processes is a good place to start. In my mind, a capability is something an organisation requires to meet a particular need. When the first banks started to spring up in Italy in the thirteenth and fourteenth centuries, they needed a capability to lend money as do banks now. While the basic steps in the process are not that different, the tools, technologies and resources available to fulfil the process are very different. And so it will be in a digital world. Businesses who choose to provide education services in the future will need to register students, share knowledge and content, assess understanding and recognise achievement. They will need to design processes that use the most appropriate tools and technologies to deliver this capability, which will be different to the tools that have been used in the past. Gone are the days when hundreds of students crammed into a lecture hall.

So in practical terms, the first step is to understand the "reimagined" customer journey, and for each step in the process, you must determine the right mix of technology and people capabilities to fulfil that step. And remember, technology doesn't just mean software and hardware.

Once you've determined what resources will be required to fulfil each step, the next step is to:

- Understand the types of technology required and how they will fit into a technology architecture.
- Understand the skills, knowledge and abilities the people require to fulfil the step.

The next step is a question of scale. How much demand will there be? What will be the load placed on the system? How many people will be needed? Where should they be located? Who are the partners that are best able to help? These are all the same design considerations discussed in Chapter 10. The only difference is that the scope and scale are much greater. Following through these points will determine the size of the team, the relevant spans of control, success criteria for individuals in roles, the grading and reward levels, etc.

In many ways, what appears to be a daunting task is something organisations have had to deal with for, in some cases, centuries. The main difference is the pace.

With that in mind, what do "operations of the future" in traditional service businesses look like from my perspective? A trite answer might be "a lot smaller". There is a school of thought that we are heading towards "zero operations". I subscribe to the view that what we do today will be barely visible in the next 10+ years, not just in the operations function but across all major functions: sales, product, service and support. My sense is that the Run Teams across all functions will largely be focussed on exception handling, with the bulk of the work delivered digitally whether that is generating sales leads, responding to service requests, assessing risk, running month-end financial reporting, onboarding staff, etc. Roles involved in exception handling will be relatively more complex than the typical role in the function today, and they will be enabled by "intelligent operations"—tools and technologies that make handling these exceptions far easier with a corresponding increase in productivity.

Most of the current BAU work will be managed and monitored through command/control centres. These will be small groups of people with deep understanding of how the systems and processes come together to deliver the customer experience, and they will be tasked with making sure it's "always on". With metrics targeted at reducing mean time to fail and accelerating mean time to recover, their role will be enhanced by predictive analytics. They will know when a platform is about to reach its operating capacity threshold but in sufficient time to do something about it. They will be able to manage customer expectations far more precisely by being able to reach smaller and smaller subsets with specific messages related to their actual experience in real time. These teams will need deep process knowledge, a detailed understanding of the range of technologies and how they fit together, data extraction and analytical skills as well as exceptional problem-solving and communication skills with a real sense of urgency and "can-do".

So far this seems like a drastic reduction in the workforce: a small number of people handling exception, probably some servicing teams with outstanding EQ and a small group of people staffing the command centre. What about everyone else?

The opportunity is to point the people that have demonstrated their ability in the techniques in this book towards generating new revenue and enhancing service. To succeed as a Run Team in this type of environment, the skills and knowledge you will have acquired will help to position you to actively participate in the workforce of the future. Whether that is to find new opportunities through analysis, supporting and maintaining robots, designing new features as part of an Agile squad or enhancing connectivity across an ecosystem, the options are limitless.

Our role is to create value. We do that by understanding customers and what they value and then finding ways to meet these needs by using the resources and technology at our disposal in the most commercially viable way. The foundations are there—it's just a question of allowing our mind-set to shift from value creation through manual service delivery to value creation through other means.

Chapter summary

For a book that is largely focussed on managing the here and now, this chapter has taken a different perspective and focussed on the future.

Specifically, it has described how a leader of a Run Team can prepare their team to be part of the workforce of the future.

The environment is challenging, to say the least, and requires a significant degree of resilience both in the individuals that make up the team and that of the leader. The negative impacts associated with workplace stress exact a very heavy toll, but fortunately, there are techniques that can be learned that will help build resilience.

Trying to determine precisely what the future looks like and the types of skills that will be required is more art than science. It's also easy to be bamboozled by the job titles themselves. When you dig a little deeper, it tends to be more of an evolution than a revolution, which bodes well for reskilling existing team members.

Given there is so much uncertainty, what is required is workforce flexibility and a willingness to adapt, learn and create value for customers in a way that is different to that of today. This mind-set does not come easy to everyone, and it is tempting to buy in talent rather than reskill existing teams. This approach, in my mind, is short-sighted. By developing a growth mind-set amongst team members and enabling and facilitating workplace learning, transitioning people to new roles is eminently possible. To do this takes time and capacity—the team needs to be Match Fit.

Some digital transformations will lead to a reduction in roles. Leading teams through a downsizing program is extraordinarily difficult. There are, however, case studies of this being handled exceptionally well, with outstanding results for all stakeholders. These lessons must be learned.

Designing your workforce of the future is no different to any other process design problem. Start with the customer. What do they value? From there it's simply a series of decisions to configure the most appropriate mix of technology and people to create and deliver this value.

Finally, I reiterated the importance of communication when leading a change program. It is practically impossible to overcommunicate during a major transformation, and leaders who role model in this aspect will be amply rewarded.

Checklist:

Checklist Item	Status
Are your team change ready, and do they practice resilience techniques?	❑
Do you know the types of skills and roles you will need in the future?	❑
Do you have a plan in place to acquire these skills either through retraining existing people or bringing in new talent?	❑
Do you have a plan in place to help build the careers of those people who will no longer be part of your team in the future?	❑
Do you have a list of the capabilities, tools and technology required for your workforce of the future, an understanding of how your team will create value in the future and a plan to get there?	❑

Part 4 – End-of-Season Review: Stay the Course

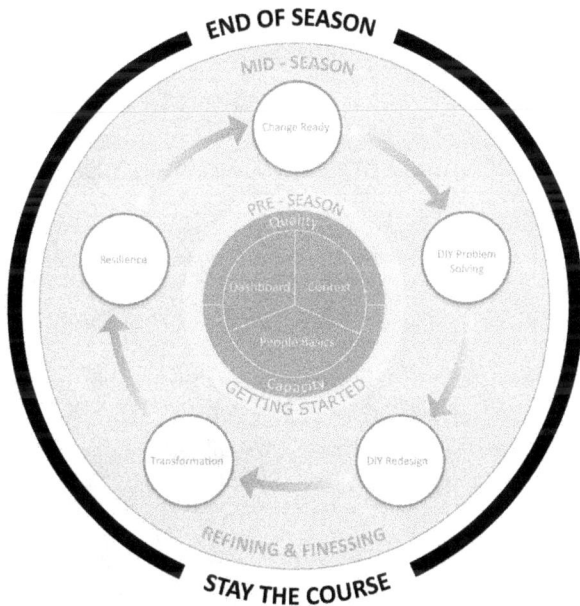

Chapter 13
Hold the Line

"Winning takes talent, to repeat takes character."
— John Wooden, UCLA basketball coach

Throughout the book, I have focussed on what it takes to get Match Fit in the pre-season, refining and enhancing performance throughout the season and setting the team up for success as it approaches those critical last few matches. At the end of the season, the players take a break before preparing for the next pre-season, preferably with some new silverware in the trophy room. Having one winning season is not enough. The challenge is to improve—even when you are clearly the best—and build a legacy.

There are many examples of clubs winning back-to-back championships. There are examples of clubs with winning streaks spread over 5–10 years: the Chicago Bulls in basketball in the 1990s or the West Indies not losing a single test series in cricket for 15 years in the 1980s and early 1990s. Very few have maintained, over decades, a level of success like the All Blacks.

Trying to emulate the longevity and performance of the All Blacks is, for many, beyond aspirational. For mere mortals, there are lessons that can be adopted. Discipline, a focus on the team, humility, passion and training in match-like conditions are just a few. Add to this an in-the-moment intensity juxtaposed with a forward-looking view underpinned by a relentless focus on excellence. And then there's getting the basics right but with a mind-set that says, "There is always room for improvement."

It is the same in an organisation. Change Teams are constantly looking ahead, introducing the new techniques and technologies, pre-empting changing customer needs and responding to competitor behaviour. Run Teams are focussed on the here and now, getting the basics right, honing their skills and always looking to improve. Collectively, they are bound by the organisation's culture, a common purpose, a clear mission with the rites, rituals, symbols and stories reinforcing the value of being part of the journey and preparing to hand on the baton to the next cohort.

Making this sustainable within an organisation requires a mix of the practical and the aspirational. There are things you can do and things you need your CEO to do for you. The foundation of sustainability is discipline and routine. You create that with an operating rhythm.

Establishing an operating rhythm

Getting Match Fit, in many ways, is about discipline. Throughout the book I've suggested that various techniques should be locked into an operating rhythm. What do I mean by an operating rhythm? In simple terms, it's a routine—a calendar of events repeated at various frequencies throughout the years. It's what you and the team will do each day, week, month, quarter, etc. By formalising an operating rhythm, it brings a level of predictability to what is a very unpredictable operating environment. It may sound counterintuitive, especially given early references to the team developing responsiveness skills like free-form jazz artists. Even jazz musicians work off charts capturing chord progressions and patterns. A good operating rhythm works in a similar way. It is not so rigid that it constrains but provides enough structure to facilitate and simplify the day-to-day running of the team.

It should incorporate the critical events and meetings covering communication updates, control cycle events, innovation and improve-ment meetings.

The core of the operating rhythm is the planning cycle covered in Chapter 7. The example in Figure 51 highlights the main components:

- Management hierarchy.
- Time horizon.
- Operating rhythm event.
- Cascading.
- Communication and other.

	TEAM LEADER					MANAGER					SENIOR MANAGER					EXECUTIVE				
	D	W	M	Q	Y	D	W	M	Q	Y	D	W	M	Q	Y	D	W	M	Q	Y
FORECAST	●	●				●	●				●	●							●	●
PLAN	●	●				●	●				●	●							●	●
Active Management Control — Check-In	●					●					●					●				
Active Management Control — Check-On	●					●					●					●				
Active Management Control — Check-Out	●					●					●					●				
REVIEW	●	●				●	●				●	●							●	●
COACH	●	●	●	●	●	●	●	●	●	●	●	●	●	●	●			●	●	●
IMPROVE		●	●				●	●	●			●	●	●					●	●

D: Daily   W: Weekly   M: Monthly   Q: Quarterly   H: Half-Yearly   A: Annually

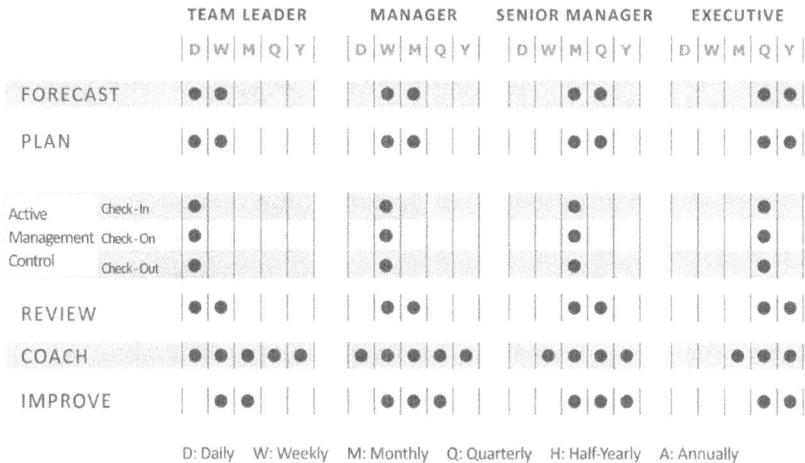

Figure 51 – Operating rhythm example.

Management hierarchy – For most people, a bad operating rhythm is more memorable than a good one. The leaders in the middle of the organisation feel the consequences firsthand. They are constantly having to reschedule meetings as a more senior leader has moved their meeting and now there is a clash. This is particularly the case in heavily matrixed organisations. Everything appears to be in constant Brownian motion with no structure. A good operating rhythm is far more structured and disciplined. It is set from the top and can be oriented around board meetings, which tend to be scheduled well in advance. The dates are published and each layer in the organisation can then schedule their relevant meetings that feed into the overall operating rhythm. Having said that, if your organisation doesn't have a formal operating rhythm, that's no excuse not to create one for your team. With more and more organisations looking to "flatten" structures and empower Agile teams, there is a question of whether this is still a relevant concept, but even if there are only four or five layers between the frontline staff and the CEO, there still need to be some mechanisms to connect the layers.

Time horizon – As we covered in Chapter 7, there are various time horizons to consider from the daily to the annual. The more senior the leadership forum, the longer the horizon term. As you would expect, there is significant overlap. The further out the horizon, the greater the focus on forecasting and strategic planning. The shorter the time horizon, the greater the focus on planning and control. All time horizons are inextricably intertwined. Once again, digital is changing the perspective and the time horizons are being reduced. What were 5 year horizons are at most 2-3 years and quarterly horizons are now weekly or monthly. Executives can no longer just think in the long term, they must also have an eye on the short-term trends that can change so quickly.

Operating rhythm event – Figure 51 highlights the key events. Forecast and plan are combined, and control is split into three: check in, check on and check out to reflect the importance of making adjustments when you recognise your planning assumptions may not hold true, then constantly checking on the revised plan before signing off on the time period and taking the learning into the formal review. The example also highlights two critical events not covered in Chapter 7—the importance of coaching your people and the need to schedule improvement activities.

The need to provide coaching should go without saying. While the example above suggests formal coaching on at least a monthly basis, including formal performance reviews, this doesn't preclude the need to provide continuous coaching. "In the moment" feedback is nearly always more helpful to understanding. In terms of improvement, the third part of this book has focussed on the need for Run Teams to improve. This is not an ad hoc activity. For it to be material, it needs to happen at scale, and the way to do this is to lock it into an operating rhythm (i.e., it is a scheduled activity).

Cascading – Cascading reflects the fact that most leaders will interact with the operating rhythm as both the leader of their own team's operating rhythm and as a participant at their line manager's operating rhythm events. This is an essential part of the feedback and learning loop to ensure effective communication flows up and down the hierarchy. It also reflects an underlying roll up of performance.

Communication and other – The operating rhythm is a communication tool. The example shows the core events, but there are others that need to be included that are less frequent. In Chapter 4, I covered the critical questions that you need to ask, and this sets the context for other items that may need to appear on the calendar you create. It may include things like customer visits, supplier reviews, transformational project steering committees and working groups, town halls, risk reviews and other meetings, etc. Essentially, whatever you need to do on a regular basis that is critical to the health of the team must be added to the operating rhythm calendar.

Having designed the rhythm and the calendar, the next thing is to make sure people stick to it. Meetings, whether virtual or real, are still an important part of running an organisation, yet they are one of the biggest drags on capacity. There are many, many video clips, blogs and articles on the topic of meeting effectiveness. In summary, my thoughts are:

- Every meeting must have a clear agenda with a named speaker for each agenda item.
- The meeting should only go for as long as is needed to cover the agenda. If that means 10 minutes, make it 10 minutes. Don't default to 30 minutes or an hour.
- Make sure any materials and briefing papers are available in sufficient time for people to read them and are accessible.
- Make sure the communication equipment works and joining instructions are available in the invite and on any papers.
- Be punctual. Start the meeting on time and ensure participants start on time.
- Ask habitual latecomers to open the meeting to ensure they do make it there on time.
- Only invite those that are needed, and if you're invited you must contribute.
- Hold people to account. If someone said an item would be complete on a specific date, make sure it is. Past due should not become the rule.
- Summarise action items at the end of the meeting.
- Schedule the meeting to conclude at a time that allows people enough time to get to their next appointment (e.g., 5 or 10 minutes to the hour).
- Record the action points in the meeting and share them immediately.
- If you're the chairperson, make sure you manage the energy and get everyone to participate. Your body language and tone of voice count.

- Be present and make sure everyone else is too. Switch your phone to silent and stop checking it every two minutes.
- Follow up on action items, and make sure they are completed.

There is nothing revelatory in this list, but it sets the tone. Remember, this is about consistency and discipline. Operational excellence is exactly that—excellence. It's not about being sloppy, humdrum or thinking that okay is good enough.

What can you do to make it sustainable?

Once you have a formal operating rhythm in place, there are several actions you can take that will increase the likelihood that you will be able to achieve the outcomes identified in this book on an ongoing basis. The first of these is down to you as a leader.

Always role model these behaviours and practices – This is very difficult to do as you will be under constant scrutiny. It is easy to let your guard down and express your frustration or exasperation with something. If you do lapse, as we all do, you must use this as a coaching moment for your team. Let them know that you are fallible, you do make mistakes, why what you did was a mistake and what you plan to do better next time.

Share the love – At this point you may feel that you are carrying the weight of the world on your shoulders, so the next step is to share the burden. Give as many people as possible a leadership role in bringing the system to life. This is over and above their core role. It may include things such as recognising someone as an expert in a technique. Ask them to ensure best practice is in place and that they be the go-to person for tips and advice. Another task may be ensuring dashboards for the daily huddle are up to date or coordinating the next social event. Whatever it is, the team need to feel that they are an intrinsic part of the system. It is not "us and them"; it is all of us together.

Get Match Fit – At the start of the book, I mentioned that many of the tools and techniques discussed within the book would not necessarily be new to you. However, you will only achieve the outcomes articulated here if you look upon the book as a whole system. You can't cherry-pick. You have to do it all, which means you need to train your people in all of the topics covered. Your team must understand the importance of setting the context, getting the people basics right, establishing listening posts and a scorecard, implementing a quality program, managing capacity, learning how to identify and implement innovation and improvement opportunities and work effectively with the Run Teams.

Celebrate your successes – Some days you may feel like you are shovelling sand in the desert and all that you can see in front of you is more sand. But you must take time to look back and see how much sand you've already put behind you. Taking time to celebrate and reflect is a critical component of adopting any new practice. Creating a focal point for your journey and progress are both incredibly important. At one end of the scale, it can be something Lean practitioners would refer to as an Obeya—a dedicated room or space that highlights all aspects of the change underway and progress towards the goal. At the other end of the spectrum, I have seen progress charts set up to resemble a race around the world.

Glossary of terms – One of the great things about new people joining a team is when they introduce new skills, techniques and ideas from their previous experiences. I've seen teams make huge leaps forward by disseminating one novel approach to a problem that has been plaguing them for months. The downside is that new people frequently bring with them new language and terminology they used at their prior workplace. At face value, a different word introduced into a corporate lexicon infers newness, but as with so much jargon today, it may just be a different term for an idea or technique already in practice. So before you roll out another new thing, just check that it's not something you already do under a different name. The best way to manage this is with a glossary of terms. List all the terms, describe what they are, and then if there are multiple terms for the same thing, highlight the preferred term.

Share the story – Invite other teams and leaders to visit your team and provide them with a briefing note on what it is you are trying to achieve. Outline the key themes, the benefits to the organisation and its customers and why the particular guest will benefit. Internal social media platforms are perfect for this. Where possible, ask your invitees to cross-promote.

Manage the system – What you will create is a management system. It needs to be governed and maintained. Changes need to be discussed, considered and introduced carefully. This is particularly the case when the approach will span different divisions, functions and locations. If you don't have a central governance body, each individual leader will adapt the system to meet their own needs. One of the major benefits of this approach is it facilitates the movement of people around the organisation without the need to learn a new way of working. Allowing individuals to set their own agenda will greatly weaken the value of the overall proposition.

Stay the course – While there are many benefits that will accrue relatively quickly, it does take time to embed this type of approach at scale. There will undoubtedly be challenges along the way, but it is important to work through these and not start chopping and changing. This can be particularly difficult when new senior leaders join the organisation with an intent to establish their own approach. The only way to avoid this is to demonstrate how well the system actually works. It won't always be enough, but it's a far bigger risk for the new leader to throw out an existing system that works than introduce one where nothing exists.

What can a CEO do to help?

Whenever the CEO or a senior executive is on a site visit, they invariably ask the question, "What can I do to help?" To my mind, this is not a rhetorical question. Nor is it the CEO lost in reverie musing on what they might do. It is a direct request. Unfortunately, leaders and team members rarely seem to take the CEO up on the offer. Here are some of the things I think should be on the wish list (see Appendix 13 for how I would like CEOs to help). Obviously, it's important for you to approach these topics with respect. Your CEO will have more than enough issues to deal with and compounding them will not help your cause.

When the CEO asks, these are some of the things you can reply with:

Change the message – The most important request is for the CEO to communicate that the Run Team is as much a part of the digital transformation as the Change Team. For the CEO to communicate this and explain how the different missions are co-dependent is a powerful signal to the organisation. The key message is that for the transformation to succeed, both the Run Team and Change Team must succeed.

Recognise success – When a Run Team hits a major milestone, for the CEO to share the news is a powerful reinforcement of the importance the Run Team plays in delivering the transformation. Your role is to provide the CEO's communications team with your successes. They need to be material and aligned to the strategic agenda. Given that a lot of what the Run Team do is small change, you will need to bundle several improvements together across multiple teams and deliver a "benefit" package.

Presence – Nothing pumps up the tyres like a visit from the CEO or the senior executive team. In organisations where service is delivered from remote or offshore centres, the commitment it takes just to turn up is not lost on the team. Seeing the CEO walking the floor, talking to team members and handing out awards is a remarkably powerful motivator. To improve your chances of finding a slot in the CEO's diary, make it worth their while. Unveiling a new solution and demonstrating major improvements that have led to greater customer satisfaction or facilitated the transformation are all good reasons.

Resolve conflict – If you are faced with conflicting objectives and expectations from other senior leaders that are impeding progress, raising awareness to the CEO is a good way to get things moving. This is a very delicate positioning exercise. Under no circumstances can you be seen to be criticising the relevant senior leaders. You can't appear to be going over their heads. A simple statement like, "We're going a little bit slower than we would like, as we need to do both A and B" should prompt the question, "Why are you doing two things?" The CEO can then work with the respective leaders to create a more aligned position.

Issue awareness – CEOs and senior executives are not always immediately aware of the implications of policy change. For example, it makes no sense if one location has a hiring freeze and another higher-cost location compensates by increasing its hiring. If teams do not release surplus capacity and hang on to precious resources because hiring policies make it almost impossible to bring on people quickly when demand picks up, the organisation is missing an opportunity. Careful use of facts, data and examples are a great way to raise the CEO's awareness of issues that are getting in the way of a team meeting their goals. A particularly delicate example is the impact of frequent restructuring and changes of direction. One leader I met very politely laid out all of the strategic packs that the various senior executives had shared with his team over the last three years. Each pack had a list of the executives and what they expected of the team. Added together there were over 30 objectives, and many of them were conflicting with each other. The team just kept doing what they thought was right. Remember that tact and diplomacy are of the utmost importance.

Pitch perfect – Asking the CEO to get involved with your team's work is a great way to help them understand the role the Run Team plays in supporting the transformation. The type of activity will vary depending on the personality of the CEO, but you must take the opportunity to reinforce the message that what you do both enables the Change Team to do their job and supports the overall digital transformation. You must use the language of digital transformation in the messages you relay back to the CEO so that they see you are on the same page. Some of the options I've seen are:

- Ask the CEO to watch a team member perform a task—this should be carefully chosen to highlight the challenges the team must overcome daily (e.g., learn how to operate 15 different systems). Better still, ask the CEO to perform the task— with some guidance, of course.
- Invite the CEO to join a problem-solving session. Walk the CEO through the problem, the root cause and what you are intending to do about it.
- Ask the CEO to participate in a panel to review initiative proposals from the team. Each group gets 3–5 minutes to pitch their initiative to the CEO. This is especially useful if there are initiatives that will make a significant difference but require some funding/resources outside of your control—you may get lucky.

Focus on the people – The challenges you are facing are probably being experienced by many of your peers, particularly when it comes to reskilling your people. Find the common ground with your peers and use this as an anchor point to raise the profile of something that needs broader consideration. To expect a team leader to be able to put a program together to reskill their team members for the workforce of the future is unrealistic. By making the CEO aware that this is broader than just your team members, you increase the chance of it being elevated. This is one area where you can be quite explicit about what will help (e.g., engagement with third-party training providers, funding for upskilling programs, greater human resources support, etc.).

Seek advice – CEOs have a wealth of experience and resources to draw on. Ask them what they would do differently or how they think you can overcome particular obstacles you're facing.

Build the network – Your CEO will be well connected both within the organisation and outside of it in the broader business community. Asking the CEO who else you should connect with to seek advice on how your team can improve is a great way to extend your network and gain some valuable advice. If you've been referred by the CEO, it's highly likely that the connection will take your call.

Getting started

After reading many pages with hundreds of tips, tricks and pieces of advice, it may feel like you are drinking from a fire hydrant. There is just so much to take in. But, as with so many problems, the start point is to chunk it down. When I started thinking about this section, my initial intent was to present a basic work plan. On reflection, remembering the many varied issues I've faced when leading teams, I realised it probably wouldn't work. One size definitely does not fit all in this regard. There's no point in focussing on quality when the quality is fine, yet the team is struggling with overtime. Similarly, there's no point in trying to build a problem-solving capability in a toxic environment. However, there are two things all teams I've led have in common:

1. We started with a current state assessment—a capability audit to understand the baseline for each team.
2. We progressively worked through all elements covered in the book, but it was not necessarily in the same order. The precise sequence was based on the operational maturity of the team and the problems they were facing.

The simple answer on where to start is with a current state assessment. The checklists at the end of each chapter provide the basis for the assessment, and I have summarised them in Appendix 12. Simply rating each item as "Not Started", "Work in Progress (WIP)" or "Match Fit" will suffice. Remember to use real evidence—facts, data and actual observations—and not "gut feel" when making the assessments.

Assessment Criteria	Logical Sequence (A)	Team 1	Team 2	Team 3	Team 4	Team 5	Overall Assessment (B)	Priority Score (A x B)	Execution Sequence
Part 1 – The Need for Match Fit									
Chapter 1 Digital - An Existential Crisis	1	Not Started	Not Started	Match Fit	WIP	WIP	2.0	2.0	1
Part 2 – Pre-Season: Getting Match Fit									
Chapter 2 Pre-Season Pep Talk – Setting the Context	2	Not Started	Not Started	WIP	WIP	WIP	1.6	2.6	2
Chapter 3 Selecting the Squad – The People Basics	2	Not Started	Not Started	WIP	Not Started	WIP	1.7	3.0	3
Chapter 4 League Ladders and the Trophy Room – Getting the Scorecard Right	2	Not Started	Not Started	Match Fit	Match Fit	WIP	2.0	3.9	6
Chapter 5 Know the Rules, Read the Game – Understanding Service Quality	2	Not Started	Not Started	Match Fit	Not Started	WIP	1.7	3.3	4
Chapter 6 Skills Clinic – Quality Essentials	2	Not Started	Not Started	Match Fit	WIP	WIP	1.9	4.0	7
Chapter 7 Picking the Team – Managing Capacity	2	Not Started	WIP	Match Fit	WIP	WIP	1.7	3.8	5
Part 3 – Mid-Season: Getting Fitter, Refining & Finessing									
Chapter 8 The Need for Change	3	Not Started	WIP	Match Fit	WIP	WIP	1.7	4.7	9
Chapter 9 The 1 Percenters - DIY Problem Solving	3	Not Started	WIP	Match Fit	WIP	WIP	1.8	5.8	10
Chapter 10 Timing the Peak - DIY Redesigning	4	Not Started	Not Started	WIP	WIP	Not Started	1.6	6.6	11
Chapter 11 Re-invent Your Game – Supporting Transformational Change	4	Not Started	WIP	WIP	WIP	WIP	1.8	6.6	12
Chapter 12 A Game of Hard Knocks – Resiliency and Workforce of the Future	5	Not Started	Not Started	WIP	WIP	WIP	1.6	7.5	13
Part 4 – End of Season Review: Stay the Course									
Chapter 13 Hold the Line	2	Not Started	WIP	Match Fit	Match Fit	WIP	1.9	4.3	8

Figure 52 – Match Fit prioritisation.

If this covers the first point above, the obvious question is, "What next?" There is clearly some work to be done here, so how do you best sequence the activities given one size doesn't fit all? In Figure 52, I have assigned a preferred sequence rating from 1 to 5. In a perfect world with a good team that works well together and delivers good quality in a timely manner, this is the sequence I would typically follow. It may seem a little counterintuitive, but under these conditions, my first priority would be to find spare capacity as quickly as possible. The freed-up resources can start working on other aspects of the program. However, if your team is faced with issues, you may need to rearrange the sequence to deal with those issues first. There are some dependencies and some aspects that are trickier to come to terms with at the start of the journey. I've classified these as level 4–5 in terms of sequencing and, irrespective of the issues you are facing, tackling these items should not be an immediate priority.

By substituting the ratings with a 1, 2 or 3 score, you can derive an execution sequence that suits your team. There are more sophisticated, operational, maturity assessment tools, but I find that this approach is easy enough for any leader to implement on their own and comprehensive enough to prioritise where the team should focus their efforts.

Based on the execution sequencing, you should now be able to develop an implementation plan. It is tricky to provide guidelines for the work effort involved, as this will be different for every team. However, for a typical team with 10–15 members supporting one or two customer journeys delivered by 5–10 core processes, 6–9 months would be a reasonable time frame to complete the elements in Part 1, Part 2 and Part 4, as well as the DIY problem solving in Part 3. The balance of Part 3 could take another 12–24 months to be not only established but running in a sustainable way. If you are responsible for managing a department or function comprising multiple teams, two to three Match Fit coaches should be able to support between 250–300 FTEs depending on the diversity of the work profile and the location of the teams. As their title suggests, they're playing a coaching and implementation support role, not an execution role. It is critical that the teams take on the responsibility for doing this themselves.

Finally, I should stress the importance of being honest in your assessment. A few years ago, I was discussing the topic of world-class operations with Alan Betts from Warwick Business School and a belief that on a scale of one to five there were no financial services firms beyond a level three in their operational maturity. Yet when I've spoken to colleagues across the industry and run many assessments, most leaders rate their teams as a four or a five. There's clearly some disconnect here. This is really self-defeating. If you can't see the problem, you can't fix it, so I would encourage everyone to be objective when they go through this type of assessment.

Chapter summary

If you want a world-class organisation, a good place to start is to have leaders and people who know what to do, when to do it and how to do it. The aim of this book has always been to provide Run Team leaders with a summary of what they need to do to survive and thrive in a digital transformation. It has focussed very deliberately on the breadth of what needs to be done rather than go into great detail on any particular topic. The breadth of what is required is wide indeed. Where most organisations fall down is to think that they can cherry-pick. But to create a sustainable system, you must cover all of the bases.

Getting the right people in place, with the right attitude, who are well trained with a clear understanding of their purpose of where they fit in the organisation and the role they play in supporting the strategy, is a great start. If you add sound listening posts and a consistent approach to measuring your performance and improvement, you have the foundations in place to free up capacity. This can be done by:

1. Establishing a forecast->plan->control->review cycle and planning resources at the 85th percentile.
2. Getting the quality basics right.

The first point will immediately free up at least 15% capacity, which you can use to train your team on quality improvement techniques. By just getting the quality basics right, you will free up more capacity as you reduce the amount of rework. This virtuous circle enables you to create enough capacity to learn a range of other improvement techniques such as A3s and redesigning, which in turn frees up more capacity to enable you to second out SMEs to work on the transformation, equip your people for the workforce of the future and meet your customer obligations with far fewer resources.

Reading a book is relatively simple. Understanding the content and how to deploy the lessons learned is also relatively straightforward. Leading the transition and staying the course is not. It's far too easy to get distracted, get caught up in "shiny new toy syndrome" and always want to move on to the next big thing. This is what will impede your progress. Leading a team through a Match Fit for Transformation transition takes time, commitment, resilience, decisiveness, role modelling and presence to give it a chance of becoming "the way things get done around here".

This chapter focussed on four things: implementing an operating rhythm, things you can do as a leader to make it sustainable, support you should ask for from the CEO and senior executives and where to start.

An effective operating rhythm is a structured way to lock in the practices. It is a calendar of events that highlights repeatability and consistency. Synchronising the calendar up and down the layers of the hierarchy both facilitates the smooth running of the organisation and ensures nothing is missed, overlooked or forgotten about until it's too late.

The second section focusses on you, the leader. In many ways, this is a transformation in its own right, and you're in charge. All of the leadership behaviours that are required to lead change are just as relevant here as they would be if you were heading up the Change Team. But it should come as no surprise that the key role is to connect, collaborate and communicate. In my opinion, technology plays a relatively small role in a digital transformation of a mature services organisation. The real enabler of success will be the people involved.

While the first chapter of this book focussed on the CEO and the challenges they face, the third section of this chapter focussed on how the CEO can help you. There are many ways to do this, as long as its respectful, pertinent to the overall strategy and not seen to be adding to the list of problems.

The final section focussed on how to get started. It may appear to be a daunting prospect, but the trick is to work through a current state assessment and then create an execution plan based on the current circumstances of the team. A typical team should expect to get Match Fit within 6–9 months, and build a problem-solving capability and be well progressed on the "getting fitter" path within another 12–24 months.

Following this approach will free up between 15–25% of capacity by fixing the basics in the first 6–9 months and a further 20–30% p.a. by getting the improvement mind-set and skills right. In addition, your customers will be far happier, and your people will have learned how to survive a digital transformation and be ready to thrive in the workforce of the future.

That's what it means to be Match Fit!

Checklist:

Checklist Item	Status
Do your team have a comprehensive operating rhythm in place that covers major events, spans the different time horizons and aligns up and down the hierarchy?	❏
Do you and your team understand the disciplined activities required to make the program sustainable, and are they underway?	❏
Do you and your team know what support you need from the CEO and senior executives to make this program sustainable, and is it underway?	❏
Do your team have a road map of how it will become Match Fit, showing progress to date?	❏

Appendixes

Appendix 1
Calculating Percentiles

Throughout the book I refer to percentiles. For those of you who haven't used percentiles before or have forgotten how they are calculated, this is a quick refresher.

Imagine you tracked your team's productivity on a daily basis over 100 days. The chart might look something like the one below (Figure 53):

Daily Productivity

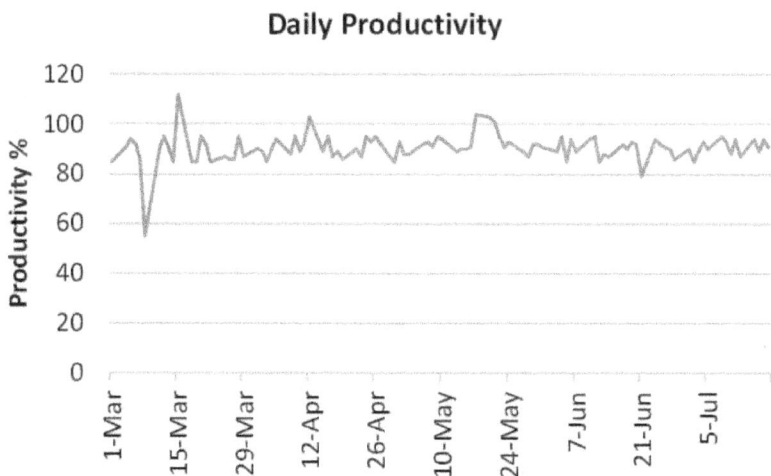

Figure 53 – Calculating percentiles, daily productivity example.

If you sorted the daily values from the least productive day to the most productive, the table would look like this (Figure 54):

Rank	Value	Rank	Value	Rank	Value	Rank	Value	Rank	Value	Rank	Value	Rank	Value	Rank	Value	Rank	Value	Rank	Value
1	55%	11	85%	21	87%	31	89%	41	90%	51	90%	61	92%	71	93%	81	94%	91	95%
2	79%	12	85%	22	87%	32	89%	42	90%	52	91%	62	92%	72	93%	82	94%	92	95%
3	85%	13	86%	23	87%	33	89%	43	90%	53	91%	63	92%	73	93%	83	94%	93	95%
4	85%	14	86%	24	87%	34	89%	44	90%	54	91%	64	92%	74	93%	84	95%	94	95%
5	85%	15	86%	25	87%	35	89%	45	90%	55	91%	65	92%	75	94%	85	95%	95	95%
6	85%	16	86%	26	88%	36	89%	46	90%	56	91%	66	92%	76	94%	86	95%	96	101%
7	85%	17	86%	27	88%	37	89%	47	90%	57	91%	67	93%	77	94%	87	95%	97	103%
8	85%	18	87%	28	88%	38	89%	48	90%	58	91%	68	93%	78	94%	88	95%	98	103%
9	85%	19	87%	29	88%	39	89%	49	90%	59	92%	69	93%	79	94%	89	95%	99	104%
10	85%	20	87%	30	88%	40	89%	50	90%	60	92%	70	93%	80	94%	90	95%	100	112%

Figure 54 – Underlying data sorted from lowest to highest.

The 25th percentile is the number that is the 25th in the list (reading from the top left)—that is a daily productivity level of 87% in this example. The 75th percentile is the number that is 75th on the list. This is a simple example as there are 100 items in the list. You need to adjust it to allow for the number of items. For example, if there are 50 items in the list, the 20th percentile is the 10th item from the top.

Appendix 2
People Basics

If you are to get Match Fit, you must create the right work environment for your team. This starts with the people basics:

- **Safety** – It goes without saying that physical and psychological safety are essential ingredients for a high-performing team. As the leader, you need to know that the workplace is safe, everyone knows the emergency procedures, workstations are set up correctly and there are clear policies in place that are understood by all team members concerning bullying, discrimination and workplace harassment.
- **Job titles** – Job titles matter. Changing someone's job title may appear trivial, but beware. A title change can be a big deal to an individual, as it confers status. Does everyone have a job tile? Are they consistent (i.e., do people doing the same job have the same title)? Does the title reflect what the individual does?
- **Contracts** – Contracts are there to protect both the employer and the employee. Does everyone on the team have a contract? Are they the same? In mature organisations, long-tenured staff may have very different contracts to more recent hires. Do the different contracts change the visible requirements to a team member's terms of employment (e.g., does it require them to work more or fewer hours than others doing the same job)?
- **Reporting line** – Does everyone know who their line manager is? Do team members have multiple or matrix line managers? Who sets the goals and performance targets? Who conducts the performance review? How are the matrix managers connected? Who takes precedence? Is there a "hard" and a "dotted" reporting line? What

difference does this make? Do team members performing the same job on the same team have the same line manager?

- **Hours and conditions** – Does everyone know how many hours they are contracted to work? Are there part-time team members or contract staff? Does everyone know what their scheduled working days are? Does everyone know what their entitlements are? Are there job shares in place? Do the people working the job share have the same understanding of how the job share works? Are there flexible working conditions? Can staff work from home? If so, do they need to give notice or have a dedicated workspace at home? Do people doing the same job have the same benefits (e.g., does everyone have a laptop provided or a smart phone)?

- **Grades** – There are few things that irritate staff more than when they are doing the same job as someone else, but they are doing so at a lower grade. Are grades consistent across the jobs? Are the grades appropriate for the level of work? Are there differences between grades based on gender, age or tenure?

- **Remuneration** – While keeping remuneration details confidential is a standard inclusion on any employment contract, it is remarkable how often people know how much their peers get paid. If people are getting paid differently to their peers doing the same job, is there a clear reason? Is the difference based on performance? Is the difference based on different conditions? Team members always know who the star performers are, and there is nothing that impedes the overall performance of a team more than people knowing the worst performers are paid more than the better performers.

- **Secondments, absences and vacancies** – What you see is not always what you get. In many teams, there are individuals on the payroll that are on extended leave (e.g., maternity leave, long service leave and sick leave). There are others that are backfilling roles on secondment who will be returning to their home business unit at a specified period, and on the flip side, there are people from your team currently on secondment to a different team but with an expected return date. There will also be vacancies—some of which will be at various stages of being filled and others will have been left vacant for some time. A leader needs to be aware of all these permutations to make sure that everyone is included and engaged, because getting Match Fit requires a great deal of flexibility. The key questions are: do you know who is currently costed to your team but currently absent? Do you know when they will return? Do you know who is notionally part of your team but seconded out to another team, and when they are expected back? Do you know how many roles you have and how many are vacant? Do you know which vacancies will be filled and when? Have offers been made to prospective employees yet to start?

- **Job descriptions** – It is very hard to drive performance if the expectations are not clearly set. Every team member must have a job description that clearly articulates the parameters of the role: the scope, responsibilities, authority, skills, competencies and behaviour that is expected in the role.
- **Key performance indicators and targets** – While the job description sets the parameters of the role, the targets are typically set on a more regular basis. The targets set the basis for how an individual's performance will be assessed, and every individual needs to know how they will be measured before the performance period begins. The key questions are as follows: Are performance reviews in place? Does everyone know their targets? Are they individual or shared targets? Does everyone know how their performance will be measured and evaluated? Do they know how frequently it will be measured and reviewed? Do they understand how they can influence the performance metrics? Do they understand who will be performing their review? If they disagree with their performance review, do they know who to speak to?
- **Individual development plans** – While the performance plan focusses on the team member's current performance, every team member needs to have an individual development plan, which is a formal document that outlines what the individual needs to work on to progress their career and what support they will need. The key questions are: Does everyone have an individual development plan? Are planning sessions with the responsible line manager held on a regular basis and is progress tracked? Does the training budget support the cost of the resource commitments made in the development plans?
- **Succession plan** – For many new leaders, especially those new

to the organisation, a nightmare scenario is a sudden flurry of staff resignations early in their tenure. This is particularly concerning if staff are exiting critical roles. One mitigant is to have an active succession plan in place, particularly one that lists potential "caretakers". These are individuals who can step into a role at a moment's notice, with little or no training required, and can perform the role at the required level. Beyond the caretaker level, it is also an indication of bench strength (i.e., the depth of the talent pool). The key questions are: Have critical roles been identified? Is there a succession plan for all critical roles? Are there caretakers identified for all critical roles? Do the individuals on the succession plan know that they are on the succession plan? Is it in their individual development plan? If there are gaps, is it clear how critical roles will be filled? What are the alternative sources of talent? Can roles be split or enhanced to attract talent?

- **Success profiles** – A success profile is an attempt to describe the ideal candidate's knowledge, experience, skills and competencies for a specific role. Using a success profile during the recruitment process increases the likelihood of finding the right candidate, and using them as part of the individual's ongoing development plan (both for the team member's current role and aspirational role) in conjunction with their performance plan makes for a far more structured and meaningful development conversation. The key questions are: Are there success profiles for critical roles? Are they used consistently so it is easier to target the right people to hire?

- **Employee milestones** – One of the greatest faux pas a new leader can commit is to miss a critical employee milestone, such as an individual celebrating 20+ years with the organisation. On the one hand, how can the new leader be expected to know, but from the perspective of the team, they are expected to know. Do you know the critical milestone dates for your team?

- **Induction program** – Last but not least, every new team member should go through an induction program. As well as orienting the individual about the physical aspects of their new workplace and guiding them on specific training that they need to undertake, it also provides an opportunity to set the context, as discussed in Chapter 2.

Appendix 3
Structure Charts

The structure chart in an organisation is a veritable treasure trove of insights for any leader, particularly a new-to-role leader.

Usually one of the first documents a new leader asks for, the structure chart can reveal far more about the organisation than who's on the team. The checklist below may provide some insight into precisely what you have got yourself into.

- **Availability** – Is there a structure chart? In smaller teams, where everyone knows everyone else and everyone is very clear about who does what, not having a formal, documented structure chart may be a sign of a healthy team (i.e., no one on the team feels the need for it). In my experience, however, this is rarely the case. The structure chart is a critical communication tool—even if it is a cartoon or screen full of avatars—clarifying who does what, how many people there are on the team, how work is organised, how the team is expected to interact and how matters should be escalated. If it's not written down, this usually masks a wide variety of team issues.
- **Access** – How long does it take to get access? From the time you ask to see the structure chart, how long it takes for you to receive a copy or access to an online version will provide clues. A delayed response may hint at a level of bureaucracy (i.e., the sender needs to get permission to share, there is a lack of transparency or the team are scrambling to pull one together).
- **Current** – Is it current? When was it last updated? Many structure charts are out of date and do not reflect the current makeup of the team because people move into new roles, leave

the organisation or take long-term career breaks. So it is a good idea to ask how often it is updated and when it was last updated. A dated chart and the current situation can tell a completely different story.

- **Format** – What is the format of the structure chart? Is it paper based, file based or online? This will present clues in terms of the overall technology environment to expect.
- **Tone** – What is the tone? Is it serious and formal or is it light and jokey? I've seen charts depicting the team as avatars, as characters in a comic book or as cartoon sketches. Most commonly, the chart is a traditional chain-of-command structure—all of which say something about the culture of the team.
- **Role titles** – Does it provide the role title? Do the role titles help explain what an individual does? Some organisations have obscure role titles or role titles designed to impress, but don't necessarily reflect what the role is responsible for.
- **Embedded hierarchies** – Are there embedded hierarchies? Do people doing similar roles have the same role titles? The chart may show one hierarchy, but the role title infers another, which is embedded within an organisational level (e.g., Analyst and Senior Analyst both reporting to the same manager).
- **Staff mix** – Does it show part-timers, temps, absences and secondees? A flexible workforce is critical to becoming Match Fit, but it's rare that the structure chart highlights the flexibility. This can deliver both a pleasant surprise and a nasty shock.
- **Location** – Does the chart identify the location of the individual or team? Running teams out of multiple locations as a virtual team presents specific challenges—especially if there's a travel budget freeze!
- **Names** – Does it include the names of the people on the team? It is important to design a structure around the required roles to fulfil the objectives of the team, rather than around the skills and attributes of the people on the team. A chart that doesn't include the names of the team members usually infers either a high staff turnover or a value statement (or lack of value) perceived by the leader of the people running the team.
- **Formality** – How formal are the names? Where names are

included, the way the name is written can indicate the degree of formality (e.g., does it just have the given name, a nickname or the full name? Is it given name first then family name (very formal) or the other way around? (Obviously, the latter also depends on local or organisational and culturally sensitive ways of addressing individuals.)

- **Qualifications** – Are there indications of qualifications? Does the individual's name show their qualifications (e.g., B. Com., MBA, Dip. Eng.) or their title (e.g., Prof., Dr., etc.)? This may indicate that the organisation values formal qualifications highly.

- **Grades** – Are role grades clear? Again, this can help explain team behaviour and dynamics around implied seniority, even though two individuals may share the same leader. Where there is a wide span of grades, it will also suggest the complexity of managing the team. Managing a team of roughly equal maturity, seniority, role size and scope is far easier than one where these attributes vary widely. One other observation here is the type of grade hierarchy—is it quite simple or broken down to a very fine level? Organisations that have many grade levels and sublevels tend to be bureaucratic, and creating a flexible workforce is quite difficult. If Priyanka takes a three-month career break, and Sid was offered the opportunity to fill the role, he may resist because the grade is lower (even though the title suggests the role is more important than his current role).

- **Comprehensive** – Does it list everyone or just a subset of people on the team? This also hints at who is considered to be important and who less so. For example, support teams may be left off even though the rest of the team may be dependent on them.

- **Shape** – What shape is it? Some teams operate within a traditional, functional structure, some operate as a matrix where each team member has at least two line managers, others have a team-based structure and others work as a network. Matrix organisations are notoriously difficult to work in and require a degree of maturity from both the matrix leaders and the employee. Issues of who sets priorities, how to deal with conflict and even simple things like double-booking team meetings can make for a stressful workplace.

- **Presentation** – What does it look like? Are the boxes representing peers all at the same level? Some charts infer seniority and hierarchy by placing roles which report to the same person in boxes that are slightly higher or lower, to subtly highlight status that neither the role grade nor title imply. Another way to imply seniority is to increase or reduce the size of some boxes.

- **Reporting lines** – Are the lines joining the boxes consistent? Use of "hard" lines and "dotted" lines is very common in matrix organisations to show who has the real power (the hard line) in the relationship. A dotted line responsibility for team members, who are co-located with the hard-line leader but not the matrix manager, may be a difficult relationship to manage.

- **Vacancies** – How many vacancies are there? A lot of vacancies can suggest low team morale but can also indicate organisational policies (e.g., a recruitment freeze). It is important to understand the reason why the vacancies exist. Taking over a team that is significantly understaffed when a recruitment freeze is in effect is extraordinarily challenging.

- **Diversity** – How diverse is the team? Is there a heavy gender or ethnic skew? (It is difficult to tell sometimes, but the name of the individuals on the chart may hint at a bias.) It is important to understand why the bias exists and what the implications are. I can't recall working with a team where increasing diversity hasn't improved the performance.

- **Number of direct reports** – How many team members are direct reports? The "right" number depends on the nature of the work (Koonz, 1966).

- **Spans** – Are the reporting spans consistent? Lopsided teams may create a power imbalance, for example, if a manager has many direct reports but another manager has only one or two.

- **Consistency** – Do charts for different teams look and feel the same? Where there are multiple teams making up your overall team, inconsistently drawn structure charts may highlight less than optimal consistency and standardisation on a broader basis and reflect that the teams are not working closely.

Appendix 4
Dashboard Design Tips

Tracking progress without a good dashboard is practically impossible. The keys to good dashboard design are:

- **Keep it simple** – Depending on the time frame, there should be no more than 4–6 metrics for daily reporting and 8–12 for monthly and quarterly reporting.
- **Trends matter** – Avoid using point data and single numbers or tables of numbers showing the current period only. It's the trend that matters, so use line (run) charts that show performance over time.
- **Less is more** – Ignore the fancy graphics options such as 3D, overuse of colours, etc. A dashboard is not an infographic. The intent is to help the reader focus on the content, not the format.
- **Keep it current** – It needs to be kept up to date. A daily dashboard that is three days old is a waste of space and effort (for those looking at it), as is a monthly dashboard that is two months old.
- **Keep it visible** – Everyone on the team should be able to see it. Buzz meetings/check-ins/daily huddles/scrums should be around the dashboard and should refer to the dashboard as the key input.
- **Exception handling** – If the business is running the way we expect it to, the metrics should be stable, so there's no need to intervene. A quick glance at the dashboard should reveal the exceptions and where you need to act.
- **Targets and tolerances** – If the objective is to deliver stable and consistent outputs, then you need to show these on the charts (i.e., a target line and an upper and lower tolerance threshold).
- **Performance icons** – These are the ticks and crosses, traffic lights or up and down arrows that frequently appear on

dashboards. They are very good at helping readers quickly assess performance. However, make sure that everyone understands how the icons are calibrated. As above, a one-period movement does not constitute a trend!

- **Target setting** – It's very easy to shoot from the hip when setting targets. If a senior executive asks you to reduce expenses by 10%, you may not want to argue, especially if your peers all sign up. But to change an outcome you must change an input or the process. So before you set targets or impose them on your team, make sure you are clear about what you are going to change that will lead to a change in the outcome.

- **Standard definitions** – This is needed where one leader's metrics shows something different to another leader's metrics, even though they purport to measure the same thing. The trick is to define them clearly (and their source) and make sure the definitions are always to hand.

- **Actionable** – The design must draw your attention to the "so what" quickly. It needs to force a "call to action" where the metric is not in line with expectations, and those actions need to be recorded with an accountable person and a time to complete.

Appendix 5
Useful Operational Metrics

The metrics in the body of the book are the core minimum metrics you must have. The following are also important depending on your team's circumstances. It is by no means a definitive list, but it is merely a list that I've found useful in my time as an operational leader. In some cases, I've provided the Excel formula to help explain the calculation.

Category	Metric	Comment
Process	Cycle time	This is the time between one piece of work completing and the next. If you complete 60 items in one hour, the cycle time is one minute.
	Throughput rate	This is the number of items delivered within a period of time. In the example above, it would be 60 items per hour.
	Takt time	Similar to cycle time, this metric calculates the time between one service request arriving in the queue and the next. In a perfect world, takt time and cycle time should match. In services, the easiest way to do this is by adjusting capacity.
	Straight through processing (STP) rate	This is the proportion of service requests that are completed with no manual intervention and is a useful lead indicator of quality and efficiency.

Category	Metric	Comment
	Automation rate	Related to STP, this is the proportion of the process that is automated. It allows for the fact that in some jurisdictions there may be other requirements impeding full automation of a process (e.g., regulatory requirements).
	Forecast accuracy	The better your forecasting, the easier it is to plan. Divide the absolute variance by the forecast (e.g., in Excel the formula is 1 — ABS [Actual—Forecast]/Forecast). You use the ABS function to ignore whether you are under- or over-forecasting.
	Demand volatility	This is useful to understand how hard it is to forecast and plan resources. The more volatile the demand pattern is, the harder it will be to forecast (assuming the demand pattern is random). To calculate, divide the standard deviation of the last 30 periods of data by the mean for the period (e.g., if there are large seasonal swings, this will affect the calculation—as will one-off extreme data points).
	Rework	This is the proportion of items that must repeat part of the process. It is calculated as number of items reworked divided by total items output, expressed as a percentage. In service organisations, this can be significant—anything over 5% is not uncommon and represents a material improvement opportunity.

Category	Metric	Comment
	Process adherence	This is the proportion of items completed that have followed the defined process. Process mining or workflow tools are typically required to calculate this on an ongoing basis. As a one-off calculation, it's a very useful indicator for quality. If everyone follows the process and there are still errors, fix the process. If most people are doing their own thing, train the team on following the process.
	Elapsed time	This is the time it takes from a work request arriving to completing. Note it should include any pauses in the processes, even if they are caused by the customer, as it provides a true reflection of the customer experience.
	Work content time	This is the amount of time it takes to complete all steps. The difference between this and the elapsed time is the time the item sits in queues waiting.
	Process cycle efficiency	This is the ratio between the time taken to complete value-added steps and the time in the system. Note that the value-added time will typically be less than the work content time, as the work content time includes both BVA and NVA steps. This is usually a very low number in services—I've seen some processes that are less than 0.01% process cycle-efficient!
	Systems availability	This is the proportion of time, in the specified operating window, that a system is actually available.

Category	Metric	Comment
	Aged WIP Profile	An aged WIP profile tracks the number of items of WIP by allocating them to various time periods, e.g., 0–2 days, 2–5 days, 5–10 days, etc. This is a useful measure to ensure items are not being overlooked. Long-dated items have a tendency to incur penalties or losses.
	Service availability	This is the proportion of time that all systems required to deliver a specific service are available. It's hard to calculate, as many services require multiple applications and systems to be available, but it is much more customer oriented.
	Mean time to fail	This is the average time between failures and can be calculated at either a system or a service level. This is a very powerful metric for measuring resilience.
	Mean time to recover	This is the average time it takes to get back to normal operation from the time a service or system becomes unavailable. Together with mean time to fail, this provides a great indication of the resilience of the service.
	Process capability	This is typically calculated as the difference between the upper and lower specified service limits divided by six times the standard deviation. For most services that I've been involved with, this is a very sobering calculation.

Category	Metric	Comment
	Grade of service (GOS)	This is a contact centre approach to measuring service levels. It measures the percentage of calls answered within a particular time frame. It is often abused and doesn't necessarily reflect the service level of individual customers. For example, if it is reported on a daily basis and the morning is busy but the afternoon quiet, on average the GOS may be within the specification, but the GOS during the morning would, in all likelihood, have been appalling. I prefer to measure the proportion of 10- or 15-minute blocks throughout the day that GOS was within specification. It is a far harsher metric but a better reflection of the customer experience.
	Average speed of answer	This is how long the customer must wait before the call is answered. I think the definition should be from the moment the customer calls to the time they are connected to the person that can solve their enquiry. A receptionist answering quickly and then farming out the call to another queue is giving a false impression that the customer is being dealt with promptly.
	Abandonment rate	Another contact centre metric measures the proportion of customers that give up prior to their call being answered. What it doesn't measure is how many repeat abandoned calls an individual customer may have.
	Average handle time (AHT)	This is a common but abused metric in contact centres. It pushes staff to finish the call quickly and not necessarily completely. This sometimes results in an additional call and a very poor customer experience.

Category	Metric	Comment
Customer	First call resolution	This is a good contact centre metric trying to avoid the issues of AHT (i.e., answer the customer's enquiry in full without a hand off to another team member).
	Client satisfaction	This can be measured in many different ways, such as through surveys or an approach like the Net Promoter Score.
	Complaints	This is measured as both an absolute number and a ratio of the total number of items delivered. Be careful and consistent in your approach to counting complaints, as some complaints are nested (i.e., a customer complains about multiple issues within one overall complaint).
	Praise	A great morale booster, displaying positive comments and praise is very useful.
	Defects	Defects can be measured in many ways at each stage of the process or at the point they impact the customer. They can be measured as a ratio, as in the Six Sigma DPMO, or as an absolute number. Remembering the distinction between outcomes and experience, this is one area where I've seen teams struggle to get the right definition of quality.
	Service level agreements (SLAs) and timeliness	This is the proportion of items completed within the time specified. I prefer to set the time specified as a range and not just an upper boundary (i.e., if you say between two and three hours then deliver in one, it is just as bad as delivering in four hours). SLAs come in for some criticism as the minimum level of acceptable performance.

Category	Metric	Comment
People	Engagement	This may be calculated as part of the annual employee opinion survey but is too important, in my opinion, to be derived only once a year. Using a continuous cultural pulse check is a far better approach to understanding how people on the team are feeling. It can be set up in a similar way to the Net Promoter Score, asking a sample of team members every week or month to rate how they are feeling about the team and what they would like to see done differently.
	Capability	There are many sophisticated tools and assessment methodologies you may use when doing a major restructure; however, on an ongoing basis, leveraging the skills matrix to derive a capability score is more than adequate. Calculate the average score for the team and track improvement over time.
	Staff flexibility	The skills matrix data is a simple way to measure the proportion of people that are skilled in more than one task, more than two tasks or more than three tasks. Remember, it should be relative to a target—trying to train everyone in everything is both expensive and will deliver diminishing returns. If a team member is not applying the skills regularly, they will forget and more than likely make mistakes.
	Absenteeism	This is a standard human resources metric to calculate the ratio of hours lost to absenteeism to the available work hours, and it is a good indicator of staff morale.

Category	Metric	Comment
	Turnover	This is the ratio of people voluntarily leaving compared to the average number of people employed. It is another indication of poor morale or that there are better opportunities elsewhere.
	Grade profile	This is the proportion of staff by grade type. It is particularly relevant if you are trying to change the mix of work the team perform (e.g., from clerical to analytical).
	Labour rate	This is the average cost per worked hour. It is useful to also break this down by location, and it is particularly common for organisations using offshoring as one of their cost management techniques.
	Annual leave	This is the average number of days of annual leave accrued per person. This can be a good indication of fatigue if the number builds, and it is also an easy way to reduce costs by asking people to take leave.
Financial	Direct costs	These are the costs incurred by the resources within a specific business unit associated with the work they directly undertake. Direct costs are often called controllable costs, as the leader responsible for the cost centres where these costs are incurred can make decisions that impact them directly.
	Allocated costs	Allocated costs are incurred elsewhere in the organisation (e.g., corporate centre costs are allocated back to the respective business unit based on the activity undertaken by the business unit). Managing allocated costs is more a question of influence but is still important.

Category	Metric	Comment
	Total costs	This is the sum of direct and allocated costs.
	Discretionary expenses	Discretionary expenses include costs such as travel, entertainment, training, etc. They are direct costs attributable to the business unit but not necessarily a direct cost of production. When cost reduction is on the agenda, this is usually the first area to come under investigation.
	Cost of poor quality	As discussed in the chapter on quality, the cost of poor quality can be broken down into four categories: prevention costs, appraisal costs, internal error costs and external error costs.
	Unit costs	This is the cost per work request completed. It is a topic of great debate, specifically around the cost allocation process, and it is particularly challenging in a mixed service environment with sketchy operational data at best.
	Overtime	Overtime is an excellent indicator of overall health. As suggested earlier in the book, some overtime can be a cost-effective way of keeping up with demand, but too much makes for a stressful and unsustainable workplace.
Risk	Operational losses	These are costs incurred directly as a result of a process failure (e.g., customer refunds).
	Business continuity planning (BCP) ratio	This is the proportion of time the business is operating in BCP mode relative to normal BAU mode. It is a key indicator of the stability of the system.
	Failed control testing	This is either the number of control test failures or the proportion of all controls that failed.

Category	Metric	Comment
	Audit ratings	This is an assessment by internal auditors of the health of the business, which is usually accompanied by a report identifying items for remediation. Having an independent team review your processes is an excellent way to find improvement opportunities.
	Compliance breaches	Tracked as an absolute number, this is a simple metric that is useful as a lead indicator of process design and adherence health.
	Near misses	This is the absolute number of events where failure has occurred but addressed prior to impacting the customer.
	Risk events	This is the absolute number of risk events of all types and is a good indicator of the robustness of design.

Appendix 6
Metrics Tips, Tricks and Red Flags

There are a number of things to look out for when reviewing dashboards. The "Tips and Tricks" are more about the design. The "Red Flags" are based on the actual data and highlight potential issues that must be addressed promptly.

Tips and tricks

- **Data source** – Do you know the source of the data and is it credible? If it's an electronic feed, so much the better—it is far less open to "fiddling". If it's manual, keep your eyes open and look for "non-random" patterns in the data.
- **One-period trend** – Because the data represents the performance of a system with inherent variability, it will move around from one period to the next. Just because the customer satisfaction line moves up one month, it is no reason to break out the champagne, nor is it appropriate to fire anyone if it moves down the following month. How many points are required is tricky to answer depending on the data, but it's at least three.
- **Watermelons and avocados** – Many dashboards use performance icons (symbols that indicate whether the performance is good or bad). Sometimes the icon will show the performance as "good", but other listening post sources will seem to contradict this (e.g., the team report they are delivering good quality, but the rising level of complaints seems to contradict this assessment). These are "watermelons"—green on the outside and red on the inside. What you need are "avocados"—green on the outside and the inside. This is nearly always driven by the definition of the metric rather than

an out-and-out attempt to undermine the reporting. For example, during an outsourcing project, I set a metric of "handling customer enquiries within 24 hours". The team was reporting at 99%, yet the level of customer noise was overwhelming. Reviewing how the metric was being calculated showed that to score a positive hit, all the team had to do was to look at the enquiry—not resolve it. Changing the metric to "resolve customer enquiries within 24 hours" saw the metric drop to a level that reflected reality. We could now see the problem and figure out a way to fix it.

- **Scaling** – Reading the scale on a chart is essential. The picture can show a significant upward trend with the line moving from the bottom left corner to the top right corner, but if the bottom of the vertical axis is 60% and the top of the vertical axis 61% when the target is 90%, the reality isn't so rosy.

- **Messy charts** – Too many data series, too many scales, too many colours, too many data points, cluttered labels—the aim of the chart is to provide clarity. Less is more!

- **Bias** – In some cases, the producer of the report may use bias to try and curry favour or support a specific viewpoint. For example, they may use one subset of a team that is performing well to infer the performance of the overall team (e.g., reporting on the quality of one service while ignoring the quality performance of the other services the team delivers).

- **Omission** – What's not reported tells as much of a story as what is reported.

- **Beware percentages** – Even though 99% sounds good, if the services you provide are critical and high volume, then a 1% defect rate implies many irate customers. Also watch out when people talk about a percentage improvement—a 10% improvement of not very much is simply not very much (e.g., a 10% improvement in customer satisfaction sounds great, but if only 5% of your customers are currently satisfied, you've now moved the dial to 5.5%, which doesn't sound so impressive).

- **Apples v oranges** – Sometimes data on a chart is represented on two vertical axes, usually when the scale is vastly different. I used to show domestic payments and cross-border payments on the same chart; the former was measured in millions and the latter was measured in tens of thousands, so showing them on two scales made sense. However, the scaling issue above can become a real problem when you have two scales and significantly distort the picture!

- **Re-baselining** – A great way to make your performance look good is to reset the baseline. Project status reporting is an area to watch here. Sometimes there are legitimate reasons for doing so (like when the environment has changed so dramatically it no longer makes sense), but a cynic would urge caution, particularly if it's close to performance review time.
- **Chicken v egg** – Once you've agreed on your strategy and selected your metrics, you must stick with them—even if you don't like the story they're telling. Unfortunately, and once again around performance review time, if the metric and the chart don't fit the intended narrative, for the less scrupulous, changing the metric is easier than changing the narrative.

Red flags

- **Absenteeism** – High levels tend to indicate a poor work environment and mean the team are always struggling to find resources and keep up with demand.
- **Staff turnover** – High levels are another indication of a poor work environment. Constant hiring and training of new staff is very expensive, both directly and indirectly, through the effects of poor quality.
- **Overtime** – High levels over a prolonged period will lead to burnout, impact morale and affect quality.
- **Budget shortfall** – If you've taken on a team where the expenses are exceeding the budget or revenues are below budget, you will be under scrutiny, under pressure and your options to innovate and experiment will be restricted.
- **Service levels and backlogs** – If you are behind in your service levels, you will be feeling pressure from the sales and relationship/account management team and customers directly. This will create additional work responding to "status" enquiries, further exacerbating the problem.

- **Complaints** – Like poor service levels and backlogs, but far more serious, is when poor performance leads to significantly higher levels of complaints. Handling complaints is expensive, and a sudden increase will put increased pressure on the operating budget.
- **Customer defections** – In a mass market environment, you will need to rely on the data—metrics such as customer churn should help. In a market based around a small number of large customers, you will hear firsthand from relationship managers. The pressure and intensity to address whatever is causing customers to leave will be immense.
- **Operational losses** – Arising from poor quality, these not only impact financial performance directly, but they also increase the level of scrutiny from other areas of the bank such as risk and compliance, which creates more work.
- **System stability** – One of the most challenging issues to deal with is operating in an environment where there is significant instability. Not knowing precisely when the system will go down will lead to high levels of rework, defects and downtime, as well as team frustration.
- **Rework and poor quality** – Nothing bad happens if you focus on quality. But ignore it at your peril. The cost of poor quality in service organisations is extraordinary and one of the greatest opportunities any team can have. In my experience, the more concerning and common issue is when quality isn't measured.
- **No metrics** – Possibly the biggest red flag is a lack of operational metrics. The lifting of the fog of war rarely reveals a pretty picture when you finally develop the metrics and you can see precisely what is happening.
- **Spans of control** – Where the ratio of team members to leaders is more than 1:20, it's highly likely the team member is not getting enough management attention, which can lead to poor quality, slow development, missed opportunity, misalignment with the strategy, etc. This ratio falls substantially the more complex the task of the team member.
- **Human resources issues** – Many of the obvious ones have been covered in the people basics section—if someone feels they are

underpaid or not graded correctly, if staff are leaving, etc., you will find out, either directly or indirectly. Other issues such as bullying and harassment can be harder to uncover and require you to spend time with the team, walking the floor, out of your office/away from your desk observing and listening. A healthy work environment should have a "buzz"—a silent workplace or one that is filled with pandemonium, cacophony and chaos are clear red flags.

- **Outside intervention** – This may be in the form of regulatory scrutiny, whistle-blower events or emergency services intervention; all require immediate attention.

- **Projects** – There are several events that merit concern with projects, particularly if the accountable leader is in a different team or division. Reprioritisation of projects and lots of new projects all create work—who and what's driving the demand? Sudden changes to schedules, particularly "go live" dates, when the project is not ready to be implemented can lead to some very difficult sponsor conversations—remember the Run Team pick up the pieces if the project deployment does not operate as intended. Another red flag to watch for is changes to scope, where items critical to delivery are de-scoped and moved to a later stage in the project. In my experience, there is a good chance these later phases won't get funded, and if the benefits are predicated on them, you may have to deliver the benefits without the enabling functionality. Very tricky!

- **Your diary** – It may seem like an unusual place to look but stepping back and looking at who is trying to make time in your diary, and the subject of the meeting, will give you a good indication of potential red flags. A large number of risk and compliance meetings indicates obvious concerns and an inflow of account and relationship manager meetings will typically point to quality problems. A series of human resources or supplier meetings will also point to issues in these areas. As a new leader, many people will just want to meet you; hence, don't be alarmed if your diary fills up fast—only be concerned if it's particularly skewed. Even for the general catch-ups and introductions, asking the meeting participant how you can help them and what they would like you to focus on will give you a reasonable indication of how the team is performing. Remember, in the early stages of your tenure, your stakeholders know far more about your team than you do.

- **Policy changes** – Sudden cuts to investment budgets, new financial targets, cuts to the travel and training budgets and recruitment freezes are all stress indicators. One of the many benefits of networking is to try and get ahead of the curve if these announcements are in the wings. When your unaware team find out, it can make for both difficult conversations and challenges to how you lead the team.

- **Authority events** – In many large organisations, the chain of command is not always clear, particularly if there's matrix management in place. Arguments over decision rights, who's in charge or who has the mandate can be an interesting spectator sport, but if you serve both combatants it can be a precarious, unpleasant and difficult position to be in.

Appendix 7
Error Proofing

There are many different types of error-proofing techniques. I've broken them down into four categories: desktop, documentation, flow/queue management and quality culture.

Desktop techniques

For many staff in services, their role is based around a computer. One of the issues here is that mistakes are hard to see—it's not like a production line, where you know you have a problem when you can see many of the defects in production.

1. **Validation** – One of the most obvious forms of error proofing techniques is to ensure fields on electronic forms are restricted where possible to allow valid data only (e.g., an input mask for a telephone number, drop-down boxes and pick lists).
2. **Dual blind keying** – Rather than have one person input data and a second check the input, have one person key and a second rekey critical fields to check they match—this is a good way to maximise input quality. A variation on this theme is to have one person read out the details to be inputted, another key and then swap roles to playback what has been keyed and compare to the original. This is time and resources intensive, but it may be by far the cheapest option—depending on the consequences of getting it wrong.
3. **Green screen masking** – Limiting the fields that can be accessed is another reasonably common approach. I've even seen a low-tech version using a sheet of paper taped over a screen with slots cut out in the area where data needs to be keyed.

4. **Spell and grammar check** – It seems obvious, given how often we use these tools, but the trick is to switch them on as a default! Make sure the language is the same across all centres and that teams performing the process are using, for example, the same regional form of English—US, UK, Australian, etc.—and that all team members have auto-check set as the default.

5. **Alarms** – This can be anything from setting reminders and notifications to pop-up messages for critical tasks. For example, when having a final check before sending an email, which could potentially create privacy breaches, a pop-up box might ask: "Are you sure you want to send X data to person Y?"

6. **Dual monitors** – These are relatively common now—one monitor displays the work request (e.g., an online form) and the other is used to process the request. This avoids having to remember what is being asked. It can also help where team members require access to multiple applications. Setting out the "windows" in a logical flow reduces the risk of pasting data from the clipboard to the wrong application.

7. **Generic mailboxes** – A common request from premium clients is to have a named contact. The issue here is that emails may go unanswered if the relevant contact is ill or on leave. Generic mailboxes are far safer and using the prioritisation tips above will ensure the right team member is allocated to the task.

8. **Structured input** – Where possible, capture data in forms, not unstructured emails, and preferably with typed rather than handwritten data. Not only does it reduce the risk of errors, it also dramatically increases optical character recognition read rates. With inputs that include images, ensure the resolution is set correctly to allow operators to zoom in without the image becoming too blurry.

9. **Templates** – An obvious solution for teams that are responsible for communicating with customers is to use stock templates (where applicable) that can be auto-populated or have validated fields to personalise. This is a great way to ensure consistency of language, tone, grammar, etc. It is particularly useful where team members are not native speakers of the template's language.

10. **Form design** – Where there is a requirement to enter data into a system from a form, laying out the form fields in the same sequence as they need to be keyed into the system makes the input role far easier and reduces the risk of missing something when going backwards and forwards.

Documentation

One of the most common causes of errors is a lack of standardisation. Driving standardisation is not easy, but it always starts with good documentation.

1. **Process and value-stream mapping** – Documenting processes and overlaying the failure points and relevant statistics is usually as good a place to start as any. Visualising a process nearly always reveals the blatantly obvious that somehow isn't quite so obvious when you're in the process day after day.
2. **Work instructions** – As ridiculous as they may seem, one of the simplest fail-safe techniques is to write down what you expect a team member to do (in detail). The mere process of getting all this information out of the experienced team members' heads will not only help get new hires up to competency far faster and making far fewer mistakes, but it will also provide significant benefits in simplifying and standardising the process. Without a reason to talk about what they do and a "system" to enforce process adherence, each team member will naturally create their own version of what to do.
3. **One-point lessons (OPLs)** – OPLs are ideal for tools such as video conferencing, phones, photocopiers and printers. Ideally, they are a simple infographic on a piece of laminated paper saved next to the device that provides relevant work instructions on how to use the device.
4. **Tags** – Using tags to make searching for documents easier is an extraordinarily simple fix for the perennial problem of lost hours trawling through shared folders. Ensure you have a standard library of tags and train your team to use them, not make up their own.

5. **Checklists** – I cannot overstate how critical checklists are. Most importantly, make sure your team members who are performing the same process share the same checklists. When one team member finds a way to improve it, they must share that with the others.

6. **Training** – This is an interesting one. On the one hand, in an ideal world and with human-centred design, the process should be so simple and so intuitive that people (customers or team members) don't need to be trained to operate the process defect-free. However, for most organisations with complex legacy processes, training is essential and a moral obligation to your staff. Anyone who has stared helplessly at a screen, willing the answer to manifest itself because they are too embarrassed to ask their supervisor for the umpteenth time what to do, will recognise just how crucial training is. Remember, team members move on to new roles, so training is not a set-and-forget activity. It must be a continuous process of skilling and embedding knowledge.

Flow and queue management

Many of these techniques are about meeting your service level objectives. Given the fluctuating nature of demand, this is one of the trickiest problems to solve. The goal is the "Goldilocks" service: not too soon, not too late, precisely when the customer expects you to deliver the service. To achieve this goal, consider using the following:

1. **Prioritisation** – Most teams have prioritisation rules for specific clients, segments, work types, due dates, etc. Many workflow tools allow you to make these settings in the system so that the highest priority work is always at the top of the queue. The rules capability in most email applications allows you to set up prioritisation rules. If you don't have a system-enforced way to pop the most important task to the top of the queue, simple things like using coloured paper or different coloured inboxes will help reduce sequencing errors.

2. **Colour coding** – In both paper and electronic environments,

setting the background colour of the "paper" for different customers can help with prioritisation.

3. **WIP windows** – A simplified combination of Little's Law and some statistical process control can quickly help you draw charts that set upper- and lower-level control limits for what is an acceptable level of WIP (queue depth). If your queue is within the control limits, you can expect to meet your service levels (under normal operating conditions).

4. **Kanban, short interval control and Heijunka** – These are a range of similar techniques to ensure you smooth out production and get through your work. They break the load (number of work requests) down into smaller time intervals—instead of thinking, "How many must we do today?", think, "How many must we do between 9 and 10 a.m.?" Checking in at the end of each shorter time period allows you plenty of time to take corrective action if you get behind. Heijunka boxes (essentially stacked in trays) with each inbox representing an hour's worth of work are a great way to manage throughput and pace. This is moving from a "push" system to a "pull" system.

5. **Visual controls** – Make the work visible and the team will respond when the problems become obvious. This means dashboards, wall charts, ticker tape displays and a whole host of other techniques—just make sure everyone can see them and they're not buried in the manager's computer. Creating physical representations of the workflow can have a dramatic effect—I've seen clothes racks with "pegged" work requests hanging from them. All the information was in the system, but—with the clothes racks in the middle of the floor—everybody could track progress easily.

6. **Runners, repeaters and strangers** – This is typically associated with optimising throughput and flow. This technique of triaging work requests then separating them into simple requests, more complicated requests with known variants and unique, highly complex requests means that you can allocate resources based on skill level. As a result, you don't put less experienced staff in the unenviable position of working on requests beyond their current capability.

7. **Single point of entry** – Many quality issues arise from upstream teams choosing their own entry point into a process. This may be sending a specific work request to someone they know in the general function rather than the capture point for the start of the process. All work requests need to enter at the start of the process—not halfway through.

Quality culture and other

At the heart of a quality culture are people who care about the customer and take pride in their work. They are empowered and equipped to solve quality problems as they arise and do not walk away from a problem. Disneyland is a great example where keeping the park clean is everyone's problem. If there's a piece of litter on the ground, the nearest member of staff will bend down to pick it up, regardless of whether they are the most junior or senior member of staff in the park.

1. **It's everyone's job** – The most critical element here is for everyone to recognise their role in delivering a quality service ("It may not be my fault, but it is my problem.") It doesn't matter which function you are in, you have a role to play in making the service defect-free. Typical examples include sales staff sending in customer orders that are incomplete or inaccurate, technology providing services with unacceptable levels of latency or dropouts and product teams designing products with manual work-arounds.
2. **Don't hand on poor quality work** – If you receive a work request that has defects, under no circumstances do you keep working on the request and perpetuate the error down the line. Fix the defect by returning the request to the source or contacting the supplier of the defect to fix and solve the issue at source. There are obviously practical and policy challenges with potentially contacting customers, but the principle applies and must be addressed.
3. **Provide space** – One of the major causes of human error in services is associated with the operating environment. Expecting staff to multitask and accept interruptions or rushing them will

only lead to defects. Create a safe environment that is conducive to delivering a quality output.

4. **Lean 5S** – A place for everything and everything in its place. The Lean toolkit provides a range of tools to ensure the physical environment is set up for success—clean, uncluttered, right tools to hand, etc.

5. **Computer clock meetings** – Using the clock on the computer to run meetings avoids the risk of people having their own watches and smart phones set to different times.

6. **Preventative maintenance** – This may sound like a manufacturing or technology task, but there are many ways that it can be implemented to ensure the operations environment is set up to minimise failure. For example, set regular cycles for restocking the printer with paper and toner, make sure there are always adequate stationery supplies, swap out computers and laptops at the end of their useful life before they break down, have chargers available in meeting rooms, conduct routine maintenance on conferencing equipment, etc.

7. **Redundancy** – Most people will be familiar with the idea of redundant capacity from a technology perspective. This can include having two communications cables coming in and out of a building in case one gets cut, having spare laptops and peripherals, or using multiskilled teams to provide spare capacity if a specific team is hit with sudden turnover or illness.

8. **Multisite** – Running a multisite operation is an extension of the redundancy concept. If an operation has three locations running the same process and loses one due to adverse weather, transport strike, etc., the other two should be able to pick up the slack—at least for a short time.

Appendix 8
Capacity Management Challenges

These are some of the elements that make capacity management challenging:

- **Defining capacity** – It is particularly tricky in services to define what we mean by capacity. Usually it is defined as "the sustainable amount of output that can be produced under normal operating conditions over a period of time". But defining it in terms of output in services is difficult given the range of possible outputs, so we typically use an input measure such as how many people we have.
- **Units of measure** – It may sound obvious, but balancing the equation requires you to be able to count the demand and capacity, and they need to be defined in the same way. The most common problem is that the sales or product teams that prepare forward forecasts may only forecast in dollars and not units. But even if you get a forecast in units, it may be different to how you're measuring capacity. For example, if your demand forecast is based on the number of customers who complain, and you measure capacity in terms of the number of complaints, there's an obvious mismatch where some customers may lodge multiple complaints or multiple customers lodge the same complaint.
- **Duration** – This may also seem obvious, but any definition of capacity requires you to be clear about the measurement time frame. If you are forecasting demand as payments per month but measure capacity as payments per day, you need to agree on a common duration and then convert one side of the equation into the other. Simple as it may sound, allowing for the different

numbers of working days per month because of public holidays that are in different months from year to year (like Easter) can have a material effect.

- **Service mix** – Most service teams produce more than one type of output, so it's rare that you can aggregate the things that get done and make it meaningful. Similarly, for a manager that looks after a diverse range of teams outputting things as diverse as credit assessments, processed payments, resolved enquiries, updated account details, etc., trying to add these things up and come up with a meaningful number is nonsense. As suggested above in "Defining capacity" the solution is to ignore the output part of the definition and count inputs instead (e.g., how many resources you have available to deliver the output required, i.e., the number of FTEs).

- **Multiple input resources** – Most teams require a range of resources to deliver their output, each of which has their own capacity limit (e.g., the number of desks, computers, telephones and people or the amount of bandwidth). You may have worked your charm and caught the company accountants at a moment of weakness, and they've said you can have more people, but if you've nowhere to seat them, or if there aren't enough phone lines, you're no better off.

- **Time horizon** – All capacity is flexible (i.e., you can wind it up and dial it down—it just depends on the time horizon). It's pretty easy to ask your team to stay back for an hour or two every now and again, but it's another thing to find new premises because you've run out of space. If demand rises by 5–10%, most teams can respond promptly. Demand rising by 15–25% is more challenging and you may need more people. A 50–100% increase will probably require a whole lot more infrastructure and navigating the vagaries of the investment planning cycles, so it's critical that both the demand and capacity sides of the equation are talking about the same time horizon.

- **Leakage** – There's a vast difference between theoretical capacity and available capacity. You might have a full complement of staff available, but you must factor in training, team meetings, unexpected CEO visits, rework, complaint handling, training new hires, absenteeism, systems latency and outages. Some of this may be deliberate and known (e.g., targeting a particular utilisation rate—time spent on core work—to ensure staff are fully trained and briefed), while other leakage factors can be quite random subject only to Murphy's Law.

- **Individual productivity** – Given we're now measuring capacity as inputs (e.g., how many FTEs we have), you need to understand individual productivity to be able to calculate capacity. We know that "all animals are equal, but some animals are more equal than others", but not only does the productivity between individuals vary, the productivity of each individual will vary from day to day. There's a great saying: "Don't waste a crisis." Essentially, if you want to see what your people are truly capable of producing (i.e., their maximum capacity), check their productivity the day after a crisis (e.g., when you've been in BCP mode, struck by a bout of sickness, etc.). You'll be amazed at how much more they can produce. The issue is whether it's "sustainable". So if we have no idea what we're going to get on any given day, how can we come up with a capacity measure?

- **Standard time** – To turn work into hours or FTEs, we must multiply the number of work items by the time it takes to process them. This is typically referred to as standard time. It sounds pretty straightforward, but when no two items are the same and the rate at which the service consultant operates varies (see Leakage above), standard time is anything but standard.

- **Output specification** – Another interesting trait of services is that it's a common but false assumption that the specification of the service is consistent. In reality, particularly in peak periods, we may change that specification just to get the work done and avoid the ignominy of backlogs or missing a customer deadline. For example, the team may take shortcuts where there is a hard deadline (e.g., in payments processing, the team may skip some of the checks). If you measure capacity in the last hour of the day, it's different to the first hour of the day with the same number of people on the team because they are doing less work for each item!

- **Forecasting** – If all the other pain points were not enough, knowing how much capacity you had yesterday is not particularly useful. It's more helpful to know how much capacity you will have tomorrow, next week, next month and next year. You now need to forecast and, as Neil Bentley once pointed out to me, "There are only two types of forecast: lucky and wrong."

Appendix 9
Capacity Management Strategies

There are three basic capacity management strategies, but it's not unusual to mix and match elements from all three.

Level scheduling

This is where the team aims to produce the same amount each day/shift. It works well in a manufacturing environment as the producer can use finished goods inventory as a buffer. When demand is higher than capacity, the organisation draws down from the finished goods inventory and when demand is below the current capacity level, the producer makes to stock. Smoothing out production helps these organisations create a more stable and predictable production environment, which in turn allows techniques like "just in time" supply chains to work more effectively.

This approach is practically impossible in a service environment, as services cannot be made to inventory—you can't answer a customer enquiry before the customer calls. Where service organisations adopt this approach it typically means periods of idleness and customer queues. Monopoly services sometimes take this approach. The more critical the service is to customers the more likely there are to be periods of idleness as staffing is towards the peak. Conversely, where the service criticality is less important, staffing is towards the trough and customers must wait.

Manage demand

Options to manage demand are:

1. **Pricing** – This is the "happy hour" scenario and can be positioned as a carrot (e.g., a discount to the base price) or a stick (e.g., a

surcharge to the base price). In the intraday scenario above, offering a discount to customers who send in their work in the morning may shift the afternoon peak.

2. **Promotions** – In the month/year chart, running promotions during the off-season months could help smooth out the trough, but it very much depends on the type of service you're providing.

3. **Specifications/service level** – You can change the service level to offer a fuller/faster turnaround time for customers sending their requests in during quieter periods. Intraday basis service levels, such as "Order by noon and get same day service", are quite common, as is offering a free wrapping service in a retail outlet during quieter periods. As a side note, be extremely careful of setting "same day" service level expectations—essentially you are saying that you can reduce the time to manufacture as the day progresses. A customer sending in a request at the start of the day gives you around eight hours to produce the service, whereas the customer sending it at the end of the day gives you minutes to manufacture the service. You would be destined to fail!

4. **Reservation systems** – Booking systems obviously help smooth out demand but do present additional problems such as "no shows" and cancellations when it's too late to rebook the same slot. In a service centre environment, these tend to be restricted to specialist resources.

5. **Large customer negotiation** – Where demand is driven by a relatively small number of large customers, negotiating one-on-one to smooth the demand out is feasible and can make life far easier, but there may be constraints on the customer side.

6. **Complementary services** – The first five options obviously require input from product, marketing and sales functions, whereas the operations team can use this option directly. The trick is to find other teams that have complementary demand profiles and cross-skill. For example, a team that was busy in the morning and then quietened down in the afternoon is a perfect complement to a team that is quiet in the morning and busy in the afternoon. I used to manage an inward and an outward payments team. The inward team received a lot of their work overnight, which was piled up when they arrived in the

morning, while the outward team received most of their work in the afternoon. Combining the two teams effectively smoothed out each team's peaks and troughs.

Chase demand

Options to chase demand are:

1. **Creating a flexible base** – The first task is to review the demand profiles for your team and create a "base" team template. When you look at the demand profiles, it should be obvious that applying a flat capacity model (e.g., 10 full-time equivalents), day in and day out, really doesn't work. The main lever you use here is the mix of full-time and part-time staff adjusted for shift schedules. This becomes your "base" plan. Note that you need to do the exercise for all the time periods.
2. **Simple flexing** – With a base plan in place, it's still likely that you will need adjustments, which is where the other levers come into play, such as leave management, loaning and borrowing resources from other teams, flexitime and overtime. Don't be afraid of overtime; it is sometimes the most cost-effective way of meeting demand but be mindful of pulling this lever too frequently and/or too hard.
3. **Setting the target productivity level** – As discussed earlier, one of the challenges is that, unlike machines, the productivity level cannot be calibrated by turning a dial. For people, the number will go up and down predominantly in line with the volume of work. By using the 85th percentile of the productivity levels the team has achieved over the last few weeks and not the average productivity level in planning your resources, you will give yourself a productivity free kick. This is not asking too much. The team are quite capable of operating at this level. What you are doing is putting a check in place to stop them operating at the lower level when there isn't enough work.
4. **Handling one-off spikes** – Many teams must deal with one-off spikes in demand. If you know when the spike is coming, you can hire temporary employees/contractors or even use

a third-party organisation. If you get hit unexpectedly with a spike, you will need to combine a range of actions, including prioritising work and adjusting service specifications.

5. **Managing individual differences** – Occasionally you can ask the team to work harder—if there is enough trust and the team see the need, they will typically respond positively. However, increasing individual productivity is one of the outcomes of managing capacity effectively. You can deliver a significant boost to team productivity by tracking the variability of individual productivity. You then work with the individual to smooth out variability, settling towards the upper quartile of what they have shown they are capable of. Every team member is different, and working closely with each one, recognising their needs and current capability, understanding how their home and work environment is making them feel and making sure they have enough to keep them busy but not overly stretched is at the heart of effective capacity management. People drive productivity, not machines! Leaders who do this well are true alchemists.

6. **Adjusting the workload: diverted time** – Besides core work, for a team to operate effectively, there are other activities that are required to be performed. These have the effect of shrinking available capacity and are typically referred to as diverted activities. They include things such as one-on-one conversations, team meetings, training, continuous improvement activity, etc. They are essential, but not time critical, and so they can be scheduled to help smooth out the core work peaks and troughs. This is commonly called "utilisation" and on the teams I've managed, trying to set this level for normal conditions between 80% and 85% works well, rising to the mid-90s for extremely busy periods.

7. **Adjusting the workload: work-in-progress (WIP)** – Where service levels allow the luxury of being able to hold WIP from one day to the next, run down WIP in quiet times and run up WIP in busy times. Bear in mind the impact on service levels. Keeping WIP within a nominated range is essential to delivery consistency for the customer.

Appendix 10
Building a Capacity Management Plan

Building a capacity management plan involves the following steps (Figure 55):

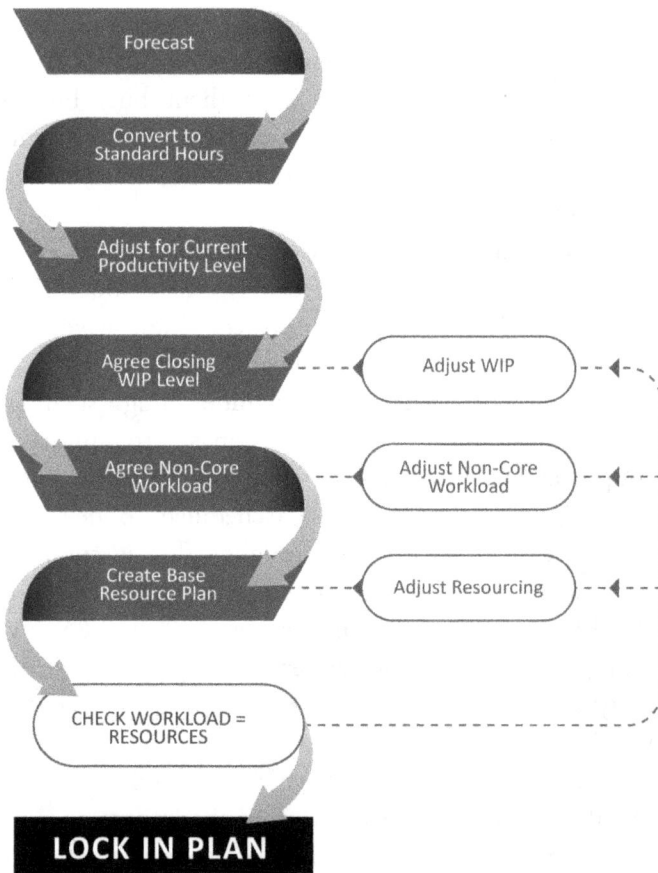

Figure 55 – Building a capacity management plan flow.

1. Create a forecast

The first step is to create a forecast. In some cases, this will be a forecast of the actual tasks your team is responsible for; in other cases, it may be a driver of the work your team do. For example, if your team is responsible for assessing credit, the agreed forecast may be for the number of mortgages, and for every mortgage application you know that a proportion will result in a manual credit assessment. You forecast the number of mortgages and then apply the ratio to determine how many credit assessment tasks to expect.

This is a great opportunity to connect different functions within the organisation and get them to agree on a common forecast. There is usually a political dynamic at play here. Sales teams may lowball forecasts; otherwise, their targets will increase. On the other hand, some sales teams may be overly ambitious to demonstrate their confidence. Both have ramifications for the delivery team and the implications need to be made clear.

One other point when bringing in the sales and product teams is that they may want to forecast in revenue terms. You will need to translate the dollars into units of work. For example, $10m worth of insurance premiums may be equivalent to 100,000 new policies. It's the number of new policies that create the work for the service delivery team. For example, if the driver is the number of new policy applications, for each application you may need to do 1.1 data entry tasks (because of rework), 0.95 assessments (some customers drop out), etc.

In terms of creating a forecast, there are many different techniques you can use. Explaining how and when to use each of these is well beyond the scope of this book. However, in the very short term, a combination of the demand profiles, data for the last month and getting input from the team doing the work usually provides a fairly accurate answer. In the absence of any additional information, it's fair to assume that next Tuesday's work volumes will be the same as this Tuesday's. If you ask the team, you'll quickly get feedback if they disagree (e.g., "Yes, but remember the second Tuesday of the month is always the busiest." Or, "All the sales representatives are at a conference next Monday and Tuesday, so they'll be quieter, but Wednesday will be busier.")

Be more cautious using this approach for longer-term forecasts. If you don't have access to forecasting tools or specialists, then it's fairly easy to do a

12-month moving average in a spreadsheet and plot this on a chart to show if there's a trend. It flattens out the trend, so sharp changes will be hard to see, but it will give a good indication of direction. It's also worth noting that there are a lot of low-cost tools available that are relatively simple to use. Simply copy the historical data into the toolset and it will generate forecasts for you. You do need to be judicious in how you apply the results, as each technique has its own peculiarities and flaws. In fact, some practitioners run a range of forecasts using different techniques and then take the average of all of them.

2. Convert to standard hours

Once you have a unit forecast, you will need to convert this into the amount of time you expect to take to do the work. Each task you do should have a standard time. The precision is not really material, as it will get adjusted for the actual productivity level your team hits, and this calculation is relative to the standard. If you pick a low value for the standard time, your team's productivity will be less than 100%, which will reflect that they couldn't do the work in that time. If you set a high value, your team's productivity will be more than 100%, which will reflect the fact that your team can do the work quicker than the standard.

For each task, you must multiply the forecast number of tasks by the standard time for that task. This tells you how many hours of work there are "at standard" for each task. Add up the individual task hours and you will come to the total core work required in standard hours.

3. Adjust for current productivity level

Once you have converted the forecast to standard time, you then need to make an adjustment for how long it will really take you to do the work. This adjustment is made by dividing total core work required (in standard hours) by the current productivity level. For example, if there are 100 hours of core work, and your team's productivity performance in recent times is 80%, then you will need 125 hours of resources to do the work.

The productivity figure you use should be the productivity figure at the 85th percentile of what your team has typically achieved over the last 30 days. This ensures that you are not dragged down by the quieter days, and you can use this extra capacity for training and improvement opportunities. Figure 56 highlights the difference in planning for a productivity level of 80%, which is the example team's average over the last 30 days, and the productivity level of 90%, which is the 85th percentile of what they've achieved over the last 30 days.

Weekly Load Plan	Mon	Tue	Wed	Thu	Fri
Forecast units	1,000	1,200	1,120	960	800
Forecast hours @ standard (a)	500	600	560	480	400
Hours required @ 80% productivity (b = a ÷ 80%)	625	750	700	600	500
Hours required @ 90% productivity (c = a ÷ 90%)	556	667	622	533	444
Capacity benefit achieved (b – c)	69	83	78	67	56
Core work required (c)	556	667	622	533	444
Diverted work effort - training, team meetings, 1:1s, etc. (d)	52	64	36	28	72
Total hours resource required (c + d)	608	731	658	561	516

Figure 56 – Example day/week load plan at the 85th percentile.

4. Agree on a closing WIP position

The amount of work that needs to be done depends on where you want the closing WIP position to be at the end of the period.

Closing WIP = Opening WIP + Work In – Work Out

In busy periods, you may be able to run closing WIP up so that you don't have to complete as much work out. And vice versa in quieter periods. This should all be within the limits set by the WIP window policy—that is the upper and lower levels of WIP you will maintain to ensure you meet your service level.

5. Agree on a non-core workload

As well as the core work, your team must also do non-core/diverted work.

Total Work = Core Work + Non-Core Work

Utilisation is the ratio of core work to total work and is measured as a percentage.

Non-core work includes activities such as team meetings, one-on-one conversations, training and continuous improvement activities. These are all important activities to maintain a healthy team, but they are not time critical. Therefore, they can be rescheduled as a way of adjusting the overall workload that your team must handle. Typically, 80–85% of your team's total work should be core work. It's okay to run this up to the high 90s for a short period but certainly not for more than a few weeks. A utilisation figure of below 70% for more than a few weeks would suggest that the team have too many resources.

6. Create a resource plan

Having completed the work required plan, it's now time to turn to how you will resource it. You start with your staff complement and then adjust for who's on leave, who's been seconded or loaned out and who has been borrowed/seconded in. You add in any expected overtime. One of the more controversial decisions is whether to allow for downtime (e.g., system outages or unplanned absences). The argument in favour is that this potentially gives you a more realistic position of the resources available to do the work. The argument against is that you are willing this upon yourself and essentially creating an artificial buffer. For me, the answer depends on how consistent the downtime is. If it seems to be 10 hours every day, then plan for it. If it's more random, then don't.

7. Check for balance

With a base work required plan and a resource plan, the next step is to check if they balance. That is:

Work Required – Resource Available = 0

If not, as is usually the case, the next step is to make adjustments to bring them into balance.

A warning note here: the level of precision in service teams is nowhere near as exact as it is in manufacturing teams. Don't spend lots of time debating where you will find one more hour from a team of 20! The team will absorb it, as it's only three minutes extra each—no need to ask someone to do overtime.

8. Adjust

Depending on the size of the imbalance, there are three options:

- **Adjust WIP** – Remember to stay inside the WIP window; otherwise, this may lead to service-related issues.
- **Adjust non-core activity** – Remember that these are important activities, so you can't keep putting them off.
- **Adjust resources** – A cross-skilled team is very valuable in this context. Cancelling someone's leave and doing overtime should be last-resort choices.

All of these are valid options. See Figure 57 for an example.

Resources Required				Resources Available			
Item	Base Plan	Adj	Adj Plan	Item	Base Plan	Adj	Adj Plan
Opening WIP (hrs)	100	0	100	Staff complement (hrs)	600	0	600
Forecast work in (hrs)	550	0	550	Annual leave	-48	0	-48
Plan work out (hrs)	550	-50	500	Loan/borrow	-32	24	-8
Closing WIP (hrs)	100	50	150	Flexitime	0	0	0
Diverted work effort - training, team meetings, 1:1s, etc.	52	-26	26	Overtime	0	6	6
				Temps	0	0	0
				Downtime	-24	0	-24
Total resources required (hrs)	602	-76	526	Total resources available (hrs)	496	30	526
Balance					-106		0

Actions:
Allow WIP to increase by 50 hours, reducing work-out by 50 hours
Reduce team meetings by 30 mins, saving 26 hours in diverted time
Agree not to lend out 24 hours
Run 6 hours overtime if required

Figure 57 – Balanced capacity plan.

9. Lock it in

Once you have a plan that is reasonably balanced, it's time to lock it in. This means sharing the plan with the team. Explaining what it means for each individual and gaining their commitment.

Appendix 11
Enabling Effective Capacity Management

There are three categories of enabling factors that need to be included in any effective capacity management program. These are:

- Capacity management toolkit.
- People and structure.
- Process.

They are covered in more detail below.

Capacity management toolkit

1. **Capacity management system** – For one or two teams, you can build a system in Excel, but anything more significant requires an industrialised system (to help with all the number crunching, amongst other things), and there are lots of vendor solutions available.
2. **Operating rhythm** – Effective capacity management is about establishing an operating rhythm around forecasting, planning, controlling and reviewing over the relevant time horizons. It takes discipline, but without a stable operating rhythm, you're wasting your time.
3. **Visual management** – Unfortunately, most service operations work is buried deep in computer systems. You need to make the state of play visible to the whole team—the simpler, the better.
4. **Outlook matrix** – One aspect many leaders struggle with is where the demand v capacity mismatch varies by time horizon.

The outlook matrix is a great tool to help manage any perceived inconsistencies (Figure 16):

People and structure

1. **Organisational alignment** – Natural evolution in many large organisations leaves a disparate legacy. This may be in the naming of teams and work or where co-dependent teams in different divisions have different objectives. A large part of the success in this area comes from finding complementary teams and doing similar work with leaders who are focussed on the same objectives and are willing to share.
2. **Consolidation** – Small, separated and fragmented teams make this very hard to do. Physically co-locate and consolidate teams where possible. Where physical consolidation is not possible, run like teams as a single virtual unit.
3. **Skills matrix and cross-skilling** – An ability to lend and borrow is dependent on being able to cross-skill some team members (but not everyone), which requires you to call like tasks by the same name and use the same skills matrix.
4. **Multiskilled teams** – A very powerful approach is where base teams are set to the minimum and a small group of the most talented, motivated and cross-skilled resources are grouped together and assigned based on the peaks and troughs across teams. I have seen leaders set their base team resourcing to just above the minimum level of demand. All surplus resources are held in a pool by the manager, and every day/week, the team leaders "bid" for additional resources from the pool. Any resources left over work on continuous improvement initiatives. Needless to say, the pool resources must be multiskilled.
5. **Active management** – Getting the most out of the team is not a "set and forget" task. It requires active management throughout the day, week, month and year.

Process

1. **Continuous improvement backlog** – There may be times when you have excess capacity on hand. Having a prioritised list of continuous improvement activities for people to work on during these times ensures this time is put to productive use.

2. **Stable production environment** – Managing capacity effectively is extraordinarily difficult if the core production systems are not stable. If the team do suffer significant periods of downtime, make sure there is a good continuous improvement backlog (see 1 above).

3. **Line balancing** – Capacity is typically lost when the production stages are not balanced. In a service environment, this is usually a question of appropriately allocating resources to each stage of production. If task A takes 10 minutes and task B takes 5 minutes, you need twice as many people working on task A than task B.

4. **Bottlenecks** – If the process has a bottleneck, this will drive capacity leakage upstream and downstream from the bottleneck. Focus on bottleneck management techniques to manage the impact.

5. **Runners, repeaters and strangers** – This is a very effective technique for triaging and assigning work at the front of a process and to speed up throughput and ensure effective resource allocation based on skills and experience.

Appendix 12

Current State Assessment

Assessment Criteria	Logical Sequence (A)
Part 1 – The Need for Match Fit	
Chapter 1: Digital – An Existential Crisis	1
Is business/digital transformation on your CEO's agenda and do your team know about it?	1
Do your team understand what a business/digital transformation is?	1
Do your team understand how a business/digital transformation is different to other transformations and how it impacts them?	1
Is there a dedicated transformation team, do your team know about them and are resources being redirected towards them?	1
Do your team understand what Match Fit means?	1
Do your team know how Match Fit applies to them, and do they have the tools, techniques and skills to get Match Fit?	1
Do your team know how Match Fit will benefit them?	1
Part 2 – Pre-Season: Getting Match Fit	
Chapter 2: Pre-Season Pep Talk – Setting the Context	2
Do your team have a clear purpose statement and understand how their work supports it?	1
Do your team understand their role in executing your organisation's strategy?	2
Do your team understand how they fit into your organisation's operating model?	2

Assessment Criteria	Logical Sequence (A)
Do your team understand the organisation's priorities and how they support them?	2
Do you have a clear communications plan to share the context frequently with your team in an authentic way?	1
Chapter 3: Selecting the Squad – The People Basics	2
Do you know your entire team, and do they know each other?	1
Do you know the level of trust in your team and do you have a plan to enhance it?	1
Have you addressed all hygiene factors on your team?	2
Have you identified the roles and skills required, designed an appropriate structure, assessed the current capability of your team and made a plan to address any gaps?	2
Does each individual on your team have a plan showing them how they can enhance the team's success?	3
Chapter 4: League Ladders and the Trophy Room – Getting the Scorecard Right	2
Do your team know the key questions to ask to help them understand what's important?	1
Do your team know the listening posts and data sources that will help them find the answers?	2
Do your team know the specific strategic and operational metrics required to manage their performance?	2
Do your team understand the design of each dashboard in use for the different periods of time?	2
Do your team know the baseline for each of the metrics?	2
Do your team know which metrics are cascaded down to each individual?	2
Have you checked the reporting for any design flaws that may impact interpretation of your team's performance and for any red flag indicators present?	3

Assessment Criteria	Logical Sequence (A)
Chapter 5: Know the Rules. Read the Game – Understanding Customer Quality	2
Do your team understand that processes underpin everything they do and that customers expect consistency?	1
Do your team know the customer journeys they support and how customers evaluate quality?	2
Do your team know what outcomes and emotional experience your customers expect, how what they do affects the customer experience, and the impact of variability and how SLAs work to manage this?	2
Do your team understand the cost of poor quality for the work they do?	3
Chapter 6: Skills Clinic – Quality Essentials	2
Do your team know which processes they are responsible for and who owns them?	1
Do your team have access to adequate process documentation (SIPOC, process map and work instructions)?	2
Have your team removed excess steps, decisions, handoffs, systems and process variants from your processes?	3
Do your team have a skills matrix and a training plan for each individual in place?	2
Do your team understand the key risks associated with the processes they are responsible for, have they completed an FMEA for each major process and have they developed a treatment plan for prioritised failure points?	2
Have your team identified and implemented preventative maintenance and error-proofing options across major processes?	3
Chapter 7: Picking the Team – Managing Capacity	2
Do your team understand the challenges in managing capacity and why it is so important?	1

Assessment Criteria	Logical Sequence (A)
Do your team understand the demand profiles for the respective time periods, how well you currently manage capacity and the levers you can pull to adjust demand and capacity?	2
Do your team understand and have a capacity management planning cycle in place, including how to forecast, adjust capacity, control the plan and review it?	2
Do your team know how to build a plan, and do they do so routinely planning at the 85th percentile?	2
Do your team have all the enablers in place to support effective capacity management?	3
Does each team member understand their individual productivity performance, what's causing the variability and do they have a plan to improve?	3
Part 3 – Mid-Season: Getting Fitter, Refining and Finessing	
Chapter 8: The Need for Change	3
Do your team understand why you need to innovate and improve?	2
Do your team have a catalogue of all change initiatives underway that impact them categorised into problem solving, redesign and transformation?	3
Do your team have a change calendar in place that outlines the impact of all changes, when the changes must be adopted and has this been factored into your capacity plan?	3
Is there a clear communication plan that your team understand to the extent that they know when, where and how change will be introduced and what is expected of them?	3
Chapter 9: The 1 Percenters – DIY Problem Solving	3
Do your team operate in a safe environment to freely raise issues without blame?	3
Do your team follow a simple, standard approach to solve problems?	3

Assessment Criteria	Logical Sequence (A)
Do your team know how to generate improvement opportunities, and is there a current list of problems to solve?	3
Do your team practice a simple and effective way of filtering out and prioritising which problems they will work on?	3
Do your team have a toolkit to solve problems?	3
Do your team schedule time for solving problems regularly and deploy techniques to maintain momentum?	4
Chapter 10: Timing the Peak – DIY Redesigning	4
Do your team understand the options available in terms of where to start your redesign journey, and have you agreed on the prioritisation criteria?	3
Do your team understand the stages in the redesign journey, what each means and how they will impact the team?	2
Do your team understand the factors that must be considered when deciding how to redesign?	5
Have the team that will be running the redesign been selected and do they have the breadth of skills and support to run the redesign effort?	5
Have your team committed to the redesign benefits plan? Do they know how the changes introduced will release the expected benefits?	5
Chapter 11: Reinvent Your Game – Supporting Transformational Change	4
Do your team know the role they play in supporting the transformation?	2
Do your team understand the new terminology introduced to support the digital transformation and how each aspect will impact them?	4
Do your team understand the challenges that the digital transformation will bring, and do they have a plan to address the challenges?	4

Assessment Criteria	Logical Sequence (A)
Do your team know the options available to get closer to the digital transformation, and are they utilising the options effectively?	4
Do your team understand how to interact effectively with the digital transformation team and role model these behaviours in practice?	4
Chapter 12: A Game of Hard Knocks – Resilience and Workforce of the Future	5
Are your team change ready, and do they practice resilience techniques?	3
Do you know the types of skills and roles you will need in the future?	5
Do you have a plan in place to acquire these skills either through retraining existing people or bringing in new talent?	5
Do you have a plan in place to help build the careers of those people who will no longer be part of your team in the future?	5
Do you have a list of the capabilities, tools and technology required for your workforce of the future, an understanding of how your team will create value in the future and a plan to get there?	5
Part 4 – End-of-Season Review: Stay the Course	
Chapter 13: Hold the Line	2
Do your team have a comprehensive operating rhythm in place that covers major events, spans the different time horizons and aligns up and down the hierarchy?	2
Do you and your team understand the disciplined activities required to make the program sustainable, and are they underway?	3
Do you and your team know what support you need from the CEO and senior executives to make this program sustainable, and is it underway?	3
Do your team have a road map of how it will become Match Fit, showing progress to date?	1

Appendix 13
How the CEO Can Help

Every CEO wants to be proud of the legacy they leave behind. We live in an age where the legacy of CEOs of many large organisations will be defined by their ability to lead their organisation through a digital transformation.

A digital transformation of a large, mature organisation is like no other initiative. The pace, depth and breadth of the change are overwhelming. Getting up to speed with the jargon, technologies and methodologies is a challenge in its own right.

For a transformation with technology at its core, this is everything but a technology transformation. As tempting as it may be, it's not all about the transformation team, with their strange sounding job titles, new acronyms and innovative technologies, bringing with them the promise of a bright future. Unless the CEO is planning to build from scratch, and allowing the new business to cannibalise the old, the BAU teams are integral to the transformation.

The BAU teams will keep customers engaged and satisfied, buying the transformation team some time. They will help fund the transformation by running their teams with far fewer resources. They will continue to innovate and improve with limited investment funding so that a larger share can be allocated to the digital program. They will help the transformation team by quickly providing insight for the new hires into the processes that create value for customers today. They will make the task of the transformation team easier by consolidating, standardising and simplifying processes. They will do so mindful of the fact that the new hires are probably paid considerably more. And they will do all this knowing that their future is uncertain.

The risk of an "us and them" environment, which could jeopardise the enterprise, is very real. To deliver the CEO's legacy, both the BAU teams and the transformation teams need to collaborate and work seamlessly together. To achieve the common goal, they need to acknowledge the different role each other plays and that neither can succeed without the other. The CEO must pay as much attention to the BAU teams as they do to the transformation team. The BAU teams are just as mission critical and their task is just as hard, if not harder. They need their fair share of management attention, support, acknowledgement, recognition and reward.

With the CEO's support, attention, recognition and trust, the people tasked with leading the BAU teams through this transformation will deliver.

References

12 reasons why digital transformations fail [Article] / auth. Boulton Clint // CIO. - Framingham, Massachusetts : IDG, 20 May 2019.

2018 Global CEO Outlook The Australian Perspective [Report] / auth. KPMG. - Melbourne : KPMG, 2018.

4+1: Embedding a Culture of Contnous Improvement in Financial Services [Book] = 4+1 / auth. Jones Dr. Morgan L., Butterworth Chris and Harder Brenton. - Wamberal : Action New ThInking Limited, 2017. - 978-0-987347-1-8.

5 Questions We Should Be Asking About Automation and Jobs [Article] / auth. Kolko Jed // Harvard Business Review. - Boston : Harvard Business Publishing, 19 December 2018.

5 Ways to Boot Your Resilience at Work [Journal] / auth. Fernandez Rich // Harvard Business Review. - 27 June 2016.

Agile at scale, explained [Report] / auth. Relihan Tom. - Boston : MIT Sloan School of Management, 2018.

Banking Customer 2020: Rising Expectations Point to the Everyday Bank [Report] / auth. Accenture / Accenture. - Dublin : Accenture, 2015.

Behind The Silver Fern: Playing Rugby For New Zealand [Book] / auth. Johnson Tony and McConnell Lynn. - GB : Birlinn General, 2017.

Blink [Book] / auth. Gladwell Malcolm. - London : Penguin Books, 2006. - 978-0-141-01419-5.

Build for Change: Revolutionizing Customer Engagement Through Continuous Digital Innovation [Book] = Build for Change / auth. Trefler Alan. - Hoboken : John Wiley & Sons, Inc, 2014. - 978-1-118-93026-7.

Digital Banking: Stretch Your Boundaries Toward the Everyday Bank [Report] / auth. Accenture / Accenture. - Dubin : Accenture, 2015.

Digital Transformation Is Not About Technology [Article] / auth. Tabrizi Behnam [et al.] // Harvard Business Review. - Boston : Harvard Business Publishing, 13 March 2019.

Don't Just Tell Employees Organizational Changes Are Coming — Explain Why [Article] / auth. Galbraith Morgan // Harvard Business Review. - Boston : Harvard Business Publishing, 5 October 2018.

Emotional Intelligence: Why It Can Matter More Than IQ [Book] = Emotional Intelligence / auth. Goleman Daniel. - London : Bloomsbury Publishing, 1996. - 978-0-7475-2830-2.

Executive Perspectives on Top Risks 2019 [Report] / auth. North Carolina State University's ERM Initiative; Protiviti / Enterprise Risk Management ; NOrth Carolina State University. - Chapel Hill : North Carolina State University, 2018.

Exploring Coporate Strategy: Text & Cases [Book] / auth. Johnson Gerry [et al.]. - Harlow : Pearson Education Limited, 2017. - 11th Edition. - 978-1-292-141512-9.

Four Types of Problems [Book] / auth. Smalley Art. - Boston : Lean Enterprise Institute, 2018. - 978-1-9341-0955-7.

Fresh Air [Interview] / interv. Gibson William. - [s.l.] : NPR, August 1993.

Getting Your Employees Ready for Work in the Age of AI [Article] / auth. Sage-Gavin Eva, Vazirani Madhu and Hintermann Francis //

MIT Sloan Management Review. - Boston : MIT Sloan School of Management, 27 February 2019.

Global Retail Banking 2016: Banking on Digital Simplicity [Report] / auth. Grebe Michael [et al.] / The Boston Consulting Group. - Boston : The Boston Consulting Group, 2016.

How DBS Bank Purused a Digital Business Strategy [Article] / auth. Sia Sien Kien, Soh Christina and Weill Peter // MIS Quarterly Executive. - Bloomington : Kelley School of Business, 2016. - June 2016.

How to beat the transformation odds [Report] : Survey / auth. Jacquemont David, Maor Dana and Reich Angelika. - Seattle : McKinsey & Company, 2016.

How to Break Down Work into Tasks That Can Be Automated [Article] / auth. Jesuthasan Ravin and Boudreau John // Harvard Business Review. - Boston : Harvard Business Publishing, 20 February 2019.

How to create an agile organization [Report] / auth. Ahlbäck Karin [et al.] / McKinsey & Company. - Seattle : McKinsey & Company, 2017.

How to Help Your Employees Learn from Each Other [Article] / auth. Palmer Kelly and Blake David // Harvard Business Review. - Boston : Harvard Business Publishing, 8 November 2018.

How Winning Organizations Last 100 Years [Article] / auth. Hill Alex, Mellon Liz and Goddard Jules // Harvard Business Review. - 27 September 2018.

ING's agile transformation [Article] / auth. Jacobs Peter and Schlatmann Bart // McKinsey Quarterly. - Seattle : McKinsey & Company, 2017. - January 2017.

Keeping us up at night The big issues facing business leaders in 2019 [Report] / auth. KPMG. - Melbourne : KPMG, 2018.

Leading agile transformation: The new capabilities leaders need to build 21st-century organizations [Article] / auth. Smet Aaron de, Lurie Michael and George Andrew St // McKinsey Quarterly. - Seattle : McKinsey & Company, 2018.

Leading Digital: Turning Technology Into Business transformation [Book] = Leading Digital / auth. Westerman George, Bonnet Didier and McAfee Andrew. - Boston : Harvard Business Review Press, 2014. - 978-1-62527-247-8.

Lean Management - New frontiers for financial institutions [Report] / auth. Roggenhofer Stefan, Ilebrand Nicklas and Mitcho Seth / McKinsey & Company. - Seattle : McKinsey & Company, 2011.

Lean Six Sigma For Service [Book] / auth. George Michael L.. - New York : McGraw-Hill, 2003. - 0-07-141821-0.

Legacy: What the All Blacks Can Teach Us About The Business Of Life [Book] / auth. Kerr James. - GB : Little, Brown Book Group, 2013.

Make Customers Happier with Operational Transparency [Article] / auth. Buell Ryan // Harvard Business Review. - Boston : Harvard Business Publishing, 5 March 2019.

Making Hard Decisions: An Introduction to Decision Analysis [Book] = Making Hard Decisions / auth. Clemen Robert T.. - Belmont : Wadsworth Publishing Company, 1996. - 2nd Edition. - 0-534-26034-9.

Making Learning a Part of Everyday Work [Article] / auth. Bersin Josh and Zao-Sanders Marc // Harvard Business Review. - Boston : Harvard Business Publishing, 19 February 2019.

Making Theory Operational: The Span of Management [Journal] / auth. Koonz Harold // Journal of Management Studies. - Hoboken : Wiley-Blackwell, October 1966.

Managing Services: Marketing, Operations, And Human Resources [Book] = Managing Services / auth. Lovelock Christopher H.. - London : Prentice-Hall International, 1988. - 0-13-551383-9.

Metamorphosis [Book] / auth. Kafka Franz / trans. Muir Willa and Edwin. - [s.l.] : Penguin Books Ltd, 1961.

Mindset Changing The Way You Think To Fulfil Your Potential [Book] / auth. Dweck Dr Carol S.. - [s.l.] : Little Brown Book Group, 2017.

Operating Model Canvas [Book] / auth. Campbell Andrew, Guttierez Mikel and Lancelott Mark. - Hertogenbosch : Van Haren Publishing, 2017. - 9789401800716.

Operational Transparency [Article] / auth. Buell Ryan W. // Harvard Business Review. - Boston : Harvard Business Publishing, 2019. - March-April 2019.

Operations and Process Management [Book] / auth. Slack Nigel [et al.]. - Harlow : Pearson Education limited, 2015. - 4th Edition. - 978-1-292-01784-6.

Operations Management [Book] / auth. Slack Nigel, Brandon-Jones Alistair and Johnston Robert. - Harlow : Pearson Education Limited, 2013. - 7th Edition. - 978-0-273-77620-8.

Operations Strategy [Book] / auth. Slack Nigel and Lewis Michael. - Harlow : Pearson Education Limited, 2002. - 0-273-63781-9.

Optimizing Your Digital Business Model [Article] / auth. weill peter and Woerner. Stephanie L. // MIT Sloan Management Review. - Boston : MIT Sloan School of Management, 2013. - Sprin 2013.

Prioritize Which Data Skills Your Company Needs with This 2×2 Matrix [Article] / auth. Littlewood Chris // Harvard Business Review. - Boston : Harvard Business Publishing, 23 October 2018.

Putting The Service Profit Chain To Work [Journal] / auth. Heskett James L. [et al.] // Harvard Business Review. - 2008. - pp. Jul-Aug.

Quantitiative Analysis [Book] / auth. Brandon-Jones Alistair and Slack Nigel. - Harlow : Pearson Education Limited, 2008. - 978-0-273-70848-3.

Realigning global support-function footprints in a digital world [Report] / auth. Chheda Hiren [et al.] / McKinsey & Company. - Seattle : McKinsey & Company, 2018.

Reframing the Future of Work [Article] / auth. Schwartz Jeff [et al.] // MIT Sloan Management Review. - Boston : MIT Sloan School of Management, 20 February 2019.

Resilience Is About How You Recharge, Not How You Endure [Article] / auth. Achor Shawn and Gielan Michelle // Harvard Business Review. - Boston : Harvard Business Publishing, 24 June 2016.

Rise Of The Robots: Technology And The Threat Of A Jobless Future [Book] = Rise Of The Robots / auth. Ford Martin. - Philadelphia : Basic Books, 2016. - 978-0-465-09753-1.

Service Operations Management: Improving Service Delivery [Book] = Service Operations Management: / auth. Johnston Robert, Clark Graham and Shulver Michael. - Harlow : Pearson Education Limited, 2012. - 4th Edition. - 978-0-273-74048-3.

Should business put purpose before profits? Companies are starting to think so [Article] / auth. Edgecliffe-Johnson Andrew // Australian Financial Review. - Sydney : NIne Publishing, 11 January 2019.

Six Sigma For Financial Services: How Leading Companies Are Driving Results with Lean, Six Sigma, and Process Management [Book] = Six Sigma For Financial Services / auth. Hayler Rowland and Nichols Michael D.. - New York : Mcgraw-Hill, 2007. - 978-0-07-147037-7.

Sponsor Success: The WHATs and HOWs for business improvement projects [Book] = Sponsor Success / auth. Jones Dr. Morgan L. - Wamberal : Action New Thinking Limited, 2012. - 978-0-9873477-0-1.

Spreadsheet Modeling and Analysis [Book] / auth. Ragsdale Cliff T.. - Cincinnati : South-Western College Publishing, 1998. - 0-538-88130-5.

Statistics For Business And Economics [Book] / auth. Newbold Paul. - Englewood Cliffs : Prentice-Hall, Inc, 1991. - 0-13-850645-0.

Stories for Work - The Essential Guide to Business Storytelling [Book] = Stories for Work / auth. Dolan Garbeielle. - Milton : Wiley & Sons Ltd, 2017. - 9780730343295.

Tapping into the Transformative Power of Service 4.0 [Report] / auth. Rehse Olaf, Hoffmann Stefan and Kosanke Christoph / The Boston Consulting Group. - Boston : The Boston Consulting Group, 2016.

Technology operations: A flywheel for performance improvement [Report] / auth. Berruti Federico, Taylor David and Weinberg Allen / McKinsey & Company. - Seattle : McKinsey & Company, 2019.

The Checklist Manifesto: How To Get Things Right [Book] = The Checklist Manifesto / auth. Gawande Atul. - New York : Picador, 2010. - 978-0-8050-9174-8.

The Decision Book: Fifty models for strategic thinking [Book] / auth. Krogerus Mikael and Tschäppeler Roman. - London : Profile Books Ltd, 2011. - 978-1-84668-395-4.

The Five Dysfunctions Of A Team: A Leadership Fable [Book] = The Five Dysfunctions Of A Team: / auth. Lencioni Patrick. - Hoboken : John Wiley & Sons, Inc, 2002. - 078-7-96075-6.

The five trademarks of agile organizations [Report] / auth. Aghina Wouter [et al.] / McKinsey & Company. - Seattle : McKinsey & Company, 2018.

The Fundamentals of Leadership Still Haven't Changed [Article] / auth. Ashkenas Ron and Manville Brook // Harvard Business Review. - Boston : Harvard Business Publishing, 7 November 2018.

The Goal [Book] / auth. Goldratt Eliyahu. - Farnham : Ashgate Publishing Limited, 2004. - 3rd Edition. - 978-0-566-08665-6.

The High-Velocity Edge: How Market Leaders Leverage Operational Excellence to Beat the Competition [Book] = The High-Velocity Edge / auth. Spear Steven J.. - New York : McGraw-Hill, 2010. - 978-0-07-174140-8.

The Jobs That Artificial Intelligence Will Create [Article] / auth. Wilson H. James, Daugherty Paul R. and Morini-Bianzino Nicola // MIT Sloan Management Review. - Boston : MIT Sloan School of Management, 23 March 2017. - Summer.

The Lean Six Sigma Guide to Doing More With Less [Book] / auth. George Mark O.. - Hoboken : John Wiley & Sons, Inc, 2010. - 978-0-470-53957-6.

The Lean Six Sigma Pocket Toolbook [Book] / auth. George Michael L. [et al.]. - New York : McGraw-Hill, 2005. - 0-07-144119-0.

The Lean Startup: How Constant Innovation Creates Radically Successful Businesses [Book] = The Lean Startup / auth. Ries Eric. - London : Penguin Group, 2011. - 978-0-670-92160-7.

The Multidimesnsional Manager: 24 Way's to Impact Your Bottom Line in 90 Days [Book] / auth. Connelly Richard and McNeill Robin. - [s.l.] : Cognos, 1999.

The next-generation operating model for the digital world [Report] / auth. Bollard Albert [et al.] / McKinsey & Company. - Seattle : McKinsey & Company, 2017.

The productivity agenda: moving beyond cost reduction in financial services [Report] / auth. PwC. - [s.l.] : PwC, 2019.

The promise and challenge of the age of artificial intelligence [Conference] / auth. Manyika James [et al.] // Tallinn Digital Summit. - Tallinn : McKinsey Global Institute, 2018.

The Role of a Manager Has to Change in 5 Key Ways [Article] / auth. Pistrui Joseph and Dimov Dimo // Harvard Business Review. - Boston : Harvard Business Publishing, 26 December 2018.

The Secret to Leading Organizational Change Is Empathy [Article] / auth. Sanchez Patti // Harvard Business Review. - Boston : Harvard Business Publishing, 20 December 2018.

The Soft Skills of Great Digital Organizations [Article] / auth. Samuel Alexandra // Harvard Business Review. - Boston : Harvard Business Publishing, 5 February 2016.

The Tipping Point: How Little Things Can Make a Big Difference [Book] = The Tipping Point / auth. Gladwell Malcolm. - London : Little Brown Book Group, 2011. - 978-0-349-11346-3.

The Toyota Way [Book] / auth. Liker Jeffery K.. - New York : McGraw-Hill, 2004. - 0-07-139231-9.

The Trusth About Coporate Transformation [Article] / auth. Reeves Martin [et al.] // MIT Sloan Management Review. - Boston : MIT Sloan School of Management, 31 January 2018.

Thriving in an Increasingly Digital Ecosystem [Article] / auth. Weill Peter and Woerner Stephanie L. // MIT Sloan Management Review. - Boston : MIT Sloan School of Management, 16 June 2015. - Summer 2015.

To Be Agile, You Need Fewer Processes and Policies [Online] / auth. Nink Marco // Gallup Workplace. - 18 January 2019. - https://www.gallup.com/workplace/246074/agile-need-fewer-processes-policies.aspx.

Toyota Production System: Beyond Large-Scale Production [Book] / auth. Ohno Taiichi. - Boca Raton : CRC Press, 2014. - 2nd reprint. - 978-0-915299-14-0.

What Do You Really Mean by Business "Transformation"? [Article] / auth. Anthony Scott D. // Harvard Business Review. - Boston : Harvar Business Publising, 29 February 2016.

What is a digital ecosystem, and how can your business benefit from one? [Article] / auth. Bennett Madeline // The Daily Telegraph. - London : Telegraph Media Group Limited 2019, 12 April 2017.

What is digital transformation? A necessary disruption [Article] / auth. Boulton Clint // CIO. - Framingham, Massachusetts : IDG, 30 May 2019.

Why a One-Size-Fits-All Approach to Employee Development Doesn't Work [Article] / auth. Finkelstein Sydney // Harvard Business Review. - Boston : Harvard Business Publishing, 5 March 2019.

Why AI Underperforms and What Companies Can Do About It [Article] / auth. Moldoveanu Mihnea // Harvard Business Review. - Boston : Harvard Business Publishing, 12 March 2019.

Why Toyota's retrenched workers still love the company [Article] / auth. Samson Danny // Australian Financial Review. - 12 July 2017.

Your Company Doesn't Need a Digital Strategy [Article] / auth. Westerman George // MIT Sloan Managemet Review. - Boston : MIT Sloan School of Management, 25 October 2017. - Spring 2018.

Your Workforce Is More Adaptable Than You Think [Article] / auth. Fuller Joseph B. [et al.] // Harvard Business Review. - Boston : Harvard Business PUblishing, May-June 2019. - May-June 2019. - 3 : Vol. 93.

Index

Customer expectations, 4,
9-10, 14, 85-87, 142-143
Customer experience, 4, 7,
166, 193, 209, 220
Customer journey, 10, 12,
65, 100-101, 105, 147,
168, 170-171, 218, 237
Customer lifecycle, 86-87
Customer outcomes, 88-91, 96, 103
Customer perception, 85-87, 96
Customer satisfaction, 3, 7, 16, 27,
65, 67, 72, 113, 233, 265, 266
Customer segment, 36, 73
Customer self-service,
125, 178, 195
CVA. *See* Waste: Customer Value Add
CX. *See* Customer experience

D

Dashboard, 67-70, 73-76, 78,
81-82, 146, 155, 170, 230,
253-254, 265, 275, 296
Data scientists, 8, 213
Decision rights, 32, 100, 270
Demand profile, 119-124, 137-138,
191, 283-287, 298
Denial of service, 109
Digital masters, 7
Diversity, 50, 59-61, 237, 252
Diverted Time, 285
Downsizing, 216, 221
Dream Team, 62
DRIVE program, 216
Dual blind keying, 271

E

Ecosystem, 8, 65-66, 183, 195,
214, 220
End of season, 14
Epic. *See* Agile

Error proofing, 93, 110-113, 271-275
Ethereum, 197

F

Fail-fast, 10, 66
Failure Modes and Effects
Analysis, 109, 110, 113,
114, 179, 184, 297
Floor walk, 40, 202
FMEA. *See* Failure Modes and Effects
Analysis
Ford, 217
Forecast, 116, 117-119, 126-127,
129, 132, 135, 138, 149,
182, 227-228, 238, 256, 278,
281, 287-288, 292, 298
Fusajiro Yamauchi, 27

G

Gamification, 215
Gemba, 100
Google, 6, 12, 195-196, 199
Growth mind-set, 213-214, 221

H

Hanafuda, 27
HCD, *See* Human-centred design
Heijunka, 123, 275
High-performing team, 41, 245
Champion team, 15, 17,
19-20, 38-39, 51, 59-60, 108
Team of champions, 38
Holden, 217
HR. *See* Human Resources
Huddle. *See* Buzz
Human-centred design, 169,
184, 193, 274
Human Resources, 30, 49, 53-55, 57,
62, 77, 80, 235, 261, 268-269

Acknowledgements

The list of people I've met and worked with that have influenced me or shaped my thinking is very long. In some ways, every job I've done, every course I've been on, every business book or article I've read has led to this book. So, to everyone who has helped me along the way, my gratitude. Thank you for influencing, encouraging, counselling and challenging me, making me think and sharing your insights.

I am particularly indebted to those people who helped with the editing and publishing process, reviewing the content, writing the foreword, providing testimonials and a whole raft of advice, but of course any errors are mine. So, in alphabetical order, my heartfelt thanks go to: Alan Jarrold, Amanda Murray-Johnson, Andy McDermott, Carina Parisella, Danny Samson, David Cecil, Donna Dainton, Graeme Hosking, Neil Bentley, Nina Muhleisen, Patricia Kot, Richard Jeffery, Rob Walliser, Roger Marsden, Sonja Steiner, Steve Gallagher, and particular thanks to my 'editor-in-chief', Katy Adams.

Contact Nigel Adams and Support Materials

There are a range of supporting materials including a current state assessment planning tool, team-based tools and online learning modules. Please visit www.hettonadvisory.com or contact Nigel directly.

Channel	Address
✉	nigel.adams@hettonadvisory.com
🌐	www.nigeladamsblog.com
🌐	www.hettonadvisory.com
🐦	@_NigelAdams
in	www.linkedin.com/in/nigeladams1

www.ingramcontent.com/pod-product-compliance
Lightning Source LLC
Chambersburg PA
CBHW060323200326
41519CB00011BA/1821